WALKING
BEN LAWERS, RANNOCH
AND ATHOLL

WALKING
BEN LAWERS, RANNOCH AND ATHOLL

MOUNTAINS AND GLENS
OF HIGHLAND PERTHSHIRE

by Ronald Turnbull

JUNIPER HOUSE, MURLEY MOSS,
OXENHOLME ROAD, KENDAL, CUMBRIA LA9 7RL
www.cicerone.co.uk

© Ronald Turnbull 2021
Second edition 2021
ISBN: 978 1 78631 107 8
First edition (as *Walking Highland Perthshire*) 2013

Printed in Singapore by KHL Printing on responsibly sourced paper.
A catalogue record for this book is available from the British Library.
All photographs are by the author except the one on the back flap, which is
by Thomas Turnbull.

Updates to this Guide

While every effort is made by our authors to ensure the accuracy of
guidebooks as they go to print, changes can occur during the lifetime of an
edition. Any updates that we know of for this guide will be on the Cicerone
website (www.cicerone.co.uk/1107/updates), so please check before
planning your trip. We also advise that you check information about such
things as transport, accommodation and shops locally. Even rights of way
can be altered over time. We are always grateful for information about any
discrepancies between a guidebook and the facts on the ground, sent by
email to updates@cicerone.co.uk or by post to Cicerone, Juniper House,
Murley Moss, Oxenholme Road, Kendal, LA9 7RL.

Register your book: To sign up to receive free updates, special offers
and GPX files where available, register your book at www.cicerone.co.uk.

Front cover: Crossing the Tarmachans: Meall Garbh summit ridge (Route 12)

CONTENTS

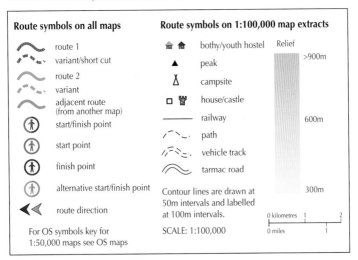

Route symbols on all maps

〜〜　route 1

〜〜　variant/short cut

〜〜　route 2

〜〜　variant

〜〜　adjacent route
　　　(from another map)

(🚶)　start/finish point

(🚶)　start point

(🚶)　finish point

(🚶)　alternative start/finish point

◀◀　route direction

For OS symbols key for
1:50,000 maps see OS maps

Route symbols on 1:100,000 map extracts

🏠 🏠　bothy/youth hostel

▲　peak

⚊　campsite

◻ ♜　house/castle

———　railway

〜〜.　path

〜〜.　vehicle track

〜〜　tarmac road

Contour lines are drawn at
50m intervals and labelled
at 100m intervals.

SCALE: 1:100,000

Relief

>900m

600m

300m

0 kilometres　1　2

0 miles　1

Route rating

The type of walk in terms of landscape encountered – low-, mid- or high-level
– length and difficulty is shown by icons (shown below) which appear at the
start of each route description. See also 'Using this guide' in the Introduction.

TYPE OF WALK

Low
Forest and riverside
walks, below 600m

Mid
Moorland and hills,
600m–900m

Mountain
Mountain walks,
above 900m

On the ridge to Beinn Bheoil, with Loch a' Bhealaich Bheithe and Loch Ericht (Route 53)

INTRODUCTION

For the Atholl highlander of 400 years ago there were two ways of treating any passing hillwalker. Arrive at teatime, and it would be a stool in front of the peat fire, eggs still warm from the midden, a glass of heather ale and a wee skirl on the pipes. That tradition continues in the main street of Pitlochry, perhaps the world capital of the nice cup of tea and slab of shortbread.

But meet him on a winter night, in his filthy old kilt and a thieving chill in his eye – you're about to lose all your livestock and maybe also your life.

The south-eastern chunk of the Grampians, filling the wide space between the Cairngorms and the Lomond-Trossach National Park, forms part of the ancient county of Perthshire. But if you think of Perthshire as little tea-shop towns like Crieff and Aberfeldy, think again. At the back of Blair Atholl you can walk over the tops for four or five days, and when your feet next touch tarmac you're somewhere north of Aberdeen. In the wilds of Rannoch Moor, your only foothold is a bleached limb of pine, bog-preserved over tens of centuries. No longer ago than 1980, a Mr J C Donaldson discovered in an old guidebook an unlisted and unrecorded Munro. It was called Ben Feskineth. At 3530ft, this secret summit was by no means a marginal Munro. And where was it? Ben Feskineth lay undiscovered in deepest, peatiest Perthshire.

JOLLY GREEN GIANTS

In the event, Feskineth turned out to be a misspelling of Beinn Heasgarnich (now, amusingly, respelled again on the Explorer map as Sheasgarnaich). Heasgarnich's high grassy sides are steep, but not unpleasantly so, and

9

Schiehallion across Dunalastair Water (Route 46)

hold snow even in unpromising winters. Perthshire's grassy, pebbly plateaus and rounded ridges are places to relax after the rigours of Scotland's rocky north and west. But relaxation is relative, when Scottish hills are concerned. These mountains may be soft-edged and noted for their wildflowers. But easy they aren't.

These hills are jolly green giants. And from Schiehallion to Atholl, from Rannoch to Ben Vrackie, there are a lot of them. Soggy grass slopes drop to peaty cols. Cross five or six brown streams, hop in and out of a hag, and get back to grips with another of the long grass slopes. In March and April that grass becomes crisp snow, ready for the kick of a stiff four-season boot or the snick of a crampon. The boggy cols freeze over, the lonely curlew comes back from the seaside, and Ben Lawers and Meall nan Tarmachan look all alpine against the sky.

If Perthshire's slogan is 'the Perfect Centre', then the centre of Perthshire is Schiehallion. Standing atop its tall tent shape of off-white quartzite, you look west along Loch Rannoch to Rannoch Moor, Argyll and Ben Nevis. Northwest, Ben Alder bulges big and serious, but is just 66m too low to be the highpoint of the former Perthshire. It's also a couple of miles outside the boundary – but included in this book for its approaches from Loch Rannoch.

Northwards lie the heather humps of Drumochter. Northeast is Atholl, and the dinosaur ridgeback of Beinn a' Ghlo – with the Cairngorms a snowy white line behind.

Eastwards, it's Loch Tummel of the bright birches and the red rowan. It's Ben Vrackie, a quick up and back from Pitlochry in time for a nice cup of tea and some shortbread. Ben Chonzie rises green and yellow like a ripening avocado. To the south, beyond Ben Lawers, Loch Tay lies grey in its long hollow. Hidden within the green moorland are the ancient shielings (summer sheep pastures), bright streams and little waterfalls, and woodlands of oak and of birch.

TREES, PLEASE!

Golden saxifrage and thyme, Loch Lyon

In this bleakest of peat, brown heather and grey stones, the civilised green of the lowlands reaches in along the rivers. Saxifrage and thyme are bright along the banks of Glen Tilt. The River Garry runs brown in autumn spate while the trees overhead are still late summer green. Glen Lyon, Scotland's longest, is where the river winds below oaks and birches, with primroses dangling above the water. And the silvery Tay runs big and surprising at the back of Aberfeldy, even bigger by the time it's got down to Dunkeld.

At the eastern side of the Highlands, these eastern Grampians have slightly more sunshine and a bit

less rain. So its valleys can be pleasingly bog-free. Green trackways from Blair Atholl, and made paths around Pitlochry or the Black Wood of Rannoch, offer low-level walking as good as any in the Highlands.

And on stormy mornings, it's time to take advantage of Perthshire's other promotional slogan: this is 'Big Tree Country'. The Douglas fir at Dunkeld's Hermitage could be Britain's tallest tree and is named after Mr Douglas from Scone, in Perthshire – although it takes its Latin name (*Pseudotsuga menziesii*) from Mr Archibald Menzies of Weem, also in Perthshire.

The Birnam Oak could have been there as a young twig when Shakespeare wrote of Birnam Wood's coming to Dunsinane to conquer Macbeth. Who hasn't heard of the Birks of Aberfeldy? And the yew at

Birnam Oak, Dunkeld (Route 35)

'REAL' PERTHSHIRE

Beinn Dorain over Auch (Routes 28, 29)

Perthshire was abolished in 1975. The name is now applied to the Perth & Kinross Council area: its tourist board is called VisitPerthshire and the council's website is www.perthshire.org. When Perthshire did exist, it extended west to include Ben Lui and Ben More at Crianlarich.

I've used 'real Perthshire' as a rough definition for this book. It lets me include the whole of the Ben Dorain group in the west, even though its main approaches are from Bridge of Orchy in former Argyll. Ben Alder is also included; the county boundary runs past Benalder Cottage, and it's a fine hill with two genuine scrambling ridges and approaches from Perthshire's Loch Rannoch.

Perthshire, however defined, is a big place; it contains one in seven of Scotland's Munros. The Lowland part of the county is represented in this book by a single route in Perth itself. Lowland Perthshire, with some fine walking in the Ochils, is covered in *Walking in the Ochils, Campsie Fells and Lomond Hills* by Patrick Baker, also published by Cicerone Press. That part of the far southwest is included in the Loch Lomond and The Trossachs National Park, and by my own Cicerone guide to it.

I've also excluded the far northeast of the county at the back of Blairgowrie. Strathardle and Glen Shee drain into the Isla not the Tay, and feel to me like Angus Glens (and eight more Munros would have meant cutting down on the lower hills, riversides and back valleys).

Fortingall is the oldest living being in Europe: according to legend, Pontius Pilate played in its shade as a child. (This is unlikely, as his mother would have worried about the poisonous berries; and anyway, Pontius Pilate wasn't Scottish.)

High striding hill ridges; quiet valleys floored with grass rather than harsh heather; big trees and even bigger rivers: these are the pleasures of Rannoch, Atholl and the south-eastern Grampians.

WHEN TO GO

April is still winter on the summits, but low-level routes offer good walking then and in May. The leaves are breaking and birds are at their noisiest.

Low-level routes are also excellent in October as the birch leaves turn gold.

May and June are enjoyable at all altitudes. July and August can be hot and humid, with less rewarding views. East Highland midges come in slightly smaller hordes than in the west but are getting worse with global warming. The trick is to keep moving, and when you stop, stop high.

Midges hang on until the first frost, normally some time in September. October brings clear air and lovely autumn colours. In between times there'll be gales. Over much of this area, from mid August (sometimes July) to 21 October, responsible access to the hills includes avoiding disturbance to deer stalking (see Appendix B).

Creag an Tulabhain of Meall Ghaordaidh from Stronuich bridge (Route 23)

Winter is a time of short days and foul weather. Snow can lie on the high tops from December to April. Well-equipped walkers skilled in navigation and with ice axe love the winter most of all, for the alpine-style ascents of Meall nan Tarmachan and the 100km views through the winter-chilled air.

SAFETY IN THE MOUNTAINS

Safety and navigation in the mountains are best learnt from companions, experience, and perhaps a paid instructor; such instruction is outside the scope of this book. For those experienced in hills further south, such as Snowdonia or the Lake District, these hills are noticeably larger and can be a lot more remote.

The international mountain distress signal is some sign (shout, whistle, torch flash or other) repeated six times over a minute, followed by a minute's silence. The reply is a sign repeated three times over a minute, followed by a minute's silence. To signal for help from a helicopter, raise both arms above the head and then drop them down sideways, repeatedly. If you're not in trouble, don't shout or whistle on the hills, and don't wave to passing helicopters.

To call out the rescue, phone 999 from a landline. From a mobile, phone either 999 or the international emergency number 112: these will connect you via any available network. Reception is good on most summits and ridges and on hillsides that have line of sight to the A9 or Aberfeldy. Sometimes a text message can get through when a voice call to the rescue service can't: pre-register your phone at www.emergencysms.org.uk.

Given the unreliable phone coverage, it is wise to leave word of your proposed route with some responsible person (and, of course, tell that person when you've safely returned). Youth hostels have specific forms for this, as do many independent hostels and B&Bs.

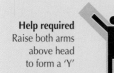

Help required
Raise both arms above head to form a 'Y'

Help not required
Raise one arm above head and extend the other downward, to form the diagonal of an 'N'

AVALANCHE DANGER

The Scottish Avalanche Information Service's website www.sais.gov.uk doesn't cover these less-frequented hills – nearest is Southern Cairngorms. Greatest avalanche danger arises after recent heavy snowfall, on moderately steep slopes facing away from the wind. After snowfall from the west, the east face of Heasgarnich could be at risk; after snowfall from the southeast, you may want to avoid the northern spur of Meall Ghaordaidh.

Being lost or tired is not sufficient reason for calling the rescue service, and neither, in normal summer weather, is being benighted. However, team members I've talked to say not to be too shy about calling them: they greatly prefer bringing down bodies that are still alive…

There is no charge for mountain rescue in Scotland – teams are voluntary, financed by donations from the public, with a grant from the Scottish Government. You can make donations at youth hostels, TICs and many pubs.

MAPS

Some people enjoy exploring in mountains that are badly mapped or not mapped at all. They should stay away from the Scottish Highlands, as they have been excellently mapped – three times over. The mapping in this book for the shorter and lower routes is from the Ordnance Survey's Landranger series at 1:50,000. For these low walks this book's mapping may be all you need. For mountain walks, however, it's advisable to have a larger map that shows escape routes and the other glen you end up in when you come down the wrong side of the hill. This guide shows mountain routes on 1:100,000 scale maps not intended for use on the hill.

Harvey's excellent British Mountain Map: Schiehallion at 1:40,000 scale covers about half this book, south of Lochs Tummel and Rannoch, and west of Aberfeldy – so Schiehallion is in the top right corner. The map is beautifully clear and legible, marks paths where they actually exist on the ground, and does not disintegrate when damp. Harvey also cover Ben Lawers in their 1:25,000 Superwalker format.

The 1:50,000 Landranger mapping, as used in this book, covers this area on sheets 42 (Glen Garry & Loch Rannoch), 43 (Braemar & Blair Atholl), 50 (Glen Orchy & Loch Etive), 51 (Loch Tay & Glen Donart), 52 (Pitlochry & Crieff), 57 (Stirling & The Trossachs) and 58 (Perth & Alloa).

The Harvey maps mark fences and walls on the open hill but not on the lower ground; Landranger doesn't mark them at all. So if you're planning

From Farragon Hill summit to Beinn a' Ghlo (Route 38)

complicated valley walks, you'll prefer the OS Explorer maps, also at 1:25,000 scale. They are bulkier and less robust than the Harvey ones, and the contour lines are less legible. But if Harvey hadn't done it better, they'd be excellent maps. Sheets 368 (Crieff, Comrie & Glen Artney), 369 (Perth & Kinross, one walk), 378 (Ben Lawers & Glen Lyon), 379 (Dunkeld, Aberfeldy & Glen Almond), 385 (Rannoch Moor & Ben Alder), 386 (Pitlochry & Loch Tummel) and 394 (Atholl) cover the ground.

COMPASS AND GPS

A compass is a very useful aid in mist, even if your skills only extend to 'northwest, southeast' rather than precision bearings. Magnetic deviation in the 2020s is close to zero and can usually be ignored; check your map for future years. GPS receivers should be set to the British National Grid (known variously as British Grid, Ord Srvy GB, BNG, or OSGB GRB36). Smartphones

have limited battery life and squinty little map extracts and aren't really waterproof; mountain rescue teams are getting fed up with people relying on them for going up hills.

USING THIS GUIDE

Basic planning information is provided at the start of each route and in the summary table in Appendix A. See the map key page for an explanation of the walk-type icons. The difficulty and timing squares are explained in the box below. Times are based on 1 hour for 4 horizontal kilometres or for 500m of height gained, with extra time where the ground is particularly steep or rough. They'll be about right, including brief snack stops, for a moderately paced party. Where a bus or train can be used to link the two ends of a linear route, this is also noted. Other public transport information is given in Appendix C.

Yellow boxes under the route information boxes make suggestions for extensions, short-cuts and route combinations elaborated on in the route description which follows if necessary.

In old numbers, 600ft was a vertical distance, while 200yd was horizontal. I've used a similar convention, so that 600m is an altitude or height gain, while 600 metres (with 'etres') is along the ground. 'Track' (rather than 'path') is used for a way wide enough for a tractor or Landrover.

Finally, the 'standard route' up a hill is the convenient and well-trodden one featured in guidebooks like Steve Kew's *Walking the Munros* (Vol 1). It's usually the shortest, and because it's so well used, also the easiest. Sometimes it is also the best and most interesting. But to avoid 90 per cent of other hillgoers, simply stay off the standard route.

Perthshire's lumpy schist is rich in brown slime and rare alpine plantlife, poor in climbing possibilities. There are only two scrambling routes in this book – and being on Ben Alder, they're not even in Perthshire. Craig a Barns at Dunkeld is the area's most notable climbing crag. It dries quickly but can be covered in pine needles; its schist is tricky even when clean and dry.

When it comes to climbs and scrambles, the eastern Grampians may not compare with other parts of the Highlands. But when it comes to walks, here are big Ben Lawers and Crieff's little Knock; Rannoch Moor and the banks of the Tay. For green mountains, for broad snowy ridges, for woodland paths, wide riverbanks, and long-striding tracks across the empty moors – Perthshire is the place.

Rannoch Station (Route 59)

LENGTH OF WALK
The length estimates are on a scale of 1 to 5:

■□□□□   up to 4 hours

■■□□□   up to 6 hours

■■■□□   up to 8 hours

■■■■□   up to 10 hours

■■■■■   over 10 hours

DIFFICULTY OF WALK
The difficulty estimates are on a rough scale of 1 to 5:

■□□□□   Clear smooth paths, with no steep sections

■■□□□   Small rough paths, some steep ground

■■■□□   Short steep climbs or long gentle ones; hill paths, or pathless ground with clear ridge lines; most of the 'standard routes' on the Munros

■■■■□   Pathless ground on grass rather than heather, navigation at the level of 'northwest, southeast'; most 'non-standard' routes on Munros

■■■■■   Featureless plateau requiring compass bearings in mist; heather tramping; remote high ground; long steep rough ascents and descents; rocky ground and scrambling

Warning

Mountain walking can be a dangerous activity carrying a risk of personal injury or death. It should be undertaken only by those with a full understanding of the risks and with the training and experience to evaluate them. While every care and effort has been taken in the preparation of this guide, the user should be aware that conditions can be highly variable and can change quickly, materially affecting the seriousness of a mountain walk. Therefore, except for any liability which cannot be excluded by law, neither Cicerone nor the author accept liability for damage of any nature (including damage to property, personal injury or death) arising directly or indirectly from the information in this book.

To call out the Mountain Rescue, ring 999 or the international emergency number 112: this will connect you via any available network. Once connected to the emergency operator, ask for the police.

PART ONE
COMRIE AND CRIEFF

Stuc na Cabaig, on the west ridge of Beinn Dearg (Route 2)

The Scots word 'couthie' means civilised, pleasant and friendly. It's altogether applicable to Crieff and Comrie, the last villages of the Lowlands along the Highland line. Well-laid, smooth-surfaced village paths venture boldly into the harsh heather, re-emerging along a wide river back to a Georgian main street. The wonders of Crieff include the monumental Hydro hotel, from the time when an exciting holiday consisted of drinking nasty-tasting healthy water. Comrie, meanwhile, boasts a white-painted church, and an encampment of historic Nissen huts, some of them listed for conservation.

But above the tea shops and hotels loom the first Munros, the schisty crags, and the heather.

1 Meall na Fearna to Ben Vorlich

Length

Difficulty

Start/finish	Glenartney church car park (NN 711 161)
Distance	26km/16½ miles
Ascent	1300m/4400ft
Approx time	9hr
Max altitude	Ben Vorlich 985m
Terrain	Grassy slopes, steep onto Ben Vorlich; some peat hags on Carn Labhruinn; small riverside paths and tracks

Omitting Ben Vorlich gives a walk of 23.5km and 900m ascent (15 miles/3000ft) – about 7½hr. Ben Vorlich can also be bagged on its own, by a long walk in up Gleann an Dubh Choirein: similar distance and ascent.

Meall na Fearna is a typical Perthshire Corbett. Once the peat hags are passed, it's a high grassy ramble. Ben Vorlich then rises steep-sided and rather rocky, an intimidating hill from this angle. In this particular case, the Munro is indeed much more than the Corbett. You plunge into the steepness of the eastern slope, avoid almost all of the trodden highway rising from Loch Earn, and earn yourself a delightful grassy ridgeline for the descent.

The riverside path from Dubh Choirein is an ancient right of way. Today just enough people walk it to keep it clear and followable for the 6km from the hill base back to Glen Artney.

See map for Route 2 for the route start. Start along the road up-valley, to cross its bridge over Allt an Dubh Choirein. Keep ahead to a white gate with a walkers' gate alongside.

Keep ahead (northwest) on the track past farm buildings. Pass below a plantation (which conceals Glenartney Lodge). In another 500 metres pass below a smaller and

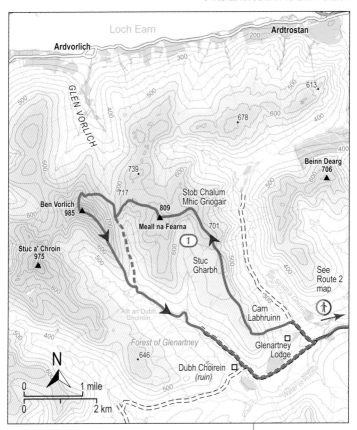

newer plantation. Now turn off left up rough grassland.
The slope steepens to the plateau of Carn Labhruinn.

Turn northwest on grass and peat hags, across **Carn Labhruinn** and the wide col behind it. Best is to keep along the tops of the east-falling steep slopes. **Stuc Gharbh** is pleasant grassy going, and this continues along the **701m** ridge and **Stob Chalum Mhic Griogair**. From the northern and main top, drop south to cross a peaty

Ben Vorlich from across Loch Earn

col at its highest point, then southwest up to the grassy top of **Meall na Fearna**.

Drop steeply north, swinging northwest as the slope eases, then bending west to the **717m** top. Now posts of an old fence lead down a spur, to the highest point of Bealach Gliogarsnaich.

To omit Ben Vorlich
Turn left and follow the stream south down out of the pass and along its wide valley. There's no path; the best going is beside the stream. You reach the valley foot and rejoin the main route at the ruin of Dubh Choirein house.

The **main route** follows the path north through the col for 500 metres, with a stream forming alongside. As Glen Vorlich opens out below, slant out to the left – leaving the path too early will land you on steep uncomfortable slopes. Head up west towards the northeast-facing hollow below the summit of Ben Vorlich. Reach the small floor of this hollow at about 700m level.

Here you have two options. One is to take a deer path which slants out to the right, passing up a grassy ramp between two small outcrops, and from the top of the ramp, turn left up the spurline Sgiath nam Tarmachan. The other is just to continue straight up the hollow. Another deer path slants out right, higher up, or you can just keep up the steepening slope, to right of stones and scree, to arrive suddenly at the path on Sgiath nam Tarmachan.

On turning left up Sgiath nam Tarmachan from either route, you soon meet the broad Munro-baggers' path up from Loch Earn. Follow it up to the white trig point at **Ben Vorlich** summit.

A delightful 100 metres of ridge lead to the east summit, just 1m lower. Continue down the well-defined southeast ridge, with a small path and old fence posts. At its foot the ridge levels, with a peat hag. Drop left for slightly easier going alongside the stream Allt a' Bhealaich Gliogarsnaiche, following it down to the ruined **Dubh Choirein** house. ▶

The route omitting Ben Vorlich rejoins here.

Remains of a footbridge start the path down **Allt an Dubh Choirein**. This path is mostly still there, and follows the left bank of the small river. After 1.2km the river has a small, tree-lined gorge. Just after this the main path heads out left, away from the river, to a bridge over a sidestream Allt na Fearna, then follows it back to the main river. In another 400 metres you pass a footbridge. Around 600 metres after that, the riverside path joins a grassy track, through a gate below a new plantation.

Ben Vorlich summit, from the east top

The track gives comfortable walking, after 1km joining a somewhat more used one that arrives over a bridge from the right. The track passes over the spur of Monadh Odhar, then drops to the farm passed on the outward walk.

If it's got dark, you can just walk back along the road.

Head through the white gate and down the driveway track. Once across the river bridge, take a gate on the left. ◄ A fishermen's path runs through riverside meadows; where it passes under powerlines it is marked with yellow noticeboards about not flourishing one's rod overhead.

As the bank steepens, the path is just above the river. Pass along more level meadows, then keep above another steep banking above the river. Just beyond this, a footbridge over a ditch leads to a gate into the church car park.

2 Beinn Dearg

Length

Difficulty

Start/finish	Glenartney church car park (NN 711 161)
Distance	13.5km/8½ miles
Ascent	750m/2500ft
Approx time	5hr
Max altitude	Beinn Dearg 706m
Terrain	Pathless grassy ridge; approach and final descent on rough tussocky grassland

Switzerland has its *röstigrabe*, east of which one eats pan-fried potatoes and speaks German. Perthshire has its heatherline, east of which one struggles in knee-scratching shrubbery and speaks Anglo-Saxon swearwords. The green ridge of Beinn Dearg is all the more enjoyable when you look across Allt Glas to the brown twigs of Ben Halton on the other side of the divide.

The green ridgeline fringed with its small crags is a delight, but the approach is across damp moorland. And the last half-kilometre of the descent shows that grass too can induce swear words, when you meet it thigh-high in July or August.

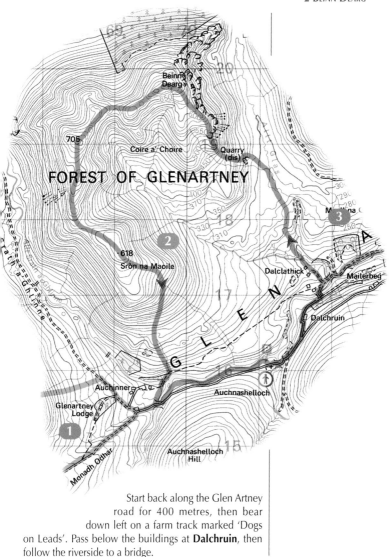

Start back along the Glen Artney
road for 400 metres, then bear
down left on a farm track marked 'Dogs
on Leads'. Pass below the buildings at **Dalchruin**, then
follow the riverside to a bridge.

Beinn Dearg from Glen Artney

The Stream of the Corrie of the Corrie; the next valley west is Srath a' Ghlinne, the Valley of the Glen.

Cross over and follow the track uphill. Where it bends left, turn off right, but at once turn up left on a smaller track. After 200 metres, as it bends left towards the hut **Dalclathick**, keep ahead, through rough pastureland. Pass right of two ruins to a gateway above the stream junction of Allt Coire a' Choire. ◄

A faint green track descends to ford the stream, then bends to right of a steep rise onto moorland. Ahead, it passes between two isolated iron gateposts. Keep following it north, as it provides a slightly more comfortable line. At a tall fence, a gate 50 metres to the left gives an easier place to wriggle between the wires.

The old track rises briefly northwest, then turns north again to **Allt Glas**. Keep to left of the stream, to the tailings of a slate **quarry**. Go up to right of this, onto the southeastern spurline of Beinn Dearg. Keep to the fairly sharp and mildly rocky crest, close to drops on the right, for an enjoyable ascent to **Beinn Dearg**. The northernmost knoll has the small cairn.

The knolly ridgeline continues around the head of a corrie overlooking Glen Artney. After an unnamed second summit (**705m**, only 1m lower than the main top) the ridge descends south for a col to a wide, grassy top at **618m** (**Sron na Maoile**). Cross this, avoiding one or two peat hags. From its end, descend southeast, to left of dense peat hags. Once below them, work downhill and to the right, to descend southwards towards Glen Artney. ▶

Aim for the tree-lined Water of Ruchill opposite, above Auchinner.

The slope levels at moraines at 300m level, and becomes heavy with rushes, tall grass and bracken. Descend to a track above the river, and turn right to a high gate with a stalking notice on the back. The track crosses a field to a bridge over **Allt Srath a' Ghlinne**. Head upstream to right of Water of Ruchill, to a stile onto the driveway below **Auchinner**.

Cross the bridge onto the start of the public road down the glen. It leads to the car park; or else, immediately after the bridge, turn left through a gate. This is the start of a fishermen's path through meadows by the river (see Route 1) that can be followed back to the car park.

3 Water of Ruchill

Start/finish	The Linn car park, Water of Ruchill near Comrie (NN 763 200)
Distance	14km/9 miles
Ascent	350m/1100ft
Approx time	4hr
Max altitude	Slopes of Ben Halton 320m
Terrain	Tracks, and a grassy meadow

Length
■ ☐ ☐ ☐ ☐

Difficulty
■ ■ ☐ ☐ ☐

A walk of parkland, moorland, and woods and fields above Glen Artney. There's a rough pasture to descend between the two tracks, and a small swamp in Ruchillside Wood. It's worth walking around this as feet will stay dry on the rest of the route.

Start back down the tarmac lane towards Comrie for 1.2km, first beside **Water of Ruchill** then between fields.

27

Oakwoods on the right-of-way track above Glen Artney

At a right bend, turn back sharp left along a gravel driveway, signed to **Aberuchill**.

Before the grand house turn left through a white gate. The track runs uphill, slanting across a field, then up again through woods and past **Tomanour** onto open hill. ◄ Follow the main track uphill through a gate, usually locked – climb it at the hinge end.

Here a track turns off right; follow it for 100 metres to a sculptural grouse butt imitating the artist Andy Goldsworthy.

The track runs gently uphill around the base of Ben Halton. After 2km it passes through another gate, now above Glen Artney and below **Dun Dubh**. A deer fence is just above. After 400 metres, just before a small quarry on the right, the wall below the track has a break where it becomes a railed fence. This is a convenient place to cross it. ▸

Head south down rough pasture. When you see **Dalclathick** hut below, head directly towards it. However, the Allt Glas prevents you from reaching it. With a streamside plantation on your right, bear left to fenced sheep handling pens. From their back left corner, a green track runs down to a smooth gravel track at the valley floor.

If you reach a gate through the high deer fence, you've gone too far.

Follow the track left, down-valley, gradually rising through woods. After 2km, it bends uphill towards **Blairmore**, but here fork right, slightly downhill, on a green track. After a gate it crosses an open field into a wood. Here it dips to cross a stream, then slants slightly uphill, becoming swampy and invisible under rushes. Recapture it beyond the swamp, where it emerges from the wood at a gate.

The track is clearer, and becomes a firm stony one. It slants gently down the valley side to **Dalrannoch** farm. Here it becomes a tarmac driveway, descending to pass The Linn car park.

4 Comrie: Deil's Caldron

Length

■ □ □ □ □

Difficulty

■ □ □ □ □

Start/finish	Field of Refuge car park, at south end of Comrie's bridge over Water of Ruchill (NN 773 218, or other car parks in Comrie)
Distance	6km/3½ miles
Ascent	250m/800ft
Approx time	2hr
Max altitude	Lord Melville's Monument 256m
Terrain	Well-used paths

Various Perthshire villages have marked and maintained paths offering gentle walks in beautiful surroundings. This is one of the best, with wooden walkways above the Deil's Caldron waterfall, and a viewpoint monument to a dodgy politician. There's also a healing spring, a quiet riverbank, and the pretty village itself.

Start across the river, turning left on the main street past the white church (now community centre). The street bends right, past another car park (School Lane). At the next bend, keep ahead into Monument Road, and in 100 metres turn right at a footpath signpost for Deil's Caldron.

The wide earth path runs around the foot of woods, then above River Lednock. Look out for a side path down right to Little Caldron, rejoining the main path above. As the wood steepens, the path runs just below the Glen Lednock road, then drops again along a wooden walkway. Turn down right to a viewing balcony above the **Deil's Caldron waterfall**.

Return up wooden steps, forking right to regain the main path. It runs up to the Glen Lednock road. Turn right alongside the road, then left at a signpost onto a steep earth path through a plantation. It zigzags through pleasanter woods above, then contours left, to level ground.

Here note a path arriving from the right, but keep ahead,

The path to the Deil's Caldron.

with a footpath sign. The path zigzags up the final rise to
Lord Melville's Monument.

> **Lord Melville** was a minister in Pitt the Younger's
> government of 1791, where his skilled political fix-
> ing delayed for 15 years the abolition of the slave
> trade. As war minister at the start of the Napoleonic
> Wars, he mismanaged the Flanders Campaign
> and bungled the siege of Dunkirk. In 1806 he was
> impeached in the House of Lords for embezzling
> public funds, but acquitted as negligent rather than
> actually criminal. An even bigger monument to him
> stands in St Andrews Square, Edinburgh.

Its waters are good
against the 'hoast' or
whooping cough, and
according to local
legend also for all
other difficulties from
poor performance
in school to dreary
Sunday sermons.

Return down the first zigzags, then bear left on the
path (previously noted) running northwest along the ridge
top under tall trees. It emerges at a smoothly bulldozed
track (the Maam Road). Turn down right, signposted
'Monument Road'.

The track slants left to a bend below a small crag.
Here keep ahead for a few steps to the 'Kinkhoast Well',
a small spring equipped with a pewter mug. ◀ Continue
down the track until it bends back left. Here take a
bracken path downhill, to a stile onto the Glen Lednock
road. Head right for a few steps, then left at a signpost
for Laggan Wood. The wide earth path leads to the riverside at Shaky Bridge. ◀ The path turns downstream, then
slants up left with a few wooden steps to the top corner
of **Laggan Wood**. Here it's joined by a right-of-way path
from the left. Follow the clear path ahead, with the plantation becoming an attractive oakwood.

A 'shoogle on the
brig' ('a shaking on
the bridge') was cure
for any indispositions
not covered by the
Kinkhoast Well. (Alas,
since rebuilding by
the Royal Engineers,
the bridge is as firm
as the Millennium
Footbridge in
London.)

After 800 metres, at a waymark post, take a side
path to the right. It passes a viewpoint on the left (the
view currently obstructed by trees), then descends steep
wooden steps towards the river. The path runs to the left,
to a bend in a smooth, gravelled all-abilities path (the
Lednock Millennium Footpath). Fork down right, soon
zigzagging down to picnic tables at the riverside. The
path continues downstream, to emerge near a car park
at the edge of **Comrie**.

Turn right, away from the car park, onto a footbridge over the river. In another 150 metres, turn left down Nurses Lane to Comrie's main street. Cross to the right into Manse Lane, down to the riverside. Turn right, to pass under Dalginross Bridge, then turn up onto the roadway above.

Cross Water of Ruchill to the car park.

5 Glen Tarken tracks

Start/finish	St Fillans car park (NN 687 246)
Distance	14km/8½ miles
Ascent	450m/1400ft
Approx time	4hr
Max altitude	Entering Glen Tarken 450m
Terrain	Tracks and a small path

Length
▓ ▓ ☐ ☐ ☐

Difficulty
▓ ☐ ☐ ☐ ☐

A short-cut track bypasses the ramble up Glen Tarken for a walk of 9.5km and 350m ascent (6 miles/1200ft) – about 3hr.

Parking is at the two pull-offs just opposite the public toilets at the west end of St Fillans. This is just below St Fillans' small hydroelectric power plant, where its tailrace flows out into Loch Earn. The walk traces the water supply up into Glen Tarken overhead. With oakwoods at start and end, and grassy trackways through the moorland above, it's a route that doesn't go anywhere in particular but has a pleasant time along the way.

Between the two pull-offs, start across the A85 up steps onto a private road at the small St Fillans Power Station (this road starts alongside the Four Seasons Hotel).

Turn left for 150 metres, then back right at a waymark post up a track. It crosses over a disused railway, then zigs back left and slants up steeply through woods. Ignore

Loch Earn from Glen Tarken foot

Roughly 100 metres beyond the gate onto open hill, the OS Explorer map marks a cup-marked rock to left of the track, but the marks aren't very visible.

two side-tracks on the right, before the gate at the top of the trees. ◀

The track slants uphill towards rocky moorland. At a junction, take the main track back up right. It soon zigs back left, through a small pass at 450m. Then it slants gently downhill into **Glen Tarken**. After 1km, a side-track turns down left: this is the short-cut route.

Short cut via Glentarken Burn

The short-cut track gives a walk of about 3hr, but its ford over Glentarken Burn could be impassable in spate.

From the junction above Glen Tarken, the side-track descends to pass below a hydro-scheme tunnel end, then goes through a gate. Now rather fainter, it contours left (south) across the top of a spoil heap (presumably from the water tunnel), then turns downhill to left of a stream. It fords the Glentarken Burn, then rises to join the main valley track beyond.

The **main track** contours along the valley side, passing some water intakes. After 3km it bends across the valley floor, before heading down-valley under the steep **Creag Dhubh**, then gently up the valley side. Where the main track turns sharply back right, take the smaller track ahead, slanting down towards Glentarken Burn.

After 1.6km, the short-cut track rejoins from the left. Now the track steepens downhill at the valley foot. It goes through a gate beside a sheep-dip complex, with Loch Earn visible below. In another 400 metres a cottage is visible across the stream. Immediately above a small pointy knoll, take a green track on the left. It crosses the stream by a ramshackle bridge, then contours out to the cottage. This building rejoices in views along Loch Earn, no road access, and the name of Jerusalem (NN 669 253).

The continuing path is invisible to start with. Contour forward (just south of east) through rushes, to pass through a fence by a gap with

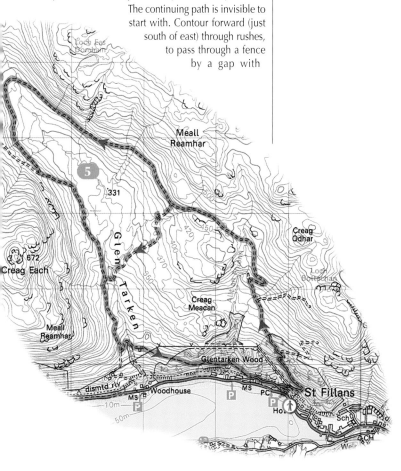

an old iron gate. Keep contouring, now through bracken, to a tall kissing-gate into a former plantation, now felled. The path is now visible, but narrow and little trodden. It continues at the same level to the start of the fine oaks of **Glentarken Wood**.

Now the path becomes a disused vehicle track, slanting gently downhill. Cross the torn-up path of tracked vehicles, a moment of World War I terrain, to continue on the previous line on a clear path.

The path crosses **Allt an Fhionn** by a footbridge, then descends with an old fence on its right. At a fork, the right branch is the disused railbed, but take the left to a bridge under the railway. Keep left on a track that weaves among the legs of a viaduct, then contours below the railway. After the first houses of **St Fillans**, the track reaches the end of the private road at the start of the walk.

Keep ahead down to the power station, and turn right down the steps to the walk start.

6 Ben Chonzie and Auchnafree Hill

Length

Difficulty

Start/finish	Loch Turret dam (NN 822 264)
Distance	19km/12 miles
Ascent	1200m/3900ft
Approx time	7hr
Max altitude	Ben Chonzie 931m
Terrain	Tracks and paths, with 4km of rougher ground including a steep ascent from Moine Bheag

Getting to the start From the north edge of Crieff, take the lane past Glenturret Distillery and over Turret Burn; at once turn left in a very small lane with 10mph markers (speed limit obedience is assured by the very rugged surface).

Ben Chonzie is possibly the easiest Munro. It is, with more confidence, the easiest enjoyable Munro. Where other 'easy' Munros are a short but steepish up-and-down from a car park (Glas Maol, for example), Chonzie offers a stroll along a reservoir track, and a little path up authentic cliffy country. And the descent is a long, high ramble along a grassy plateau with a decayed fence to do your navigation.

The warm-up over Auchnafree Hill makes things only slightly more serious. After a rough slope to start, there's a grassy Landrover track that peeps into the hollow of the Blue Crags and pauses at King Kenneth's Cairn. Back in the ninth century Kenneth MacAlpin, had he been so inclined, could have lain in the long grass here and surveyed a large chunk of his newly united Scotland.

'Dowchty man he wes and stout,' King Kenneth, according to the 11th-century Chronicle of the Kings of Alba. So he'd have revelled in the tough little ascent onto Biorach a' Mheannain, the steep grass and the deer path weaving among the chunks of crag. It's a moment of adventure that makes all the more enjoyable the gentle ramble along Ben Chonzie plateau.

Start at **Loch Turret** dam car park, and take a tarmac path to the east end of the dam. A stile and gate lead out to a Landrover track. Turn right, down-valley, for about 50 metres, then turn left off the track.

The southwest cairn on Auchnafree Hill

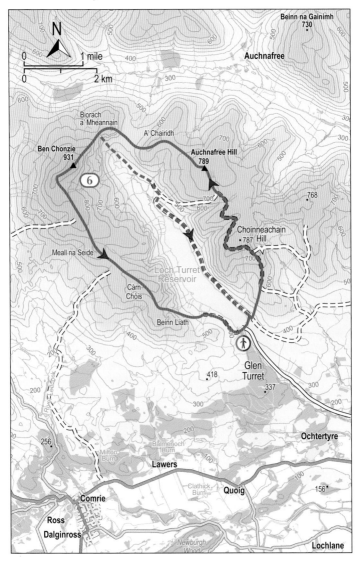

The steepish slope above the track has heather and bracken, but you start up firm grass. As the slope steepens, useful sheep paths wind up through the heather. Gain 200m of height to meet a grassy track. Turn left up this, soon ignoring a side-track down right. The main track runs above the rocky hollow Corrie Barvick, then bends left below King Kenneth's Cairn on **Choinneachain Hill**. ▶ A path leads up to the cairn on its stony base.

Rejoin the track, and follow it west for 500 metres to an even more imposing cairn above Loch Turret. The track now runs north across the top of the slope above the loch. It slants down to cross a stream, rises around a spur, then dips into a second stream hollow. After a first small stream, a peaty short-cut path lets you contour forward to rejoin the track. It now fords Gilbert's Burn (alongside remains of a bridge).

Turn up the stream's grassy banks, slightly west of north. In the peaty bog at the stream top, don't go as far as a decaying fence ahead, but turn up left (northwest) over short heather to the summit cairn of **Auchnafree Hill.** ▶ A more imposing cairn with views is 100 metres southwest.

It deserves to be the main hill hereabouts but is 2m lower than Auchnafree.

Those who say Corbetts are just as good as Munros should compare flat, featureless Auchnafree with craggy Chonzie ahead.

The route from Moine Bheag up the steep end of Biorach a' Mheannain

From the main summit head northwest over short heather, joining the decayed posts of the former fence. The fenceline has a very small path, down just to the left (west) of a peaty col, then up the slope of the grassy transverse hillock **A' Chairidh**. From its top descend grassy slopes northwest to confront the peaty col Moine Bheag and the steep nose of **Biorach a' Mheannain**. ◀

As an alternative to Biorach's steep nose, or in descent, less steep slopes are to the right, north.

This steep nose can be taken direct, zigzagging up grassy slopes between the small crags. Slant up left below the first crag, head up steep bilberry to left of it, then take a deer path across its top, across steep and slightly exposed ground. Head directly uphill (the top end of a shallow, rocky open gully is on your right). On reaching more open grass slopes, slant up right, on another deer path, to gentler slopes above another of the crags. Turn up left to the summit.

A cairn is poised on the edge of the southern drop towards Loch Turret. A path leads down from it, southwest. At the low point of the col, a worn path arrives from down left, the standard baggers' route from Loch Turret. ◀

This well-used path, and the track beyond, give a short cut back to Loch Turret dam.

Follow the path up the broad northeast flank, or keep up left of the path following old fence posts for views down Loch Turret. **Ben Chonzie** summit has a large shelter cairn.

Continue southwest, following the old fence to its corner, then turn southeast for some gentle ridgewalking. The path accompanies the old fence posts. About 2km from the fence corner the descent gets slightly steeper and peaty, before the small heathery knoll **Meall na Seide**. The path here is stony through heather, while the fence alters to less conspicuous metal posts.

The path and fence remnants cross a damp col, before rising to the mildly rocky top of **Carn Chois**. This has a trig point. Continue 300 metres to a cairn. Now descend south, close to the drops on the left, on a small grass path. A fence is crossing the ridge ahead. Before you get to it, the small path turns down left, to descend rather steeply into a grassy corrie.

The path goes through a gate in a lower fence (NN 799 271). Then it slants down to the right, crossing a small stream, to the start of a rough track above the reservoir. This track leads to the end of the dam, which you cross to regain the car park.

7 Crieff, its Knock, and River Earn

Start/finish	Car park at Turret Bridge, east side, marked MacRosty Park (NN 857 222)
Distance	13km/8 miles
Ascent	400m/1400ft
Approx time	4hr
Max altitude	Knock of Crieff 279m
Terrain	Paths and tracks, partly waymarked

Length
■ ■ □ □ □

Difficulty
■ □ □ □ □

The walk of Knock Hill alone is 7.5km with 250m ascent (4½ miles/900ft) – about 2½hr. For shorter Knock Hill walks start at the Knock End car park (NN 864 225).

The walk of Laggan Hill and River Earn is 6.5km with 100m ascent (4 miles/300ft) – about 2hr.

Crieff: the noise of heavy traffic, dangerous with its young ruffians and hoodies, stinking and squalid. That's in the 17th century, when the traffic was cattle from the whole of the Highlands, the 'hoodies' actually wore the blue bonnets of the Gaelic drovers, and the streets were ankle deep in dung. Today, on the other hand, it's a gently elegant country town. The traditional welcome to mountain men continues, with a fine set of eating places (including a surprising Islamic takeaway).

For a first view of the hills of the Highlands, or for sheltered exercise on a foul stormy day, the town has marked walks of woodland, field and river. If you only have a few moments to spare, spend them on the 1km and 77m ascent to the Knock of Crieff – Marilyn-baggers note that the true summit is in a gloomy plantation 1km further along the ridge. The route described here links five of the town walks, two small hills, a fine riverside, and alcoholic intoxication at the Glenturret Distillery.

Crieff from Laggan Hill

Start behind the car park, to head north (upstream) on the inland edge of the park, then turn right up a long series of steps. You pass a 'caleidogira', a landscape-fracturing kaleidoscope. Turn right along the park top for 200 metres, passing the Tuckie Café hut, to exit onto the road above.

Turn right for 50 metres and then back left, up Craigard Road. At its top keep ahead into unsurfaced Ancaster Road. Before reaching the **Crieff Hydro**, turn left up an earth path, to a kissing-gate signposted for The Knock. Continue up the path to another gate into a housing estate. Turn left (waymark arrow 'The Hosh Walk') to a road above. The small Knock End car park (my unofficial name) is just to your right.

> 'Hydro' comes from **hydropathic**, a late 18th-century form of complementary medicine involving drinking nasty water. Today the hotel offers a rich variety of active fun from archery to Zumba (which is leaping up and down to Latin rhythms), also afternoon teas.

Somewhere hereabouts is the Cradle Stone, a dolerite erratic on the conglomerate of the hill.

Cross the road to a signpost 'Knock Summit'. Take the wide path uphill. ◀ The path reaches a viewpoint table surrounded by benches at the 244m 'summit'.

42

Continue on a wide path past the viewpointer, northeast as before, descending to a crossing path. Keep ahead, to pass through a stile into replanted brushwood. A path leads across it to a similar stile. A rough path continues uphill, into a gloomy plantation, where some conglomerate bedrock is exposed. The path passes a sprawly little cairn at the true summit of **Knock Hill**, then

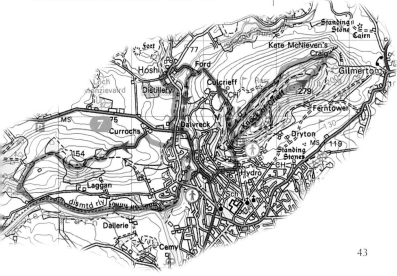

43

The crag is conglomerate (puddingstone) of the Old Red Sandstone, which makes the Knock a hill of the northernmost edge of the Scottish Lowlands. Look out for buzzards here.

descends. Bear left on an earth track to the edge of trees, where you meet a wide, smooth timber track.

Turn right on this, between felled areas. The track descends to a sharp bend down right. Here turn left into a wide fenced path, to a deer fence at the edge of the brushwood. Pass through a high kissing-gate, and turn right to the top of **Kate McNieven's Craig**. ◄

Return to the kissing-gate but don't go through it. Turn right along the outside of the deer fence, heading back west, with views across Shaggie Burn to Monzie Castle and the Highlands. The path descends alongside the forest edge. After 800 metres, the path passes through a kissing-gate into the woodland. In a few metres, fork right on the lower path close to the woodland foot, soon with Crieff Hydro's golf course below.

If you keep on ahead above the car park onto the tarmac lane, the Knock End car park is reached in another few hundred metres. (The circuit from that car park is about 2hr.)

After 800 metres the path rises a little, to join a wider path above. Keep ahead down this, to pass above a car park overlooking the golf course. This car park has a viewpoint indicator in it. ◄

Turn down through the car park to steps marked 'Celebration Woodland'. A fenced path leads down into a field assigned to woodland. Go down through a gate onto the golf course, and turn left to a tarmac lane. Turn right down this, past various outdoor Experiences and Centres of the Crieff Hydro.

Just past the golf clubhouse, as the lane bends left, keep ahead into a dirt track signposted for **Glenturret Distillery** (aka the Famous Grouse Experience). It leads down into woodland, to a three-way signpost.

'Knock Only' option
Turn left at this signpost, marked 'Comrie Road'. The broad earth path soon reaches River Turret. This is 'Lovers' Walk', and romantic even for booted hillwalkers, downstream in riverside woods. On reaching A85 (Comrie Road) cross and turn left, to a signpost into MacRosty Park marked 'Turret Bridge'. Follow this path above River Turret, then ahead through the riverside park to the walk start.

For the **full-length walk**, follow the main track down to
the right, marked 'Hoff', to its **ford** of Shaggie Burn –
there's a footbridge alongside. The track leads out to the
Monzie lane.

Turn down left, to cross Shaggie Burn on the road
bridge, with **Glenturret Distillery** just ahead. At once
turn right, signposted for Comrie Road, through old
iron gates marked 'Strictly No Dogs'. The track runs up
under trees. In open field, take a kissing-gate on the left
marked with a blue waymark as the Currochs Path. Pass
left around the field edge, along the top of wooded banking above the distillery and the Glenturret lane. At the
next field, take a kissing-gate to pass along the field-edge
fence, then down under trees to a track. Turn left down
this to join the very foot of the Glenturret lane.

Turn right across the A85 into Turretbank Road. After
300 metres, just before a street on the right, a grassy path
is signposted for Laggan Hill. The shorter Laggan Hill and
Earn walk joins at this point.

Laggan Hill and Earn option
From MacRosty Park car park cross the river on a footbridge just upstream from the road bridge. (This footbridge has wooden parapets, and circular holes as if
gnawed by a river serpent.)

Turn right on earth path for 200 metres upstream;
then fork left up a steep earth path to a street (Turretbank
Road) just above. Turn right on pavement, to pass the end
of Turretbank Drive, continue for 300 metres, and find
Turretbank Drive arriving again from the left. Immediately
beyond this junction, a footpath signpost points left for
Laggan Hill.

Whichever way you arrived here, you now take the
signed path that runs west to a gate into open field. A
faint path heads up west to the field top hedge. Turn right
along this, northwest. Before **Currochs** farm, take a gate
on the left onto a track, follow this down briefly towards
the farm, then turn left up a green track.

River Earn from Lady Mary's Walk

Left at this point is a shorter return to Crieff.

This runs up southwest, partly overgrown, then into a hilltop wood. Here it bends down left to join a wider earth track at a signpost. ◄ Turn right, signed for Laggan Hill.

The track runs through the woods of **Laggan Hill**, then descends bending gradually left with a wall to its right. After a brief rise, take a kissing-gate on the left signposted for Laggan Road. This path winds downhill, with views to Torlum Hill, to meet a wide earth track. Turn right for 50 metres, then left on a wide path signposted for Crieff by Lady Mary's Walk.

The path soon reaches **River Earn** and turns downstream. After 1.5km, at a signpost, the track bends up left away from the river, but fork right on a small riverside path. This soon bends left, to run upstream to left of Turret Burn. It emerges at the road bridge to MacRosty Park.

8 Glen Almond and the Lochan Slot

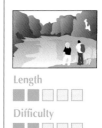

Start/finish	Sma' Glen: car parking south of Newton Bridge (NN 888 314)
Distance	22km/13½ miles
Ascent	200m/750ft
Approx time	6hr
Max altitude	Glen Lochan 450m
Terrain	Tracks, rugged path, quiet back road

Length

■ ■ ☐ ☐ ☐

Difficulty

■ ■ ☐ ☐ ☐

There is limited verge parking east of the track foot above Loch Freuchie (NN 863 388) for a pick-up or drop-off on a **shorter route** leaving out the less interesting bits. Sma' Glen to the track foot via Glen Almond and Glen Lochan gives you 14km with 250m ascent (8½ miles/800ft) – about 4hr.

This walk on tracks, paths and roads includes the most spectacular section of the Rob Roy Way, as well as some much less demanding estate tracks and 2km of quiet road.

Glen Lochan is perhaps at its best when the cloud swirls along the heather slopes, and wind rushes along the narrow hollow. This is a good, longish walk for a bad day. And if you do feel damp along Glen Almond, stop at Clach na Tiompan and consider how much worse it was in the Bronze Age.

North of the River Almond, start along the wide gravel track with SRWS (Scottish Rights of Way and Access Society) signpost for Loch Tay (14½ mile away). After 5km, fork left passing **Conichan** house. In another 1km, a cairn with interpretation board marks the ruins of the **Clach na Tiompan** chambered cairn – no chambers survive. Just along the track, a new 'stone circle' or drystane sheep fank was built under Auchnafree Hill to mark the Millennium.

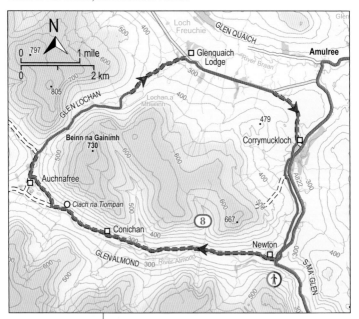

The Rob Roy Way heads into Glen Lochan

The **Sma' Glen** seems too twisty for a glacial glen, and could be a meltwater channel. This supposes an earlier River Almond flowing north to Amulree and the River Braan. With this blocked by ice, a lake would have formed in upper Glen Almond, and overflowed to carve this gorge.

Before Glenshervie Burn fork right on a smooth track, to a bridge towards **Auchnafree** house. Immediately across the river turn right on a track running up to left of Glenshervie Burn and below a plantation. After crossing the burn, the track rises steeply, then bends left (into Glen Shervie). At this bend leave it. The old path is round to the right but simpler is to take the steep small path ahead, rejoining the older path after 50 metres.

The path is barely more than a sheep trod, as it runs along the steep slope above the unnamed burn. It crosses the top of the stream, and runs through the striking V-slot of Glen Lochan.

A dry streambed runs through the slot, and while we may be unconvinced by the Sma' Glen, this is surely a **meltwater channel**, carved by a much bigger stream than the present one, the outflow of a glacier-dammed lake in Coire a' Chearcaill ahead.

The path dips to run along the left-hand shore of a small lochan. It crosses the outflow of an even smaller pool just below. Passing over a ruined fence, you see the gate of the original path just below. No longer following the old path line, the path becomes rugged stones and peat. It runs along the foot of the southern slope, with the valley now wide and flat-bottomed, the bed of a former lake of which only the tiny Lochan Uaine remains.

Cross the outflow of this lochan, with the clearest path now running on the stream's left bank, to where the valley broadens again. The path, now faint and boggy, bends left, to follow the foot of the northern slope. After 500 metres the path reaches the corner of **Lochan a' Mhuilinn**. Just ahead it joins a rough track.

Follow the track downhill (northeast) to the minor road near **Glenquaich Lodge** above **Loch Freuchie**.

Turn right, following the road for nearly 3km. Where it bends left under power pylons, turn off right in a track enlarged as the access to a pylon of the Beauly–Denny power line. After 500 metres, as the construction track turns away, keep ahead on the pleasanter old track descending towards A822. It bends right at a mobile phone mast, joining the track of General Wade's Military Road towards the ruined farm at Corrymuckloch.

The **'Military' roads** were built after the Scottish rebellion of 1715, to make it easier to control the Highlands. General George Wade started the pro-gramme of road building: its crown jewel was the fine stone bridge at Aberfeldy (Route 40). He also joined Perthshire and Speyside through the Drumochter Pass (Route 80). His successor Major William Caulfeild built the ones that now make up much of the West Highland Way.

At **Corrymuckloch** the track bends left to the A822, but keep ahead, south, to right of a wood and across open field; gates still exist along the line of the former road. Join the A822 at a lay-by to cross a stream; soon a gate lets you move down into the field on the right.

A hill track descends from the right, and from its foot the faint old track of Wade's Road runs immediately above the A822. After 500 metres the track moves up away from the road and becomes clearer. As it descends towards Sma' Glen, parts of it are soggy – Wade's drain-age has broken down after 250 years. The old road crosses a stone bridge to join the A822.

It's only 400 metres back to the start, but the main road is narrow and twisty. You can climb the awkward fence opposite, and go down under larch trees to left of the road to Newton Bridge at the walk start.

PART TWO

KILLIN AND GLEN LOCHAY

Killin, Ben Vorlich and Stuc a' Chroin, from Creag na Caillich (Route 12)

The Lomond-Trossach National Park takes a bulge to include Killin – apparently the natives anticipated a tourism boom and lots of new town paths. Glen Lochay's hills are also half in Lomond-Trossach, although their eastern approaches give an experience of long trackways, hydro pipes and big grassy slopes that's purest Perthshire.

And Perthshire perfection is Meall nan Tarmachan, a hill of narrow grass ridges, rocky knolls, and a convenient car park at the 600m mark.

9 Looking at Loch Tay: Meall Clachach

Length

■ ■ ▨ ▨ ▨

Difficulty

■ ■ ■ ■ ▨

Start/finish	Killin, central car park (NN 574 332)
Distance	10.5km/6½ miles
Ascent	550m/1800ft
Approx time	3¾hr
Max altitude	Meall Clachach 603m
Terrain	Lochside path; then a rough hill crossing on paths and moorland

Route 9 could also start at the **Longhouse car park**, omitting the shoreline stroll.

When you find yourself at the end of a really large loch the best thing to do is to find a hill that looks out straight along it. The villagers of Killin obviously agree, as they've formed a steep little path straight up the end of Sron a' Chlachain.

Before looking at the loch from the hill, examine the hill itself from the loch shore. Then get the Loch Tay view all of a sudden, sneaking up the northern side by Moirlanich Longhouse and an equally old path above it. I take it to be a peat road, used for dragging down winter fuel from the bogs above.

After crossing the Bridge of Dochart at the south end of Killin, continue 800 metres to a road bend, and keep ahead to a car park. Start through a gate at its back right corner onto a gravelled railway track. Follow this over River Lochay, then turn right through a kissing-gate.

A path (sometimes underwater) runs along the riverbank to **Loch Tay**, then turns left along the loch shore. ◄ A gate leads back onto the railbed alongside Pier Road. Turn left along the railbed path for 600 metres under trees. Just before the road bends away right move across to join it, and follow it past **Killin Cemetery** to the A827 at Coach House Hotel.

The shoreline path follows a sandbar, and it's clear that the loch once flowed right to the doorsteps of what is now Killin.

Turn right on the pavement for 500 metres, then left in the lane signposted for Moirlanich Longhouse. Pass the complex electricity substation with transformers for all the hydroelectricity off Ben Lawers, to the red-roofed **Longhouse**.

Looking down to Loch Tay from Sron a' Chlachain

Moirlanich Longhouse is a traditional dwelling for people and their livestock, last occupied in 1968 and now managed by the National Trust for Scotland. It is open on Wednesday and Sunday afternoons in summer.

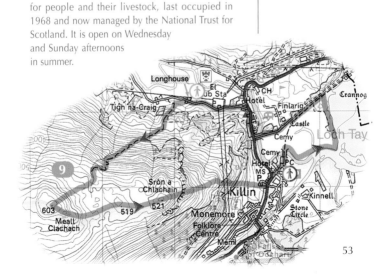

53

The original foot of the old track (a bit further on) is blocked by an 8ft electrified fence. So start through the gate opposite the Longhouse, and slant to right up a field. At the field top, a gate is between the foot of a birchwood (to left) and the top of a plantation (to right).

Beyond this, the old path appears as a sunken grassy groove, sometimes waterlogged but mostly surprisingly good. It slants to the right, heading for the summit of Meall Clachach far above. The path crosses a stream, and then a fence crosses the path – there's no gate and the fence must be stepped over. The path, little used but still clear, zigzags up fairly steep ground. As the hillslope turns from grass to heather, the path contours to the right. ◄

Over on the left at a slightly higher level is the wall leading to the summit of Sron a' Chlachain – you could short cut directly across to it.

The path turns up alongside a stream to a damp hollow (perhaps peat cuttings) at 480m. It continues up south, to left of the stream as a groove in the deep heather, but it's easier to follow the stream itself. At the stream top, turn up right. Low heather and moss lead to the small cairn on **Meall Clachach**. (Meall Clachach means stony hump, but there aren't any stones.)

Turn just south of east over a nearby knoll. Down behind it you'll find a line of old iron fence posts. A path is forming along the old posts. There's a 50-metre stretch on soft ground, with drier ground down to the right. The fence posts eventually turn away south, but keep ahead for another 400 metres to the lopsided cairn of **Sron a' Chlachain** (called Creag Bhuidhe on some maps). A small path forms for the last 50 metres or so.

The small path continues down east, along with a broken wall, to another lopsided cairn. (Coming uphill from Killin, this cairn appears to be the summit.) The path continues down steeply beside the broken wall, then dodges on rocky steps down a break in a low crag. Below, there's a slight rise over a knoll, and a very steep descent where the path is carving itself deep into the hill – a random diversion into the bracken will help prevent further erosion.

Pass under two power lines (to remind you that this is hydroelectric Scotland, not the fussily preserved Lakes). The path runs down in an oakwood to a ladder stile just above Killin. At the village edge, a few steps to the right take you to Fingal's Stone, a small standing stone repaired with mythic cement that looks a bit like ordinary Portland. The main path runs out through the decorative gates of Breadalbane Recreation Park to arrive on **Killin**'s main street at a red phone box.

Turn left (north) for 100 metres and bear right to the car park.

10 Cam Chreag and Ben Challum

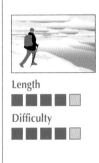

Start/finish	Car park between road and river east of Kenknock (NN 476 367)
Distance	27km/17 miles
Ascent	1200m/3900ft
Approx time	9hr
Max altitude	Ben Challum 1025m
Terrain	Tracks; pathless grassy ridges, occasionally steep
Note	Bicycle to Allt Challuim intake, 8km each way, saves 2½hr

Length

Difficulty

Up Glen Lochay's upper track, and back down the track of the valley floor, gives a track walk of 15km and 250m of ascent (9½ miles/800ft) – about 3½hr. The scenery is almost unchanging, but it lets you examine five Munros and two Corbetts as well as the big hydro pipe.

The pathless side of Ben Challum might not be enough to justify the 9km walk in along Glen Lochay. So grab the impressive Corbett Cam Chreag at the same time.

Start at a new car park 1km east of Kenknock (the traditional parking place west of the farm is now discouraged by signs and blocked by schist boulders). Walk

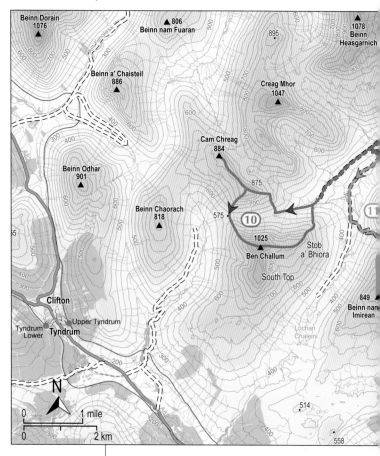

west along the road for 1.2km, passing below **Kenknock**. Follow the private road as it turns right, uphill, passing through a gate. The potholed road zigzags up the north side of the glen. Just below where it bends back right for the second time, take a track ahead.

The track crosses over the top of a massive hydro pipe, then contours along the glen side, passing in

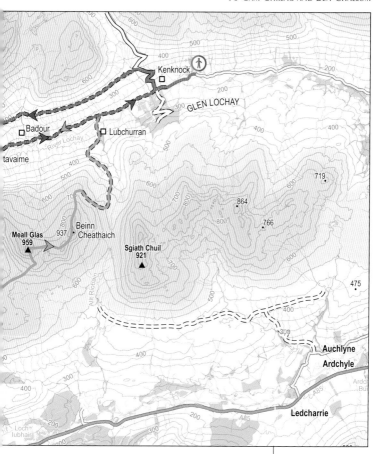

and out of deer-fenced young woodlands. After 4km, it crosses a stream above **Badour** cottage. In another 1.5km, it runs briefly downhill, then crosses another stream above Badvaim (or **Batavaime**) cottage. In 200 metres, a track turns down left at a spoil heap.

Glen Lochay track, to Ben Challum

For the Lochay tracks walk, turn down this track to the valley floor, and return alongside River Lochay.

The track enters a final woodland plantation, then ends at a gate out of the enclosed land just below the intake dam of Allt Challuim. Head up to right of the stream, just below the deer fence. At the 500m contour the deer fence turns away across the face of Cam Chreag. Head directly up the grassy slope, northwest, to reach the ridgeline above its lower outcrop.

The ridge above rises in grass and rocky outcrops. With more grass than outcrops, it's fairly easy to gain the plateau above. One way is to keep to left of the lowest outcrops, up steep grass, then slant out right at the top corner of the grass. On the grassy terrace above, slant back left to gain the plateau just above.

Head gently uphill, west, to the first knoll (**875m**). The bumpy ridgeline now runs northwest, with notable drops on the right, to reach the small cairn at **Cam Chreag** summit.

Return along the knolly ridge. At its end, the ridge broadens into a small plateau with peat pools. Turn right to descend from the southwest corner. In mist, make sure you're descending southwest, rather than south (too far left) or west (too far right). A short way down the slope is the top of an old fence and wall. Follow the fence down the steep grass spur, and across the broad col Bealach Ghlas Leathaid at **575m**. ▶

Follow fence posts up the spur ahead. They end against a slabby outcrop. Scramblers can tackle it direct; it is most easily bypassed on the left (east). Regaining the crest, you arrive below a knobby outcrop. This should be bypassed on the right (south). Above this the ridge changes its character, becoming stones and moss, and leads up directly to **Ben Challum** summit cairn.

Old fence posts down left are an escape route via Allt Challum.

South Top option

As you arrive at the cairn, a path joins from the right (south). You could use this for an out-and-back walk along the airy summit ridge to the lower **south top**, 800 metres away (1.6km there and back, 70m of ascent, about 30min).

From **Ben Challum summit** descend a steep spur east, to reach the level shoulder and slight rise to **Stob a' Bhiora**. Descend just north of east to a final knoll. The spur drops steeply below. If you're above a fringe of crag, move a few steps left. Go straight down northeast into broken ground, descending between a couple of small crags. As the ground eases, continue down the spurline until you see the deer fence crossing below. Then slant back left to the intake dam on the Allt Challuim at the end of the approach track. ▶

Continuing straight down to the valley floor involves a deer fence and ungrazed tussocks of newly planted woodland.

Return along the approach track for 2.5km to the track junction above Badvaim/**Batavaime**. Descend the winding track all the way if you wish or else, directly above Badvaim, keep directly downhill with deer fence on your left. Head down to right of the stream to an old gate and Badvaim hut. Its access track reaches the valley floor past farm sheds.

A smooth track runs down the valley to left of the river, to the road corner near **Kenknock**. Continue ahead along the road to the car park.

11 Beinn nan Imirean, Meall Glas

Length

Difficulty

Start/finish	Car park between road and river east of Kenknock (NN 476 367)
Distance	22.5km/14 miles
Ascent	1000m/3300ft
Approx time	7½hr
Max altitude	Meall Glas 959m
Terrain	Tracks, and high-altitude grassy hill slopes

The tough bits of the eastern Grampians are the bottoms. Below the 600m mark the tussocks are lumpy and the heather is high. So it makes sense to seek out walks where ready-made Landrover tracks take you up through this less likeable ground, onto the grass and gravel of the heights. It's a bonus when those tracks also give you a few miles of sheltered riverside rambling on the way in.

Beinn nan Imirean is unvisited and pathless, a couple of cairns at the summit the only mark of man. The extra 100m of height on Meall Glas mean it's somewhat rocky, and gravel replaces grass. But the main difference between 850m and 950m is Munro status, which means a trodden path, and a human being or two to chat with at the cairn.

Start at a new car park 1km east of **Kenknock** (see Route 10). Follow the public road to Kenknock drive end, where it becomes a private (hydro board) one. Where it turns uphill, keep ahead past a vehicle barrier and over a bridge. Follow the track up-valley to right of the river.

By a gatepost 1km from the end of the tarred road a strange boulder shows black starburst crystals that I take to be **graphitic schist** (NN 456 357). Later on the route the track alongside the Lubchurran Burn offers fine displays of garnets, up to the size of peas. Spot them in clean rocks turned over by track construction. The red-brown crystals are indicators of the high temperatures and pressures sustained by this metamorphic stone.

Beinn nan Imirean, to Creag Mhor

A track turns off left for the ford to Lubchurran, and will be the return route: for now, keep ahead. Pass below **Badour** and then below a mountaineering club hut, Badvaim (or **Batavaime**). At the head of Glen Lochay the track crosses two streams, and bends to the south.

As the track starts to climb towards Lochan Chailein, look out for a smaller grassy track forking down left. It fords the stream then zigzags up towards Meall Glas. Waterfalls are to right of the track. It ends in a shallow grassy bowl at 550m altitude. Turn south, crossing various feeder streams of the waterfalls, onto the north ridge of **Beinn nan Imirean**. Go up the pathless grassy ridge to the summit cairn.

Turn down east at first, keeping to right of a cairn apparently placed to guide you over the one small cliff hereabouts. Go down grassy slopes, to pass a conspicuous quartz boulder. The col below is peat-hagged on the right (southeast) side, but at its highest point a short peaty crossing leads to a series of firm hummocks. Go straight up **Meall Glas** to a shoulder to right of the summit, then turn up northwest to the top. The summit cairn is mostly made of quartz from a nearby vein.

Head east along the broad summit ridge, with a small path. The path skirts to left of the 908m top to the trig point on **Beinn Cheathaich**. Head north, on a pleasantly angled grassy ridge ideal for descent. At 680m look out for a track on the right – its start is just beyond a bare peat patch, itself just to right of the ill-defined crest line. The track contours right, southeast, across a stream, then turns downhill to left of the main Lubchurran Burn.

The track passes a small water intake, then passes to left of **Lubchurran** house. The river crossing beyond is a shallow ford – a former footbridge downstream no longer exists. Turn right on the track beyond, back to the car park.

Meall Garbh summit ridge (Route 12)

12 The Tarmachans

Start/finish	National Trust car park (former visitor centre) on high road below Lochan na Lairige (NN 607 378)
Distance	14.5km/9 miles
Ascent	850m/2800ft
Approx time	5½hr
Max altitude	Meall nan Tarmachan 1044m
Terrain	Well-built ascent path, clear ridge path with one rocky descent, small descent path and grassy track

Length

Difficulty

The multitude of small pointy summits along the ridge gives the Tarmachans a feel of miniature mountaineering. None of the tops apart from Meall nan Tarmachan itself is a Munro. Accordingly, this ridge is 'purely for pleasure'. The path weaves among the rocky knolls, and the only moment of distress may be the descent from Meall Garbh. The bare rock here isn't a natural scramble: it's been exposed by human footfalls over the years. It's in a rather exposed position, and uncomfortable or worse when wet or under snow.

Note that limited verge parking is also possible where the contouring track encountered (see end of first paragraph below) meets the Lairig road (NN 604 384). Follow the track through a gate and then for 300 metres to where the path crosses.

The pay and display car park at the 430m contour is spacious, with signboards about natural history. Start at the bottom corner of the car park, following a rough track briefly, then turning up to the right on a well-built path. After 800 metres the path crosses a contouring track.

Continue up the well-built path, into a fenced regeneration enclosure, to meet Meall nan Tarmachan's south ridge at about the 700m level. The wide path heads up the ridge, which is a sequence of grassy lumps to a top at 923m. The path descends over a ladder stile to cross a col, then rises in very steep stone steps. As the angle

*The Tarmachans
from Killin*

From Meall Garbh the gently angled but well-formed south ridge carries a little path clearly used as a descent off the ridge – avoiding both the charming ridgelet and the eroded rocky step ahead.

eases a bit, the path slants up a terrace shelf on the east side of the hill, passing just below the summit, to join the north ridge. Turn back up left 50 metres to the small cairn of **Meall nan Tarmachan**.

The ridge path heads south, then bends southwest along the knolly ridgeline. That ridgeline is decorated with a couple of pools down on the right, and decorated still more by the pointy summit ahead – **Meall Garbh**. The little peak is reached by the well-defined path zig-zagging up. ◀

Behind Meall Garbh, the path follows a short narrow ridgeline with bare rock to scramble over. Descend the still quite sharp crest, until the final drop to the col. This drop is steep, on eroded bare rock in a fairly exposed situation. Clean rock is usually preferable to steep grass. But in wet snow conditions, one may prefer the steep grass slope immediately round to the right, descending northwest from the top of the steep section.

The path continues weaving around knolls of grass and rock, then heads to the right out of a col to bypass another steep section. From the next top, **Beinn nan Eachan**, the path descends northwest, before swinging left below steep ground to a narrow col. This leads south-west for the short ascent to **Creag na Caillich**.

The traditional descent has been to return north for 200 metres, to the first dip in the ridge: here a small cairn marks a faint path descending southeast into Coire Fionn Lairige. However, a better way has developed, following the natural ridgeline south from Creag na Caillich. Descent from the ridge end will be westwards: so it's surprising that at the final knoll, the path heads out to the left – east – purely so as to contour above the brink of the crags of the ridge end.

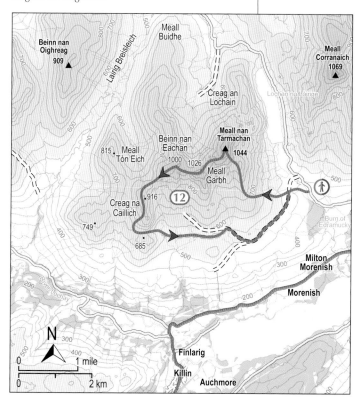

On Creag na Caillich, looking south to Loch Tay

Having teetered these brinks, the path descends grassy slopes westwards to about the 700m level. Here it bends round to the left, to pass through a small peaty col below the southern crags. ◄ The intermittent path drops down the grassy valley beyond, to an intake dam (NN 567 367).

This is the col north of Point 685m.

A grassy track contours eastwards, following a buried water pipe, with several small intakes. After a gate through a deer fence, the track bends uphill. Here fork off right over wet ground to Intake 1, and cross a concrete bridge above the small dam to the start of another track. This contours forward to meet the stony track descending from an abandoned quarry. Follow it forward around the hillside for 3km, to join the path descending from Meall nan Tarmachan.

Meall Garbh, An Stuc, Ben Lawers, across Glen Lyon from Creag Ard (Route 22)

Across Loch Tay to the Lawers group

Scotland's nine highest mountains all lie in the Ben Nevis range, or else in the great high plateau of the Cairngorms. The 10th, somewhat to our surprise, is Perthshire's Ben Lawers. There is, however, a difference. Ben Nevis and Ben Macdui have huge and celebrated crags to climb on. Ben Lawers is Scotland's biggest mountain made of grass. Grass – but also wildflowers. In high slimy corries where the sheep can't reach and minerals seep out of the mountain, little alpine blossoms make Ben Lawers into one of our largest nature reserves.

Lawers grass means you can go, in heather-free comfort, pretty well anywhere above the 800m contour. From Lochan nan Cat, any slope not altogether rocky tempts as a possible line onto the ridge. Grass is eaten by sheep, and shepherds ride quad bikes; so, on the north side, the unexplored valleys between the ridges have useful tracks, with high slopes above offering a dozen more ways to get lost on Lawers.

FIGURE IN THE MIST

A mysterious figure was seen on the summit by a respected member of the Scottish Mountaineering Club some time between the wars. The wind was so fierce that Ratcliffe Barnett was unable to stay upright. Through the mist he saw a human shape, apparently unaffected by the wind and the drenching rain, and unaware of Barnett crawling towards the cairn a few feet away. The 'man of the mist' was gathering small stones, wrapping them in newspaper, and putting them in its pocket – the sort of obsessive behaviour typical of ghosts (but also of geologists).

BEN LAWERS ROUTES

13   Edramucky Burn (from the Lairig road)
14   Up and down from the Lairig road
15   Lawers Four from Lawers village
16   The Cat's Bowl (from Bealach Dubh col)
17   Down via Beinn Ghlas to Lawers village (from Ben Lawers)

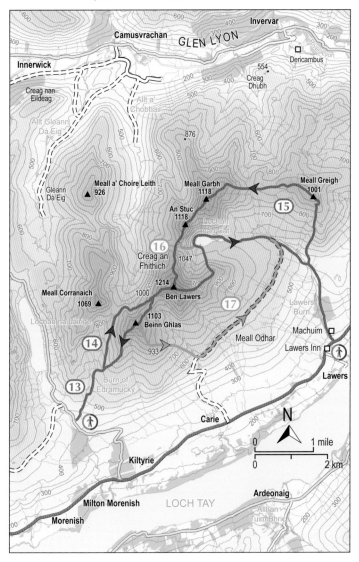

13 Edramucky Burn

Start/finish	Nature Trail car park (NN 608 378)
Distance	2.5km/1½ miles
Ascent	250m/800ft
Approx time	1¼hr
Max altitude	Top of Edramucky enclosure 630m
Terrain	Small paths, sometimes damp; big but stony path for descent

Length

Difficulty

The high car park of the former Ben Lawers Visitor Centre allows a short, easy walk at big-mountain altitude. The young woodland in the fenced enclosure gives shelter, along with a chance to enjoy plantlife uneaten by sheep. Willow and birch were planted at the start of the century, with natural regeneration to follow. Summer flowers include moss campion, yellow saxifrage, wood cranesbill, globeflower, goldenrod, marsh hawksbeard, northern bedstraw, lady's bedstraw, and alpine lady's mantle. The Nature Trail has numbered waypoints and a leaflet.

Descending by Edramucky Burn towards Loch Tay and distant Ben More

Start on the wide path through the low walls of the interpretation area, through a gate and across the road. After a short moorland crossing the path enters the fenced-in area. The main path heads uphill to left of the **Edramucky Burn**, but take the Nature Trail that turns off right to a footbridge. It heads up in the stream valley, recrossing it twice. At 540m level it rejoins the main path.

Turn left, to cross the burn, and where the path turns downhill, take the small old path uphill. Ignore a ladder stile over on the left. The old path ahead runs up to left of the stream, in places a soggy trench.

With the plantation fence (and another ladder stile) ahead, turn off right to cross a stream. Remains of old shielings are above the second stream branch, which you also cross to rejoin the well-made main path. Just ahead is where it leaves the enclosure at a gate.

Coire Odhar option

From the gate at the enclosure top, one might like to continue to the col at the head of Coire Odhar. There and back from the enclosure gate is 3.5km with 250m of ascent (2 miles/800ft) – about 1½hr. See Route 14.

From the top of the fenced enclosure, turn down the well-made but stony main path. A sign asks you not to reuse the Nature Trail path in descent, so stay on the main path back to the car park.

14 Up and down from the Lairig road

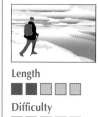

Start/finish	Nature Trail car park (NN 608 378)
Distance	10km/6½ miles
Ascent	850m/2800ft
Approx time	4¼hr
Max altitude	Ben Lawers 1214m
Terrain	Small paths, sometimes damp; big but stony path for descent

Length

■ ■ ☐ ☐ ☐

Difficulty

■ ■ ■ ☐ ☐

The combination of a high car park and a magnificent summit make this one of the most popular outings in Scotland. It's usually taken in the opposite direction (Beinn Ghlas first) but this way the ascent unfolds interestingly around the northern corrie, is only steep for the final 200m to the summit, and reserves the airy ridges of Beinn Ghlas for the descent.

Start on the wide path which crosses the road and soon enters the fenced-in stream area. The main path heads uphill to left of the **Edramucky Burn**, or you can take the Nature Trail that turns off right to a footbridge. It heads up in the stream valley, and at 540m level it rejoins the main path. Turn left, to cross the burn, and where the path turns downhill, take the small old path up to the right. ▸

The old path ahead runs up to left of fence, in places a soggy trench. With the plantation fence (and another ladder stile) ahead, turn off right to cross two stream branches, then join the well-made main path to leave the enclosure at a gate. In another 300 metres, at a tiny rocky outcrop, the path forks. ▸ The well-built left path slants gradually up the side of Coire Odhar, to the col at its head.

Through this pass between Meall Corranaich and Beinn Ghlas, the path contours round to the right, gradually climbing around the north flank of **Beinn Ghlas**. The path here is narrower and rougher. The slope is north

Here a stile on the left out of the enclosure is the way onto Meall Corranaich's south ridge.

The path ahead here is the stiff climb on good path to Beinn Ghlas.

Arriving at Ben Lawers summit

facing and rather steep, and it can hold hard old snow. The path enters the north bowl of Beinn Ghlas, drops a little to cross a stream, then slants up to the Lawers/Ghlas col at **1000m**.

The well-built path with steps and zigzags leads ahead up the first steep slope to Creag Loisgte. It's then not quite so steep to **Ben Lawers** summit with its trig point and non-functioning viewpoint indicator.

Return southwest on the wide engineered path with its steps and zigzags. After the slight shoulder at 1100m, the descent is steeper to the Lawers/Ghlas col. Here take the main path ahead up the gently rising ridge. ◄ The ridge has drops on the left, becoming pleasantly narrow for last few steps to Beinn Ghlas summit.

The spot height 1084m on older Explorer maps should be 1034m.

From the summit knoll drop southwest, on the wide, clear path down the well-defined southwest ridge. The path is engineered, with some zigzags, but it's a fairly relentless descent. From the ridge foot the angle eases down to the gate into the regeneration area around Burn of Edramucky.

The path runs down to left of the stream, then at 540m bends right (ahead, the Nature Trail shouldn't be used in descent). Across the burn the path turns downhill (reddish-brown garnets 2–3mm long are in the grey schist stones beneath your feet). The path bends right to the gate out of the fenced area. Recross moorland to the car park.

15 Lawers Four from Lawers village

Start/finish	Lawers Inn (NN 677 395)
Distance	17km/11 miles
Ascent	1550m/5200ft
Approx time	8hr
Max altitude	Ben Lawers 1214m
Terrain	Good path, grassy slopes and pathed ridges, steep near-scramble onto An Stuc

Length

■ ■ ■ ☐ ☐

Difficulty

■ ■ ■ ■ ☐

The combination of a pleasant approach path, a total of four Munros, the challenging moment on An Stuc, and the slightly sharp ridgeline off Lawers, makes this perhaps Perthshire's finest mountain walk. Or for only the three eastern summits, the Cat's Bowl descent (Route 16) isn't just a short cut but an intriguing wiggly way between the crags. Adding in Beinn Ghlas, on the other hand (Route 17), gives the fifth Munro but a very ordinary route down off it.

The lower car park at Lawers Inn is free to hillwalkers, 'on the understanding that they will spend money in the hotel afterwards'. Parking at the Horn Carvery is for customers, although others may use it for a fee.

Start down the A827 to cross its bridge at the Horn Carvery. Head up the track behind the workshop to **Machuim** farm. Pass to left of buildings on a path (signed 'hill path') above the river, to emerge onto the track just above the farm.

Keep ahead, up through a gate, on a small path under flo-riferous blackthorn. Waterfalls are seen or heard through the trees below. Reddish-brown garnets are in path stones all the way up to the footbridge. Cross a high stile into an enclosed area with plantings of larch, birch and pine. Another stile leads out at the plantation's top.

The wide, grassy path follows the top of the slot of **Lawers Burn**, among shielings. Then it slants down to a footbridge. Don't cross the bridge, but head up to right of the stream for another 400 metres to a sidestream.

Meall Greigh may mean 'hill of the bits of horse harness' – apparently horses were pastured up here. Meall Garbh means rough hump.

Go up grassy slopes to right (east) of this stream. An outcrop line runs up parallel with the stream. For plantlife, pass along the foot of this outcrop; for views pass more naturally along its top. Slopes above lead to a shoulder of Meall Greigh at 800m. A small path leads up to the cairn at **Meall Greigh** summit. ◀

Descend gently northwest, over a cairned knoll. The small, peaty ridge path continues with a derelict fence up on its right. After a col the ground ascends more steeply, with the path to left of the fence remains. The ridge narrows to the crest of **Meall Garbh**.

The path above Lawers Burn, to Meall Greigh

The path continues down the mildly rocky ridge to the col below the intimidating rise of An Stuc. Slightly

round on the left (east) flank, various paths go up in zig-zags to the rocky steepening. Here the paths are eroded down to bare rock, so becoming more and more scrambly. There are some good handholds, but the footholds are smooth and sloping, awkward in wet or especially in icy conditions, or in descent.

From **An Stuc** summit, the clear path runs down roughly south to Bealach Dubh col. ▶ Continue up the ridgeline opposite, with what looks like, but isn't, an obstacle at **Craig an Fhithich**. Just pass round to the right of this to the small cairn on top of it. ▶ Then carry on up the ridge to **Ben Lawers** trig point.

From the trig point, a well-defined ridge runs just south of east with a small path. It's pleasingly sharp, and in winter carries a cornice. After 400 metres the ridge broadens to a series of hollows, which will be confusing in mist and snow. The small path skirts to left of these, to descend quite steeply to where the ridge becomes sharply defined again.

The ridge now runs down just north of east. There's a small path down to left of the crest. At 1070m the ridge broadens and becomes gentle. Follow it down northeast to a shoulder at 950m. ▶

Take the steeper slopes down northwest, to the head of **Lochan nan Cat**. A small peaty path runs around the loch head and along the northern shore to the outflow of Lochan nan Uan (or maybe it's the Kitten Lochan). The peaty path continues to left of the stream with its small waterfalls, down to the intake dam. Here cross to the dam track, and follow it to the right for 300 metres. At a small cairn, fork down left on an old but good path.

The path follows the rim of the incised valley of **Lawers Burn**. Above the footbridge the path turns sharp left. It descends in sweeping zigzags down to cross the footbridge.

Continue down this good path, through the ruined shielings, the plantation, and a scrubby wood, to **Machuim** farm and the A827 above Loch Tay. Turn right for 500 metres to the **Lawers Inn**.

Turn down left here for the Cat's Bowl (Route 16) descent to Lochan nan Cat and Lawers Burn.

In descent: when you reach this small cairn, there's a small rocky drop immediately ahead. Divert round it to the left.

The easier, but dull, way here is to head down the main ridgeline, east, to mildly peat-hagged moorland, and join the 600m-contour track near the top of the Lawers Burn path.

16 The Cat's Bowl (descent)

Length

◼ ◻ ◻ ◻ ◻

Difficulty

◼ ◼ ◼ ◼ ◻

Start	Bealach Dubh col south of An Stuc (NN 636 426)
Finish	Lawers Inn (NN 677 395)
Distance	6.5km/4 miles (as part of longer routes)
Descent	750m/2500ft
Approx time	2hr (as part of longer routes)
Terrain	Steep grass between rocky outcrops

This is a neat little short cut back to Lawers Burn after the three eastern Munros. In the uphill direction, it also makes part of a very appealing route up Ben Lawers by shieling path, lochan and stream hollow – start from Lawers Inn reversing Route 15.

The path coming down south from **An Stuc** passes slightly down left (east) of the boggy col Bealach Dubh to cross the very top of a small stream. Turn left (southeast) down this stream. As it steepens (and perhaps goes under snow) switch to the broken spur immediately to left of it. There's a little zigzag down to the grassy bowl at 870m.

Follow the stream down to the steepening at the bowl's lip. Head down grassy slopes about 50 metres to right of the stream to reach **Lochan nan Cat**. Pass round to left of the loch, joining the previous Route 15.

Start	Ben Lawers (NN 635 414)
Finish	Lawers Inn (NN 677 395)
Distance	10.5km/6½ miles (as part of longer routes)
Descent	1150m/3800ft
Approx time	3hr (as part of longer routes)
Terrain	Big path to Beinn Ghlas; grassy slopes; track and good grassy path

Length

Difficulty

Turn Route 15 (Lawers Four) into Lawers Five. Gaining a Munro, you lose Lawers' nice south ridge and the lochan at its foot.

From **Ben Lawers** trig point, head down southwest on the wide engineered path with steps and zigzags, to the Lawers/Ghlas col. Take the main path ahead up the gently rising ridge to **Beinn Ghlas** summit.

Above Beinn Ghlas on the summit slopes of Ben Lawers

Head southwest for 50 metres, off the summit knoll onto the big main path; but then strike down left for the start of the southeast ridge. Follow this down to its final knoll at **933m**. Turn left, down grassy slopes east, to cross Allt an Tuim Bhric above where it carves itself an awkward little valley.

Slant on down east to join the well-built track

along the 600m contour – it follows a buried water pipe. Follow the track around the flank of the hill, passing above **Meall Odhar** hump. As the track turns north, you can drop off down rough grass to join the Lawers Burn path – or else continue another 300 metres to the small cairn at the top of that path.

The path runs down above **Lawers Burn**, crosses it at a footbridge, and descends to the A827 just east of **Lawers Inn**.

OTHER LAWERS LINES

The descent half of the Lawers–Ghlas standard Route 14 is sometimes used as an ascent to **Ben Lawers**, followed by the three Munros to **Meall Greigh**: return along the south-flank track at 600m then contour the hillside to the Edramucky Burn.

Already mentioned (see Route 18) are the Munro-baggers' small, damp paths from the top of the Lairig road (NN 595 416) to **Meall a' Choire Leith** and to **Meall Corranaich**. Meall Corranaich can also be reached from the Nature Trail car park (NN 608 378) by a ladder stile out of the Edramucky enclosure at NN 613 386 and its pleasant south ridge.

Beinn Ghlas can be reached from the A827 (Loch Tay) by a track from Tombreck (NN 652 378). Parking is at a lay-by 500 metres east, opposite Craggantoul track end.

Meall Garbh can be reached by its southeast flank, from the intake dam at the top of the Lawers Burn path (NN 662 427). A faint path leads up the grassy slopes northwest.

A **direct route to Meall Garbh** from Glen Lyon takes off from a track associated with the micro-hydro scheme at the Inverinain Burn (NN 655 472). To right of the stream, what seems to be a path is actually infill over the buried pipeline. At the water intake dam (430m contour), head up rough grassy slopes of Meall Garbh's north ridge.

Finally and formidably, the **seven Lawers Munros** form a natural horse-shoe from Glen Lyon, with lots of good ridgewalking, 27.5km/17 miles and 1500m/5000ft of ascent – about 10hr. From Camusvrachan (parking NN 613 475) take the track south of the River Lyon to Inverinain and up onto Creag Dhubh. Follow a fence up the ridge to Meall Greigh. Ridge paths cross Meall Garbh, An Stuc and Ben Lawers, to Beinn Ghlas. Take care on the steep descent and reascent to Meall Corranaich. Descend as Route 18.

On Creag an Fhitlich

18 Glen Lyon: Da-Eig Circuit

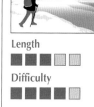

Start/finish	Camusvrachan (NN 620 477, or Lairig road top NN 595 416)
Distance	20km/12½ miles
Ascent	1300m/4400ft
Approx time	7½hr
Max altitude	Meall Corranaich 1069m
Terrain	Steep rugged ascent, then rough heather/grass/peat over the Corbett; hill paths over the two Munros

Length

■ ■ ■ ▢ ▢

Difficulty

■ ■ ■ ■ ▢

The natural way to take a horseshoe is from the valley below. Route 18, oddly, can also be entered from the **550m high point of the Lairig road**. The Munros make an enjoyable morning; the waterfalls in Glen Lyon make a great lunch spot. But 600m of ascent and the peaty ground above mean a tough afternoon. For this option, start at the road bend 100 metres east of the pull-in. A rebuilt path sets off north up a little stream valley. At the ridge crest, the path turns right over peaty ground, heading towards Meall Corranaich. Continue from the point indicated halfway through the walk description below.

The two western Munros of the group are usually taken from the Lairig road, with a Munro-baggers' path easing the damp moorland trek to Meall a' Choire Leith. Adding the Corbett Meall nam Maigheach transforms this into a grand horseshoe walk. It also demonstrates that a single Corbett can be harder work than two full-sized Munros...

There's a fishermen's pull-off just north of the River Lyon bridge, just beyond the sign 'Private Road'. There's also a large parking area above the road, 0.5 miles up-valley (west) from the track foot, occasionally used by farm lorries.

From the Lairig road start point: arrive here on the track from the east, and keep ahead.

Start along the smooth track, across the River Lyon, to a T-junction. Follow the main track to the right. ◄

The smooth-surfaced track passes a reservoir pond among birches, with the face of Creag nan Eildeag ahead full-frame. At the next house (**Balmenoch**) cross the **Allt Gleann Da-Eig** and head up alongside it, past some fine waterfalls. Join a grassy track up through a gate to a left-hand bend. Now for the direct route to

Creag nan Eildeag you bear off right up grass to the foot of the rocky spur. Pass round to the right through a broken wall. Now follow a fence up left in a grassy rake, to a little grassy col.

Above the fence, pass to the right along the foot of a crag with small trees on. The ledge has a faint sheep path as it gets narrower and steepens. After ascending alongside the crag, you turn up left for a few metres past a rowan tree to the ridge crest above.

Rough heather, grass and peat lead over the summit of **Creag nan Eildeag**, and southwards. In the col beyond, the going gets rougher, on grass with heather and peat, to the flat top **Meall nam Maigheach**, with its cairn.

Not much more than half a hill, it yet boasts **two names** – 'Meall Luaidhe' is also given on the Harvey map. Maigheach is hares, Luaidhe is lead mining, with the alternative translation 'my darling hill' implausible.

Meall Corranaich from Creag an Fhithich, Ben Lawers

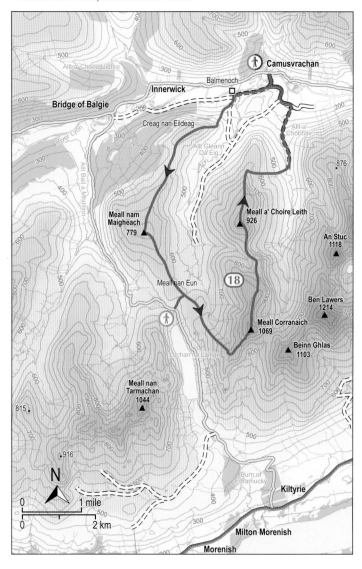

Head down the heathery slope southeast, with traces of a path. Cross a rough peaty col, and pass over the top of the hump **Meall nan Eun** for better going, following some old iron posts. Drop to the top of the rebuilt path arriving from the road top down on the right. ▶

Those starting from the Lairig road car park slot into the walk at this point.

At the ridge crest, the path turns right over peaty ground. The rough path follows the line of a few old metal fence posts, southeast then south. Passing through a dip, take a line to right of the old fencing to avoid peat hags.

The path now follows the fenceline quite steeply uphill, southeast. At the 825m level, the path and fencing turn left, slantwise across the northwest flank for Meall Corranaich summit. But it's nicer to continue uphill to the knoll at the end of the hill's southwest spur. Cross the level section of the ridge and ascend grass to rejoin the main path, worn and somewhat rebuilt. The path continues straight up to the preliminary cairn on a rock knoll, and a few steps further to **Meall Corranaich**'s main cairn with fence posts in it.

Take the gentle north ridge, which becomes quite narrow. After 800 metres from the summit the ridge dips

The north ridge of Meall Corranaich

85

and widens into a grassy plateau, where the small path disappears. Ahead is a stony summit (c990m) which you should not visit. Instead turn down northeast, to find a subsidiary ridge below – take care here in mist. The path runs above the stream on the near side of this lower ridge, than slants out right to its rounded grass crest.

Follow the new ridge down north then northwest to a col. A clear and somewhat eroded path runs up along the top of drops on the right, to **Meall a' Choire Leith**.

Continue down the gentle north ridge, a convex slope so you can't see the lower ridge you're aiming for. That lower ridge narrows, then levels into the peaty heathery plateau of Sron Eich (Horse Nose).

Alternative descent

For Glen Lyon views, but a peaty ridge: a small path threads through the peat north to the nose end. Slant down east, on steep wet grass, to cross the **Allt a' Chobhair** above its wooded, fenced-in gorge.

But for the less peaty descent, after passing through an old fence, turn down right on moderate slopes of wet grass. Another old fence runs down on your left: join it where it becomes a wall running directly downhill. Follow this wall down to a hydro intake in the Allt a' Chobhair below.

Cross below the dam to its access track beyond. Follow the track down to a new house. Turn left over the stream, past Balnahanaid and through birches. At a track junction, turn right to the start point in Glen Lyon; or keep ahead if you started the walk at the high car park on the Lairig road.

PART THREE
GLEN LYON

Carn Gorm from Meall Garbh (Route 22)

Glen Lyon is not just Scotland's longest, but also (according to Meggernie Estates and Sir Walter Scott) the loveliest and loneliest. From the head of the Lyon reservoir it's just a couple of hours' walk and a low hill pass through to Bridge of Orchy in Argyll; the glen foot, at Fortingall, is right on the other side of Scotland.

Above its 42km of river and woodland rise 20 Munros. Some of them are obscure, with Heasgarnich/Sheasgarnaich/Feskineth not even sure of its place in the alphabet. Strenuous back ways onto Ben Lawers are dealt with in Part Two; the Tarmachans are better approached from the south; and the head of Loch Lyon is embedded into the Bridge of Orchy section in Part Four. Even so, this Glen Lyon part is big on big hills, and low in low-level walks. (There are, however, some woodland walks from Bridge of Balgie – see sign-boards in car parks.)

19 Carn Mairg from Fortingall

Length

Difficulty

Start/finish	Fortingall church (NN 742 470)
Distance	19km/12 miles
Ascent	1250m/4200ft
Approx time	7¼hr
Max altitude	Carn Mairg 1041m
Terrain	Hill tracks; pathless moorland, mostly grassy, some heather; hill path between the two Munros

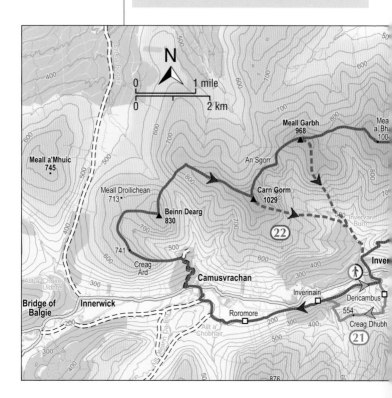

The four-Munro round of the Mairgs is a satisfying one, especially the 4km high-level stroll – we hesitate to call it a ridgeline – between Meall Garbh and Carn Mairg (Route 22). But for a pathless moorland ramble, there's also an eastern approach to Carn Mairg, with that Perthshire essential, a Landrover track to the 600m level.

Fortingall has very limited car parking. There's room for a handful of cars at Fortingall church (signed for the Yew Tree) except on Sunday mornings, when it's reserved for churchgoers. The yew tree, the oldest living being in Scotland, is in the churchyard.

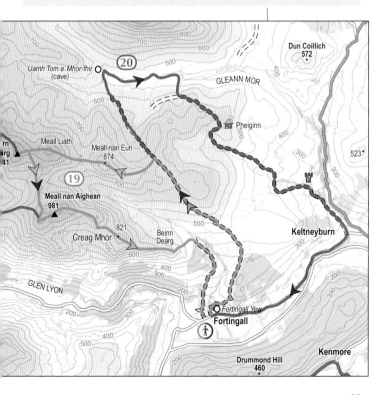

Start immediately east of the bridge over **Allt Odhar**, on the track into the housing cluster named Balnald. Pass between houses onto a hill track rising behind. This climbs northeast, then bends uphill with a plantation on its right, and exits onto moorland through a gate.

The track slants northwest up the moor. At the top a fence joins from the right, then turns away again at the high point of the track (700m) where it starts to drop to Gleann Mor at the back of Schiehallion. Here drop left off the track, across a col, with quad-bike wheelmarks to guide you initially (south). The ridgeline bends round to rise westwards, with a broken wall now as guide, and a derelict fence as well. Granite boulders speckle **Meall nan Eun**, then there's a short dip and a stiff climb onto **Meall Liath**. Its top has a small cairn with a fence post in it.

Another short drop leads to the broad saddle below Carn Mairg. This is stony rather than grassy, as befits a Munro of comfortably over the 1000m mark, and there's even a shard or two of granite bedrock. Take the boulder-fields direct, to **Carn Mairg**'s large summit cairn. ◀

To avoid boulderfields for the descent, leave the summit north, soon bending round right, to pass above a

Carn Mairg could mean 'hill of sorrow', or 'of the boundary'; but the most appropriate translation is pudding hill, because it looks like a black pudding.

stony knoll and down into the broad col. A well-marked path slants down southeast, then turns directly downhill, south, to the col leading towards Meall nan Aighean.

The path crosses this col southwards, pretending to head to the southwest top. Halfway up the path bends left for the rockier main summit: however, it's worth a preliminary visit to the southwest top for views along Glen Lyon. Then take the path east to **Meall nan Aighean**'s main summit with a lump or two of bare granite at the very top.

> 'Meall na Aighean' on Explorer maps, but 'nan' is surely correct. The Munro is called '**Craig Mhor**' on older maps and guides: that's actually the name of the outlier to the east, which looks like the main summit when seen from Fortingall.

Head gently downhill on gravel and short heather to the east summit (904m, 'Craig Mhor' on Harvey). Now descend rather steeply on heather and stones, with the best line southeast, then slanting back left into the col. Cross a lower summit (**821m**, 'Craig Mhor' on OS maps).

On the east ridge of Meall nan Aighean, looking back to it and to Carn Mairg

Then drop to an almost level heathery ridgeline, blessed with a small peaty path to the ridge tip at **Beinn Dearg**.

New plantations block the ridgeline below, so slant down left, northeast, to pick up a track just above Allt Odhar. It enters the plantation of pine and broadleaf at a gate with tall kissing-gate. Below, the track exits at a cattle grid. Keep downhill on the main track to a farmyard. Turn left towards Glenlyon House, then right down a tarred hedged driveway to the public road. Turn left to the bridge over **Allt Odhar**.

20 Back of Schiehallion

Length

Difficulty

Start/finish	Fortingall church (NN 742 470)
Distance	23km/14½ miles
Ascent	800m/2600ft
Approx time	7½hr
Max altitude	Pass on approach track 710m
Terrain	Moorland tracks, 2.5km rough riverbank, 3.5km quiet road

This is a good one to do when the cloud's at 600m. The highest ground is on tracks, so you can enjoy the misty atmosphere without major map and compass worries. And Glen More at the back of Schiehallion is even more lonely and remote with a lid of grey clag.

This forgotten bit of country is worth visiting for its own sake. A bonus is the small limestone cave, a rarity in Scotland; also a mini-gorge in the stream above. There's also a castle, gorge, and nature reserve on the return route.

Fortingall has very limited car parking. There's room for a handful of cars at Fortingall church (signed for the Yew Tree) except on Sunday mornings, when it's reserved for churchgoers.

Start as on the previous Route 19, up the track to right of **Allt Odhar**. It passes through a deer fence at 330m, then slants northwest to a high moorland ridgeline. The track continues northwest, slanting down into Gleann Mor, the big empty place at the back of Schiehallion. It becomes fainter to see, just wheelmarks in peat, as it passes above Glenmore Bothy, to end alongside Allt a' Mhadaidh. ▸

Stream of the Fox, or Wolf – Gaelic for wolf is 'wild fox'.

Cross the stream and head down its bank until a wiggle of the sidestream Allt a' Choire Glais appears ahead. Bear left up green limestone ground between shieling remains to find the cave Uamh Tom a' Mhor-fhir.

UAMH TOM A' MHOR-FHIR

The cave is fairly easy to find, about 100 metres northwest of the stream confluence at NN 7078 5337. Up to left of the sidestream's final wiggle is a patch of green ground – limestone underlies it – with low shieling remains. At the top of these shielings an

inconspicuous hole in the ground marks the entrance to the small limestone cave.

Can't locate it? There's a heathery hillock (Tom a' Mhor-fhir) immediately north of the stream confluence. From this hillock the cave bears 282° (magnetic bearing 2020s). Starting from the stream opposite the hillock the cave is 75 metres up the slope between the shielings.

Upstream from the shielings, Allt a' Choire Glais has a small limestone gorge that's worth exploring, especially when the water's warm enough for paddling.

Head down the main river, **Allt Mor**, on the right bank, with a ruined deer fence alongside. The going is grassy, with heather at one point where the stream is in a small gorge.

After about 2km, a track runs along the hillside up on the right (unless the cloud's down and you can't see it!). Here, the valley becomes more enclosed and steeper.

Limestone gorge, Allt a' Choire Ghlas

The old deer fence mounts the bank above the river, then drops steeply to a junction with a sidestream: the river drops in two steps of waterfall. Here turn up to the right, keeping to right of the small sidestream. You join the track above at its lowest point.

Follow the track left, down-valley. The track climbs gradually up the valley side, then crosses the bounding ridge and drops southeast to **Pheiginn Bothy**, a cosy wood-lined shelter.

The track runs down to join the stream Allt Coire Pheiginn – look over your right shoulder to spot a couple of waterfalls. The track is joined by another from the left, and also a stone wall. Soon it crosses the stream, contours out to the right, then runs down to right of a sidestream.

Keep to right of the stream, descending past a tower house (Garth Castle). After the Keltney Burn joins, below is a river gorge bursting with vegetation, the Keltneyburn Nature Reserve.

Apart from its fine wooded gorge (look out for dragonflies), the **Keltneyburn reserve** is noted for its patch of ancient grassland. In July or August you could spot eight species of wild orchid. There's a small car park where the track enters the reserve.

The track runs down to the valley floor, joining the road at the Keltneyburn Smithy Gallery.

The more artistic could linger here enjoying the bizarre metalworks (two shovels and a fire extinguisher make a basset hound?). The philistine of the party meanwhile walks the quiet road for 4km back to **Fortingall**. Riverside fields can sometimes be used instead, but are unpathed.

21 The Black Crag of Glen Lyon

Start/finish	Invervar, Glen Lyon (NN 666 483)
Distance	7km/4½ miles
Ascent	400m/1300ft
Approx time	2¾hr
Max altitude	Creag Dhubh 554m
Terrain	Old path, rough heather, good tracks for descent

Length
◼ ☐ ☐ ☐ ☐

Difficulty
◼ ◼ ◼ ☐ ☐

Creag Dhubh isn't even a shoulder, more of a knee of Ben Lawers. Climb Creag Dhubh and you're less than halfway up the main mountain – although you have overcome the heathery lower slopes, and are poised for a long grassy ridgewalk onto Meall Greigh.

But from Creag Dhubh you see up and down Glen Lyon, which you don't do from Ben Lawers. And you look across at the Mairgs range, rather than down on it from a great height. The old zigzag path that leads up behind Dericambus is a delight. It's a shame that it stops short of the summit, giving a half-hour of heather. But then, a hill called 'Black Crag' oughtn't to be altogether easy.

Park on the track below the road at the red phone box at Invervar.

95

Start down the track, to cross the **River Lyon**. The track bends left, then rises away from the river in two sweeping bends under birch trees. Keep ahead, signed **Dericambus**. Pass through the farm and take a gate on the right. Keep ahead, up a steep meadow, seeking out the zigzags of an old and disused path.

The path exits through a gate and zigzags up through heather, to left of the little stream gorge. At about 450m level the path crosses the stream, and continues onto damp terraces on the north face of the hill. Ahead and above is the outjutting summit, crossed by a fence. You could slant up directly to it. If obstructed by boggy bits and heather just head up left onto the plateau to find the fence, and turn right alongside it to **Creag Dhubh** summit.

Descend southwest, on slopes more grass than heather, to a rough track slanting across the hillside.

Follow this down to the right. It zigzags down the western end of Craig Dhubh, to run into a larger track not far above the top of plantations.

Keep ahead on this track as it contours down-valley above the plantation, then turns sharp left to plunge down through the trees to the valley floor. Turn right along a wide, smooth track, under birches and along a steep bank above the river, to the junction near Dericambus. Turn left down the sweeping S-bend to the River Lyon, and up to **Invervar**.

The track down the west ridge of Creag Dhubh, to Carn Gorm

22 Beinn Dearg and the Mairgs

Length

Difficulty

Start/finish	Invervar, Glen Lyon (NN 666 483)
Distance	28km/17½ miles
Ascent	1700m/5700ft
Approx time	10½hr
Max altitude	Carn Mairg 1041m
Terrain	Track, pathless grassy slopes and summits, Munro-baggers' path over the Munros

It's possible to descend to Invervar from various points around the Mairgs horseshoe. A wide path leads down the southeast ridge of Carn Gorm, and a small one from the col immediately north of the same hill. Described within the main route is the descent from Meall Garbh, combining the Corbett with two Munros and conveniently leaving Carn Mairg and Meall nan Aighean for the 'Carn Mairg from Fortingall' Route 19. Beinn Dearg to Meall Garbh and using the direct descent to Invervar gives a circuit of 22km with 1300m of ascent (14 miles/4300ft) – about 8hr.

The Mairgs offer a high-level wander of about 7km on wide, rounded ridges. With four Munros, the horseshoe route from Invervar is fairly popular, and pathed most of the way (the exception being the occasional small boulderfields of pinkish felsite).

Turn this into a more serious hill day by adding the smaller but rougher Beinn Dearg. This gives a fine viewpoint at Creag Ard, pathless but reasonably pleasant hill walking. It also gives 6km of Glen Lyon's valley floor, a counterpoint to the high path from Carn Gorm to Carn Mairg.

Park on the track below the road by the red phone box at Invervar.

Start down the track and across the **River Lyon**. The track bends left then back right in an S-bend to a junction. Turn right, signed for Inverinain. The track contours through woods above the river, then through fields and along the foot of a plantation, to pass **Inverinain**.

The track continues along the valley floor with its big river. At a gate before **Roromore**, during lambing time a diversion sign may divert you to the left, above the top edge of the field, on a sketchy path above a deer fence. Turn down right through a gate to the farm, and out on its access track. Pass two more houses, round to a junction where ahead and right are both tarred.

Turn right over a cattle grid. The track crosses the River Lyon to the valley road at **Camusvrachan**. Turn left for 600 metres. A grassy track turns back up right through two gates.

Continue up through mixed woods, and through a gate in a deer fence into dense plantations. The track is quite steep and stony. About 150 metres above a second gate, the track bends right and levels off. After 50 metres, and just before the track dips to a stream crossing, turn back left up a grassy tree gap to a gate at the plantation top.

Strike up left to the crest of the spur and follow it uphill. Pass along above **Creag Ard**, broken crags dropping towards Glen Lyon, to the summit cairn above. ▸ Continue northwest along the ridgeline over rough heathery grass past a couple more cairns. After a small area of peat hags, pass to right of a small pool to a cairn. There's a direction change here to the right, northeast, down across a wide, shallow col. Keep ahead up heather then grass to **Beinn Dearg** summit, which is of short height.

Pinkish-grey felsite (fine-grained granite) here matches the pinkish screes on the face of Beinn Dearg opposite – whose name means 'red hill'.

Head down northwards for 400 metres. Avoid swinging right too soon as the steep ground below has some small crag. Some old iron fence posts can be used to guide you down northeast to the col. The slope of Meall Droilichean above is scree and boulder, so slant up right, onto the grassy ridge of **Carn Gorm**, and follow it to the summit with its fallen trig point. ▸

The Munro-baggers' path could now lead you southeast past a smaller cairn, then down the ridgeline to Invervar Burn.

Follow the path left (north) down to a gentler ridge. (At the first col, traces of path lead down to the right for another escape route to Invervar.) The main path ahead contours the northwest slope of An Sgorr; a smaller path

goes over the top, where you'd turn down left (north). Either way you reach a second col beyond.

The path runs up ahead, with an old fence joining it on the gentler boulderfield slope above, to **Meall Garbh** summit cairn with iron fencing in it. The rounded boulders are of felsite granite.

Direct descent
From Meall Garbh summit head east-southeast, following the old fencing, to a second knoll. Turn down south to cross a third one.

Keep descending south until the slope steepens, then slant down left on a slight spur to right (west) of a burn. A little way above Invervar Burn meet a green track at shielings and an iron hut. Follow the track downhill, up to left of the stream. The track gets stony, and passes down through a gloomy wood of larch to Invervar.

For the **main route** to Carn Mairg, follow the old fencing roughly east, but as it bends right, uphill, the path contours forward then slants gradually down around the north flank of the hill. Rejoined by the fence remains, the path runs into boulderfields, again the rounded felsite. So the path's not all that clear, east along a col and over a slight

rise. Beyond this the ground becomes easier and the path clearer as it returns to grey schist.

Follow cairns and old fence poles along the rounded crest of **Meall a' Bharr**. The path contours to right of the final cairned rise, and stays down to right of the crest, which is a pile of pinkish felsite boulders again, before the final climb to **Carn Mairg**.

Head down east, on a sketchy path, then down a boulderfield to the wide flat col. The path heads down to the right, slanting around the slope of **Meall Liath** to join the spurline running down south towards Meall nan Aighean. Across the wide col, the path heads up south, as if for the southwest summit. At a slight levelling at half-height it bends left, slanting to the col between the two tops. Turn left, to the mildly rocky main summit of **Meall nan Aighean**. ▶

Return across the shallow col, and head up to the southwest summit, which has fine views to Ben Lawers and Glen Lyon. Here turn back right, almost to the arrival direction, descending north to a levelling at 900m. From here the descent ridge runs down west, with a grassy path. At about 600m the ridgeline narrows and becomes heathery. The path descends in a zigzag to the right – a sign that it's an old pony path – to a levelling in the ridge.

The Carn Mairg group, from Creag Dhubh

Aighean means red deer hinds. Harveys' map has 'nan', which seems better Gaelic than the OS 'na'.

Ahead the obvious path follows the crest, with more steep eroded descent ahead. To continue at the milder gradient enjoyed by the ponies, turn down sharp left at this ridge levelling, on a wide path used by quad bikes. This descends the south slope in zigzags. At a cairn, the quad-bike path turns away left, to slant away down-valley: don't turn with it but keep ahead, down a faint grassy groove in the heather. For these 50 metres the old path is unclear.

The old path becomes evident again, green and ter-raced, slanting gradually downhill to the right. After 250 metres of gentle descent, it zigzags back down left, then bends back to its former direction. It runs right around the slope, to join a stony track near **Invervar Burn**.

Just below, the track passes through an empty gate-way into a wood of larch and rhododendron. Noisy waterfalls are on the right and you can leave the track to visit them – they're less impressive than they sound through the trees. The track exits the plantation at a tall gate with ladder stile. After a second such gate, the track reaches the valley road through a third one, opposite the red phone box.

Start/finish	Track end east of Stronuich Reservoir (NN 512 421)
Distance	15km/9½ miles
Ascent	1000m/3300ft
Approx time	5¾hr
Max altitude	Meall Ghaordaidh 1039m
Terrain	Grassy slopes, peaty moorland, quiet road

Length

Difficulty

Meall Ghaordaidh is commonly taken from Glen Lochay: a moderately angled grassy slope for three hours up the hill, and then the same slope back down. But most hills are more interesting from the north. On Ghaordaidh's shady side, the glaciers carved out two rather rocky corries. Thus the hill becomes a horseshoe, with a bit of a ridge, a bigger bit of peaty moorland, and a return leg along the quiet cul-de-sac of Glen Lyon.

The track end access for Stronuich dam is 600 metres down-valley from the dam itself. Parking is on the road verge, with more alongside the reservoir.

Meall Ghaordaidh from Glen Lyon, summer evening

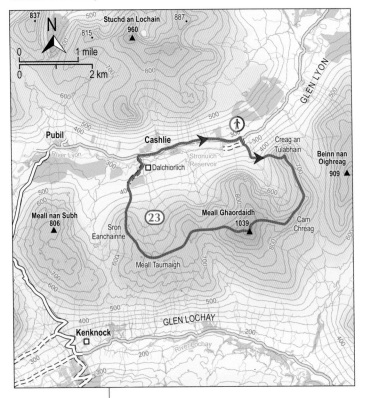

Start over the **River Lyon** on the concrete bridge, and turn left on a track to an intake dam on Allt Laoghain. There's a fence gate here. Head up to right of the stream to the lip of Corrie Laoghain at about the 400m level. Cross the stream and head up the steep western spur of **Creag an Tulabhain**. Keep to right of the lowest outcrop (500m contour), then slant left to its top. Head straight up the spur, until the final slightly rocky steepening. Here zigzag out to the right and back again. ◄

In winter this could give good crampon ground. For less steep slopes head further into the corrie, then up east.

Follow the very pleasant grassy ridge with a small path round by **Cam Chreag** to the summit cone of

Meall Ghaordaidh. The trig pillar stands in a stone shelter cairn; the views are very wide.

Head down west, across a wide col with a small pool, and then up, quite steeply at first, to the minor top Meall na Cnap-laraich. Descend southwest, over rough peaty moorland (but without hags). After 1km, you'll meet a fence starting on the top of a knoll. Follow it roughly west for 500 metres, over a second knoll (**Meall Taurnaigh**) and onto a third – this one protected in front by a small peaty swamp. Here leave the fence and head down northwest, on bumpy grassland, for a short climb onto **Sron Eanchainne**.

Descend north, and head for the top left corner of a pine plantation. Don't take the ladder stile into the plantation, but head down to left of it to a gate. Through this, a rough track slants down to the right. After another gate, the track fades: find it just ahead descending the far bank of a stream. It bends right, above a lower plantation, and runs down to **Dalchiorlich** farm. Cross to the left bank of the stream here to avoid the farmyard, to a gate leading onto its access track.

Follow the track out to the Glenlyon road, and turn right for nearly 3km to the walk start.

24 Around Loch an Daimh

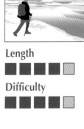

Start/finish	Below Loch an Daimh dam (NN 513 464)
Distance	26km/16 miles
Ascent	1500m/5000ft
Approx time	9½hr
Max altitude	Stuchd an Lochain 960m
Terrain	Rough, steep path, then grassy slopes and ridges; good track to finish
Parking	At foot of track below Loch an Daimh dam (with map board with stalking season routes)

Length

■ ■ ■ ■ ▢

Difficulty

■ ■ ■ ■ ▢

For a longer outing over two Munros and two Corbetts carry on over another Meall Buidhe (the one that's a Munro) to give a distance of 29km and 1850m of ascent (18 miles/6200ft) – about 10½hr.

On Stuchd an Lochain in 1590, Mad Colin Campbell of Meggernie with his faithful gillie made the first recorded Munro ascent in Scotland. Their plan was to chase the wild goats over the cliff edge. Mad Colin thought it would be even more fun to see what would happen to a human being, so ordered the gillie to leap over after the goats.

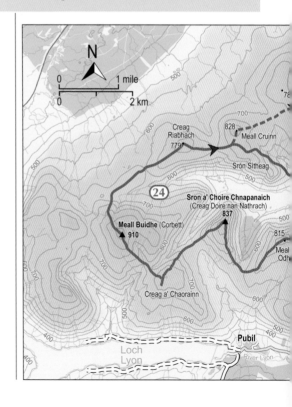

The gillie asked to say his prayers, and Colin, who was not cruel (simply crazy as a midge) allowed him this. As the man was on his knees for rather a long time, Colin wandered over to take a look down the drop. At which the gillie leapt up and pushed Mad Colin over the edge.

Today's walkers, being altogether sane and sensible, find a reason for the ascent in the shapely summit itself, rising triangular above its little lochan. And rather than back down the same way (the eroded path above the reservoir is even nastier downhill), continue over grassy humps that include two Corbetts, before returning along the north side of the loch.

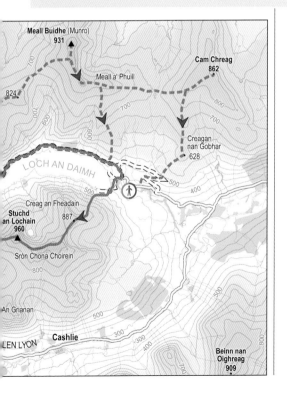

Stuchd an Lochain from Glen Lyon

Start on the road below the dam, over a locked gate, and up to the south end of the dam.

Follow a lochside track to its first bend, then head up a rough, eroded little path. It slants above the reservoir, then turns directly uphill, steep and stony, to the ridgeline east of Creag an Fheadain. There's a cairn at the path top where it joins fence remains (this dead fence will guide for more than half the walk).

A pleasant ridge path ascends **Creag an Fheadain**, then turns southwest along the ridgeline of **Sron Chona Choirein**. Path and fence skirt just to right of the summit. After a slight dip, a steeper ascent leads to the shapely summit of **Stuchd an Lochain**.

Descend west, on short grass, above rocky drops to the reservoir. A small path follows the old fence over the hump of **Meallan Odhar**. ◄ Descend southwest to a peaty col; the fence goes straight through, but easing down to the right avoids the hags. Follow the fence remains up to the jutting viewpoint of **Sron a' Choire Chnapanaich**. (Different names: Stob a' Choin on the estate's map signboard, and Creag Doire nan Nathrach on older maps.)

This path must have come about because of Cameron McNeish's Munros guidebook, which suggests a circuit of Stuchd an Lochain, Sron a' Choire Chnapanaich and Meall Buidhe (Munro).

Descending west from Stuchd an Lochain

Follow the fence down southwest into another wide, peaty col. Cross this to right of the fence, up to a rocky knoll with cairn at 680m level. From here you could contour steepish grass to the 709m col southeast of Meall Buidhe. But the watershed takes you over the extra hill, **Creag a' Chaorainn** (798m). The fence crosses the plateau but not the summit, which is a small cairn 300 metres to the east – there's another cairn at the plateau corner overlooking Beinn Heasgarnich.

Return to the fence and follow it down into the col at 709m, where it has an old gate in it. The spurline above leads to a grassy plateau corner, but more direct is to contour left for 200 metres to cross a stream, and head straight up Meall Buidhe's grassy southeast spur. **Meall Buidhe**'s summit is a stony plateau with a couple of cairns. ▶

Note that this is the Corbett Meall Buidhe (910m) – not the Munro Meall Buidhe (932m) 8km northeast.

Follow the fence down northwest for 200 metres, until an even more decayed fence bears down to the right. Keep down north, crossing a stream, until the ground steepens. Bear right to go down the spur to left of a stony gulch, to reach the flat valley that's the very head of Gleann Daimh. Cross this valley onto a broad ridgeline of peat, stones and low heather.

Follow the crest of the moor northeast, with a few boundary cairns, and a faint path formed by a scramble bike. The going is easy, so it doesn't matter if you lose the path, or bear left off it to cross the summit of **Creag Riabhach** just above.

Head down east, to the start of a faint, rough track. It passes two small pools, runs east through a wide col, and ascends onto the south shoulder of Meall Cruinn. It then runs southeast along the grassy crest. In a slight dip, it turns down left into Coire Chorse.

Follow the faint track down grassy slopes, keeping up to right of the main stream. The track runs down to left of a plantation, to ford the stream near the reservoir side and just below a small gorge. After another 200 metres the faint track joins the start of a smooth, well-built one. This runs above the reservoir to pass above the dam. In another 300 metres, the main track turns down right to the valley road.

Both Buidhes

Trouble keeping track of which Meall Buidhe you've been on? For a long but grassy outing over two Munros and two Corbetts Route 24 can be extended to take in Meall Buidhe (the Munro).

Having picked up the rough track east of Creag Riabhach, cross the col but then head up left over **Meall Cruinn**. The northern cairn is the higher (probably).

Pick a line across the head of Coire Dubh, which has grassy bits among small hags, with a grassy climb to the right-hand of two bumps beyond (**824m**, unnamed). In the col beyond is a small track that becomes a path to the summit of **Meall Buidhe**. All along this ridge there are fine views across Rannoch Moor to the wall of mountains along its opposite edge.

From the summit, it's a pleasant stroll round the top of Glas Choire to a steeper drop east. The path bears down to the right, onto the south flank of **Meall a' Phuill**, in peaty ground. Here are various paths down south to the track above Loch an Daimh dam.

...and Cam Chreag makes three

On a summer day, the energetic could add a third Corbett, **Cam Chreag**. The summer day is a long one: 35km and 2100m of ascent (22 miles/7000ft) – about 13hr.

Meall Buidhe (the Munro) to Cam Chreag is covered in Route 61. From Cam Chreag, return 600 metres to the southwest top. Descend the ridge southwest then south, with bare rock slabs leading down into the col before the slight rise to **Creagan nan Gobhar** (Craglet of Goats – Mad Colin didn't get all of them). Head southwest, aiming for a fenceline on the opposite side of the glen, to hit the track corner below. Head down to the right. From its next corner descend grass to the valley road.

25 Beinn Heasgarnich and Creag Mhor

Start/finish	Below Loch Lyon dam (NN 459 417)
Distance	22.5km/14 miles
Ascent	1300m/4300ft
Approx time	8¼hr
Max altitude	Beinn Heasgarnich 1076m
Terrain	Track, grassy slopes and ridges

Length

Difficulty

Marked as road on some maps, the **track north from Glen Lochay to Lyon dam** is a private hydro board track. It is horrendously potholed, and at the Glen Lochay end is marked 'Private road authorised vehicles only'. Various guidebooks suggest it for access to Beinn Heasgarnich and Meall nan Subh.

From the east, Heasgarnich is approached across two miles of peat, and looks like a wide flat plateau. But as so often, the north side is more interesting, with a new track around Loch Lyon giving a long but easy approach march. And the flatness of Beinn Heasgarnich is an illusion, caused by the pleasantly level ridges northeast and southwest. This route arrives on the former, and continues along the latter.

Park at the foot of the private road over to Glen Lochay, where there's a small pull-in with an estate notice board.

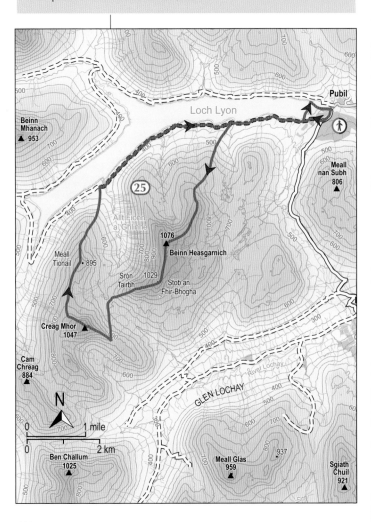

Start up the potholed road for 500 metres, then turn off right above a deer fence to short cut to the tarmac lane to the south end of Loch Lyon dam.

Creag Mhor from the north

The track beyond crosses above a tunnel inlet, then passes a Nissen hut boat shed. In another 1.5km it fords a stream, with the decaying old bridge just upstream. Once across, turn off up grassy slopes southwest. After 15 mins (450m level) cross a new sheep fence. At 600m, ease across to the right for views into the north-facing Coire Heasgarnich.

Head up to reach the level ridgeline. It is grass and outcrops, with several small pools. Head southwest along the ridge. A small path forms, leading up the steeper rise to **Beinn Heasgarnich** summit cairn.

Leave the summit on the other high ridge. After a broad grass slope down south, the narrower ridgeline swings right, and has a clear path. In mist the ridge appears to end at Point 1029m (**Stob an Fhir-Bhogha**): the continuing ridgeline is just down to the right, and runs west. It narrows to Point 971m (**Sron Tairbh**), then descends a steep spur with zigzag path.

Cross the peaty col below at its highest point to avoid peat hags. The 'standard route' between the two Munros ascends to Creag Mhor's north ridge, but we shall use that ridge for the descent. So instead contour to the left along the foot of broken ground with rocks, then slant up the grassy slope beyond, to join Creag Mhor's fine southeast ridge at its levelling (800m level) or just above. Continue up the fairly narrow, pathed ridge to **Creag Mhor** summit.

Descend west, swinging to the right (northwest) once past stony broken ground. Descend a wide grass slope to the lochans in the col north of Creag Mhor. Cross **Meall Tionail** and descend its well-defined north ridge. As the ridge eases and widens (700m contour) descend northeast. At about 550m level the spurline steepens and you work down through a few metres of broken crag. Steepish grass leads down to the shoreline track.

Turn right over the ford of **Allt Fionn a' Ghlinne** and follow the track for 6km back to the Lyon dam. Cross the dam, and at its end turn down right on a faint path to join the tarmac access track. Follow it out to the road and cross the river to the start point.

PART FOUR
BRIDGE OF ORCHY

Descending west off Beinn a' Chreachain (Route 31)

SUMMIT SUMMARY: BEINN DORAIN

Up Auch Gleann with Beinn Dorain, Beinn a' Chaisteal and Beinn Odhar and a glimpse of Beinn Mhanach (Routes 26–29)

Bridge of Orchy is in Argyll, so should these routes be in some other book? Well, the middle Munro, Beinn Mhanach, is entirely in ancient Perthshire, and modern Perth & Kinross; Achaladair and Chreachain are on the border. For once the geography matches the politics. From Loch Lyon in the east these hills are rounded, steep and green: pure Perthshire. West and north, however, their crags and corries are altogether Argyll.

For those who want to bag 'em and be off, the group breaks down into three hill days. Beinn Mhanach is achieved from Auch: a dull grassy day, but then Beinn Mhanach is like that. Dorain and Dothaidh are done up the steep path from Bridge of Orchy. Poet Duncan Ban wrote thousands of lines of flowing Gaelic in praise of Beinn Dorain; as Steve Kew dryly notes of this Orchy outing, it 'may leave the impression that Duncan's sentiments were excessive, if not altogether misplaced'.

BEINN DORAIN ROUTES

26 Beinn a' Chaisteal and Beinn nam Fuaran (from Auch)
27 Beinn Mhanach, the Monk (from Auch)
28 Dorain and Dothaidh from the back (from Auch)
29 Bridge of Orchy to Beinn Dorain, Beinn an Dothaidh
30 Beinn Mhanach long crossing (Auch to Achallader)
31 Rannoch Edge: Chreachain and Achaladair (from Achallader)
32 Beinn an Dothaidh from Achallader

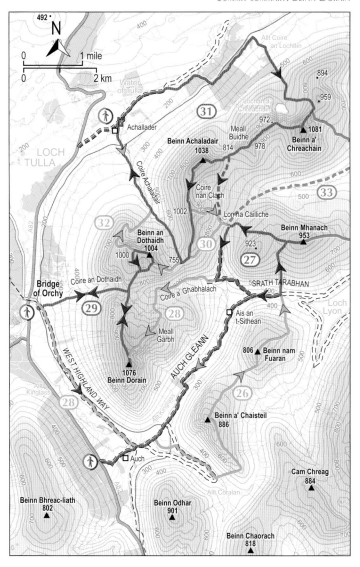

The remaining two are ascended from Achallader farm, a fine ridgeline of the cragged Rannoch edge.

But why not make all the outings into fine ones? Beinn Dorain from Auch by its back route saves the steep Bridge of Orchy path for the descent. Make Beinn Mhanach a two-car or bus-link outing from Auch to Achallader: add in Beinn an Dothaidh on the way out. Or do these Perthshire hills out of Perthshire – approaching from Loch Lyon to get that view over Rannoch Moor as a sudden surprise.

BEINN MHANACH

This section includes three ways of adding excitement to what Irvine Butterfield (author of *High Mountains of Britain*) described, a bit unfairly, as a 'tedious lump'. Two Humps and a Monk (see Route 26) adds in the two smaller hills south of Auch Glen for a day of solitude and strenuousness. Route 30 is a linear route from Auch to Achallader that is varied and interesting and could even include Beinn an Dothaidh (Route 32); meanwhile Route 33 is a natural horseshoe of the three eastern Munros from the unnatural start point of Glen Lyon.

26 Beinn a' Chaisteal and Beinn nam Fuaran

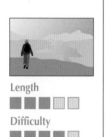

Length

■ ■ ■ ▫ ▫

Difficulty

■ ■ ■ ■ ▫

Start/finish	A82 Auch track end (NN 317 353)
Distance	19km/12 miles
Ascent	1000m/3200ft
Approx time	6¾hr
Max altitude	Beinn a' Chaisteal 886m
Terrain	Good tracks, grassy slopes

Two Humps and a Monk: to continue over Beinn Mhanach switch into Route 27 below. The full walk is 24km with 1550m of ascent (15 miles/5200ft) – about 9hr. Beinn Mhanach is a grassy lump: so why not add on two smaller grassy lumps on the way in? The result is a long and fairly energetic walk on short grass and some Landrover tracks.

The two Corbetts visited on Route 26 make for a mild sort of hill day, with a lot of solitude and spring birdsong, and a dramatic viewpoint from the top of Beinn a' Chaisteil.

At Auch track end there are a few parking spaces on the A82, with more 50 metres down the private track.

Start down the track across the valley floor, past houses and holiday cottages at **Auch**, to Allt Kinglass river. Here ignore side-tracks to right and over the bridge left, both being the West Highland Way (WH Way). Instead keep ahead on a track marked 'No Access to West Highland Way'.

In 500 metres is a new side-track along a hydro-scheme pipeline. Ignore this, and cross the ford ahead, to take an older track on the right just beyond. This leads to the left-hand end of the right-hand railway viaduct, the one over **Allt Coralan**. Dodge under the viaduct and bear uphill across grassy slopes to join the track above, the only one marked on maps as yet. Follow it up Glen Coralan to just above the waterfall marked on maps. The intake is being built immediately above this waterfall, which will presumably be a waterless waterfall thereafter.

Beinn nam Fuaran from the west

The track turns downhill here (to join the pipeline track and return to Auch) so leave it at its highest point, and strike up moderate grass slopes to reach the south-eastern ridgeline of Beinn a' Chaisteil. Follow this up, with posts of a decayed fence. A summit ridge of about 400 metres leads to the cairn of **Beinn a' Chaisteil**.

Turn right, to descend the gentle slope northeast, ideally not following the old fence too closely to avoid tangling ankles in rusty wire. The col Mam Lorn is peat-hagged. You could follow the old fence through the peat and straight up the steep slope ahead. More comfortable is to skirt to right of the peat, then slant up to the right, to gain the rather less steep southern spur to the top of **Beinn nam Fuaran**.

From Beinn nam Fuaran the route can be extended over Cam Chreag, Beinn Chaorach and Beinn Odhar for an unusual, strenuous, but not altogether enjoyable **round of five Corbetts**.

Follow the old fence down northeast for 600 metres of gentle ridgeline. Where the fence divides, follow the left branch down quite steep grass (or for less steep slopes, stay with the right branch down to about 650m level, and then slant down left), to reach the highest point of **Srath Tarabhan**. Directly opposite, the stream Allt a' Chuirn tumbles down the slope of Beinn Mhanach, with waterworks concrete at its base – here water joins it from a leat and also a tunnel, and it is diverted eastwards to end up in Loch Lyon. ◄

To continue over Beinn Mhanach, switch now to Route 27.

Turn left, on the track down into **Auch Gleann**. After 1km it joins the main track beside **Allt Kinglass**. Follow the track down over seven fords and under the railway viaduct to **Auch** farm.

27 Beinn Mhanach, the Monk

Start/finish	A82 Auch track end (NN 317 353)
Distance	20km/12½ miles
Ascent	750m/2500ft
Approx time	6½hr
Max altitude	Beinn Mhanach 953m
Terrain	Tracks, rough grass slopes with small path
Note	Bicycle to head of Auch Gleann, 6.5km each way, saves 2hr

Length

Difficulty

Mhanach means monks. Monkish life is austere, with plenty of peace and quiet, few thrills and passion. Auch Gleann is a pleasant ramble, but the grass path up Beinn Mhanach is only mildly exciting.

There are a few parking spaces on the A82 at Auch track end; more can be found 50 metres down the private track.

Up Auch Gleann to Beinn Mhanach

Start by following the track across the valley floor, past houses and holiday cottages and through a gate, to **Allt Kinglass**. Ignore tracks to left and right, and keep ahead on the track marked 'No Access to West Highland Way'.

The track runs to right of Allt Kinglass into **Auch Gleann**, passing under the left hand of the two big viaducts and over a cattle grid. The track fords the river half a dozen times. ◄ After 4km, pass farm sheds **Ais an t-Sithean**.

In 1km more, fork right on the track up **Srath Tarabhan**, beside Allt a' Chuirn. In another 1km you reach the top of the pass, with Loch Lyon ahead. Up to left the stream Allt a' Chuirn tumbles down the slope of Beinn Mhanach, with waterworks concrete at its base.

> **Allt a' Chuirn** now turns east, flowing (as Allt Tarabhan) into Loch Lyon. Its name indicates that originally it turned west, joining up with the Allt a' Chuirn running to Auch Gleann. Chuirn is a churn.

Turn up left just before the track bridge. A path runs up from the river engineering, keeping to left of the stream. It's a quad-bike track for the first few metres, then a faint grassy trod, with views to small waterfalls. It fades below the slope top, which leads out to the broad saddle between Beinn a' Chuirn and Beinn Mhanach. Turn up to the right on gentle slopes to **Beinn Mhanach**'s stony top.

Return west to the wide saddle, bearing right to pick up the corner of an old fence (NN 366 413). Follow the fence remains down to the wide peaty col **Lon na Cailliche**. ◄

Turn down to the left, on faint quad-bike tracks. Very soon a track starts beside the stream, at about 600m altitude. Follow the track down beside the stream to a dam. Cross below the dam and follow the track down left to a track junction on the approach route.

Follow the track out past **Ais an t-Sithean**, over the fords, under the railway viaduct, and out to Auch and the A82.

Garnets, reddish crystals up to 2mm across, are in some of the river pebbles.

Switch here to Route 30 for the linear route to Achallader. Lon is a local word for a pass; it means 'a strip of a field'.

Start/finish	A82 Auch track end (NN 317 353)
Distance	27km/17 miles
Ascent	1200m/3900ft
Approx time	9hr
Max altitude	Beinn Dorain 1076m
Terrain	Tracks, pathless grassy slopes and ridges, hill paths

Length

Difficulty

Starting at Bridge of Orchy would save a bit of distance, but it's better to have the WH Way track at the end – do it in the dark if necessary, or send the driver along it while the rest of you recline in the Bridge of Orchy Hotel.

A rambling way around to Beinn Dorain, which not only explores the aspects of it so enjoyed by the Gaelic poet Duncan Ban, but also passes the poet's own residence at Ais an t-Sithean.

There are a few parking spaces on the A82 at Auch track end; more can be found 50 metres down the private track.

East ridge of Beinn Dorain

Some have achieved the south spur of Beinn Dorain, directly up from here, claimed as the highest continuously steep grass slope in Scotland.

From **Auch**, start on the track down to the valley floor and across it, past houses and holiday cottages and through a gate, to the river. Crossing the WH Way, keep ahead on the track marked 'No Access to West Highland Way'. ◄

The track to right of **Allt Kinglass** passes under the left hand of the two big viaducts and into **Auch Gleann**. The track fords the river half a dozen times. After 4km, pass farm sheds at **Ais an t-Sithean**.

> Ais an t-Sithean is a barn conversion in reverse: the lower walls of the eastern half are the cottage once home of **Duncan Ban Macintyre**, the poet of Beinn Dorain. Sithean are the fairies.

In 1km more take a side-track on the left. It slants up to a reservoir on a small stream. After crossing below this, the track turns uphill, but contour forward on a rougher track to pass below a second intake dam, this one gathering Allt **Coire a' Ghabhalach** (Stream of the Forking Corrie). Head upstream on grassy slopes into the corrie. After a steepish start the stream bends left (so that upstream is now westwards) and the slope is easier.

At 600m altitude, the valley levels in what is probably a former lochan bed, with crags of Beinn an Dothaidh up on the right. Here turn up left, south, onto the northeast ridge of Beinn Dorain. Once on its rounded spur, ascend southwest to **Meall Garbh**. A pleasant ridgeline with path traces runs to the north top of **Beinn Dorain**, with a big baggers' path leading south through a shallow col to the summit.

Note that the path down left here leads straight to Bridge of Orchy.

Follow the path and ridgeline north back over the north top and down to the Dothaidh/Dorain col at the head of **Coire an Dothaidh**. ◄

The slope ahead now rises in fierce crags. Take a path slanting to the right (northeast) out of the col. It slants up a steepish slope, then fades onto soggy slopes of a shallow south-facing hollow. Ahead is the 993m top of the east ridge, and you can cross damp ground to reach this before following the ridgeline (good drops on the right) to the 1004m main top of **Beinn an Dothaidh**.

Bridge of Orchy Hotel

Even though you arrived on Beinn an Dothaidh from the Dothaidh/Dorain col, it can be tricky to rediscover the ascent path. From Dothaidh's main summit, drop west around the top of the hollow enclosed by the summit ridge. A tiny stream runs south out of the hollow. Once across this stream head down a bit west of south, to find the small path contouring to the right (west) out of the hollow.

Back in the Dothaidh/Dorain col, turn right, down a steep eroded path west. At the floor of the corrie, the path descends to left of the stream through peaty ground, to reach the WH Way track just above the railway at **Bridge of Orchy**.

To relax in the hotel, turn down through a small waymarked gate to pass under the railway just to right of the platform, and follow the tarred lane down to the A82. Alternatively turn left to return to **Auch** by the WH Way, over 6km (3.75 miles) of straightforward track, taking about 1¼hr.

29 Bridge of Orchy to Beinn Dorain, Beinn an Dothaidh

Length

Difficulty

Start/finish	Bridge of Orchy (NN 297 395)
Distance	13km/8 miles
Ascent	1200m/3900ft
Approx time	6½hr
Max altitude	Beinn Dorain 1076m
Terrain	Steep stony path to col, then enjoyable ridge path up and down Dorain, smaller one to Dothaidh

Short and sharp, this is the standard route, but one that undervalues these two fine hills.

The car park at Bridge of Orchy station is for rail users. Arrive by train or bus; if coming by car, park at the A82, or across the bridge on the minor road to Inveroran.

Coire an Dothaidh above Bridge of Orchy

Start up the road opposite the hotel. Pass under the railway just to left of the station. Ignore the track (WH Way) bending off to the right, but keep uphill to right of the stream into **Coire an Dothaidh**. The path is soft to start with, stony and eroded above, and steep in the upper corrie, until it arrives in the col between Beinn an Dothaidh and Beinn Dorain.

Which one first? Dorain is the finer hill: and if you later decide to come down without doing Dothaidh, that one is very good tacked onto a later trip over Achaladair. So take the path up to the right (south). It's a long but fairly gentle climb up an ever-improving ridgeline to Carn Sasunnaich. ▶ A slight dip leads on to the true summit of **Beinn Dorain**, perched at the ridge end.

Return to the Dorain/Dothaidh col, and continue over **Beinn an Dothaidh** and down to **Bridge of Orchy** as on Route 28.

Sasunnaich (sassanach) is foreigner or English person – this cairn is so named because it's fun that such strangers may think they've already got to the top.

30 Beinn Mhanach long crossing

Start	A82 Auch track end (NN 317 353)
Finish	Achallader farm (NN 322 442)
Distance	18km/11 miles
Ascent	900m/2900ft
Approx time	6½hr
Max altitude	Beinn Mhanach 953m
Terrain	Valley track, rough grassy slopes, small path, then rough path down Coire Achaladair

Length

■ ■ ■ □ □

Difficulty

■ ■ ■ ■ □

Longer but even better is to take in Beinn an Dothaidh and its fine northern hollow: see Route 32. Auch to Achallader via Mhanach and Dothaidh is 19.5km and 1100m of ascent (12 miles/3700ft) – about 7hr.

This route through the middle of the range by a wiggly and rather surprising line is well worth the hassle with the Citylink coach timetable or the two cars. After the long valley track and the strenuous but otherwise comfortable grass slopes of Mhanach, there's a surprising contour path across the steep end of Beinn Achaladair for the sudden arrival at the head of craggy Coire Achaladair. There's no better way of having fun on the Monk.

Start using Route 27 (Beinn Mhanach) along **Auch Gleann** to **Beinn Mhanach**; and down towards the wide peaty col **Lon na Cailliche**.

From here to the Achallader col there will be a small Munro-baggers' path that delightfully crosses the steepish grass slope. But above Lon na Cailliche it peters out, and it's not easy to find the start of it. Looking out to the left from the base of Beinn Mhanach, the slope has a couple of small dark scars. The path passes just below these, and then can be seen slanting out left around to the skyline. Carefully note its start point above the col, as this is hard to pin down when you get there.

Coire Achaladair and Beinn an Dothaidh

From Lon na Cailliche, head northeast up old fencing for about six minutes, to a larger strainer post in the old fencing. Now contour left below a line of stony humps. Once found, the path dips into a sharp stream below the waterfall over one of the black scars. It can then be easily followed as it rises gently around the slope to the Achallader col (**755m**, at the top of Coire Achaladair).

Across the col a large path sets off down to the right (north) into Coire Daingean. A steeper descent leads into the lower corrie, **Coire Achaladair**. Here the descent becomes gentler again. Cross to the left-hand side of the stream to pick up a well-marked boggy path. Emerging from the corrie, the path follows a deer fence to a foot-bridge over the railway. The track below leads down through **Achallader** farmyard to the car park. The A82 with its buses is another 1.5km down the driveway track.

If doing this route in reverse, the trick is finding the start of the contour path from the Achallader col (755m). From that col, turn to face towards Beinn Achaladair, then contour to the right out of the col (east). You pass a small cairn to find the start of the path. Follow it around the slope until it peters out. Slant down to Lon na Cailliche – in mist, the old fence posts will guide you down southeast to the col. Head up the old fencing opposite for Beinn Mhanach.

31 Rannoch Edge: Chreachain and Achaladair

Length

■ ■ ■ ☐ ☐

Difficulty

■ ■ ■ ■ ☐

Start/finish	Achallader farm (NN 322 442)
Distance	21km/13 miles
Ascent	1200m/3900ft
Approx time	7½hr
Max altitude	Beinn a' Chreachain 1081m
Terrain	Small paths and grass slopes

Riverside, natural woodland, a corrie loch and high ridgelines above Rannoch all make for a grand two-Munro day. Coire Achaladair is ruggedly handsome – however, the path down it is just rugged. For an even grander three-Munro day, add in Route 32.

Achallader farm, off the A82, has a parking area beside the ruined tower.

It's actually a route to Gorton.

Ignore a sign 'to the Hill' (for Coire Achaladair) but start along the track marked with a broken notice 'Pedestrian to Go'. ◀ Go, then, through a gate, with the broken tower on your right. The track fords the Allt Coire Achaladair

(garnets in the pebbles here), then heads up-valley, running to right of the **Water of Tulla**. After 1.5km, just before the track bends left to a bridge over the river, keep ahead, to right of the river, on a small path, with the first of the widely spaced yellow waymarkers.

The path line is faint, but followable. It stays near the river, below a fenced wood, crossing a low stile on the way along. After 700 metres comes a tall ladder stile, and the path turns uphill through Crannach wood to a bridge over the railway (NN 349 455). Across this, the path turns left to run just above the railway. After about 1km it crosses a ladder stile, and then becomes narrow through dense head-high scrub of rowan and birch. Another 1km, and the path emerges over another ladder stile onto open grassland beside the **Allt Coire an Lochain**.

A small path heads up to right of the stream, which has many waterfall steps one or two feet high due to the level lie of the strata.

At around 400m the deer fence alongside turns away to the right. Further upstream you come to the bottom corner of a higher regeneration enclosure. Ignore the ladder stile leading into it, and continue between the stream (left) and the deer fence (right). The stream's now a small gorge with trees, these supplying seedstock for the regenerating

Across Rannoch Moor to the Bridge of Orchy hills, from the West Highland Way

Lochan a' Chreachain

woodland inside the fence. The fence turns away again to the right (another ladder stile, ignore). Follow a path to right of the stream, to **Lochan a' Chreachain**.

Head up grassy slopes to the left (east). The slopes are less steep further left. At the ridgeline col (945m) turn right up the attractively sharp ridgeline southwest. At its top, bear right, south, for 200 metres to **Beinn a' Chreachain** summit cairn, which is of grey schist topped with quartz from an outcrop just to the north.

From here you can simply slant down the west flank; or else return north for 200 metres to the north end of the summit ridge, and turn down left to find a rough path alongside the escarpment. From the col below, a path passes left of the first small ridge knoll overlooking Lochan a' Chreachain. From the second col, ignore a path contouring the south flank of Meall Buidhe, as it just peters out. It's better to head up to Point **972m**. Now head along the crest with a small path and more Rannoch views.

Escape route option

It's possible to descend Meall Buidhe's northwest spur, round to the outflow of Lochan a' Chreachain. Between

Meall Buidhe and the descent route into Coire Achaladair there is no good route down to the northwest. However, from Bealach an Aoghlain, it is possible to bypass Beinn Achaladair on the southeast side: see below.

Meall Buidhe's cairn is at its far end. The path leads down southwest to the col Bealach an Aoghlain. The slope of Achaladair ahead is outcrops with grass passages among them, and quite steep. A slightly less steep ascent could be found by contouring to the left (southwest) out of the col for about 500 metres, then ascending northwest. However, the steep section of the direct ascent is quite short, with a confident zigzag path. Then more moderate slopes, with the typical steep drops on the right to Rannoch Moor, lead to **Beinn Achaladair**'s summit cairn.

To bypass Beinn Achaladair

The route round to east and south of Beinn Achaladair is just as long as the ridge route over the top but much more sheltered. From Bealach an Aoghlain (northeast of Beinn Achaladair) you head to Lon na Cailliche, the 638m col in front of Beinn Mhanach. In clear weather, just slant down diagonally south around the grassy slope to reach the peaty col. In mist, follow the dead posts of old fence, contouring (west of south) to Coire nan Clach. From the fence corner (NN 348 421) the old posts lead straight down southeast, eventually to pass through the peat of **Lon na Cailliche** col.

About 50m (vertical height) above this col, at a stout strainer post in the fence, contour southwest (leftwards for a person facing uphill) along the foot of some stony humps. Aim just below the black patches of bare rock on the slope ahead. With luck, you'll soon come across the small path of Route 30, leading forward to the **755m** col at the top of Coire Achaladair.

Beinn Achaladair's cairn is perched on the edge of the northward drop, with a fine view down to Loch Tulla. You can gaze down onto Achallader farm and see whether anyone's stolen your car yet.

To switch into Route 32, Beinn an Dothaidh, keep on ahead now.

From here, head down southwest on a gentle and pleasant ridge, turning southwards as it flattens off. It rises slightly over the lesser **1002m** top, then runs down to the pass (755m) at the head of Coire Daingean. ◄

A large path sets off to the right, down into the corrie, but soon splits into sub-paths. A steeper descent leads into the lower corrie, **Coire Achaladair**. Here the descent becomes gentler again. Cross to the left-hand side of the stream to pick up a well-marked boggy path. Where the path crosses a sidestream at 450m level, there's a single step of scrambling out of its small gorge.

The path stays up to left of Allt Coire Achaladair stream, then joins a deer fence to a footbridge over the railway. A wide green path leads to a gate into farm enclosures. Keep ahead between the buildings to **Achallader** tower and car park.

32 Beinn an Dothaidh from Achallader

Length

Difficulty

Start/finish	Achallader farm (NN 322 442)
Distance	11km/7 miles
Ascent	850m/2800ft
Approx time	5hr
Max altitude	Beinn an Dothaidh 1004m
Terrain	Rugged path, pathless hill slopes

Combine this with Route 31 for a **grand three-Munro day** along the Rannoch edge. It's 26km with 1500ft of ascent (16 miles/5000ft) – about 9½hr.

This route explores the craggy northern face of Beinn an Dothaidh, as well as the huge views over Rannoch. The descent is by a minor ridgeline and a hidden little hollow.

Achallader farm has a parking area beside the ruined tower.

Rannoch Moor from the north ridge of Beinn an Dothaidh

Follow a sign 'to the Hill' past the farm buildings. Beyond a gate a path runs south towards the big, craggy **Coire Achaladair**. The path crosses the railway on a small bridge, and runs up to right of the stream, boggy in places. The path gets less boggy, but stonier, as it climbs up **Coire Achaladair** to the col (**755m**) at its head.

Turn up to the right, south of west. The grassy unpathed ridge runs up fairly steeply, to arrive suddenly at the 993m cairn at the corner of the summit plateau. Continue north around the edge of the escarpment to **Beinn an Dothaidh**'s summit cairn (1004m). ▶

The views are northwards over Rannoch Moor, as you head on around the rim, now westwards. In 600 metres you reach the cairn (1000m) on a small rock outcrop at the plateau's northwest corner.

Head down west, with big crags dropping to the right. At the 900m level the spur bends round north, then northeast, thus enclosing a small green hollow and giving

In Gaelic 'th' and 'dh' are generally silent, so it's Ben an Dowey, meaning the burned hill.

135

views across it back to those big crags. Follow the spur right round to where it ends at a steep drop ahead. Now double back to the right, slanting down into the enclosed hollow. There's a small boulderfield to cross before reaching the grassy slopes beside the stream.

Turn down the hollow, following the stream. At the hollow's exit, keep downhill (either side of the stream). Just before the Allt Coire Achaladair, you reach the main path down **Coire Achaladair**. Turn left, down the sometimes boggy path. It stays to left of the stream, to a bridge over the railway with **Achallader** farm just below.

33 The Lyon side:
Chreachain, Achaladair, Mhanach

Length

■ ■ ■ ■ ■

Difficulty

■ ■ ■ ■ ■

Start/finish	Pubil, below Loch Lyon dam (NN 459 419)
Distance	30km/19 miles
Ascent	1550m/5200ft
Max altitude	Beinn a' Chreachain 1081m
Approx time	10½hr
Terrain	Track; grassy slopes, some quite steep, and pathed ridgeline
Note	Bicycle along Loch Lyon track, 7km each way, saves about 2hr

On OS Explorer 337, Beinn Achaladair has so many crag and boulder marks that the crucial contours are illegible; you'll also need Sheet 378. Landranger mapping is clear, but again on two sheets, 50 and 51. So if you have it, use the **Harvey 1:40,000 'Schiehallion'**.

A very natural horseshoe from the Perthshire side but without a bicycle, the walk along Loch Lyon is a big one.

About 200 metres east of the bridge over the River Lyon, a track on the north side of road leads towards farm sheds; there's verge parking at its foot.

Start along the track but turn off at once through a locked gate marked 'no vehicles'. The track rises above **Loch Lyon** dam, unnecessarily rising 100m above the water, then drops towards the reservoir shore.

At Invermearan fork down left through a gate (the track up right leads to a shed). The track turns northwest alongside the 'thumb' of Loch Lyon. In **Gleann Meurain** ▶ beyond, pass a junction on the left (to a track continuing around Loch Lyon), and in another 400 metres ford Allt Meran.

The track runs gently uphill (northeast) for 400 metres, then bends left, levels and fords a stream. Turn uphill alongside this stream, on comfortable grassy slopes. Follow the stream all the way up. At 650m, enter a peaty hollow where the stream runs underneath the turf. Crags are up on the left. Pass up the hollow north, until the ground steepens with small outcrops. Head up just north of west, alongside the stream as it tumbles over rocks and boulders.

The upper corrie, at 900m level, is Coire Dubh Beag (small black corrie), and holds a tiny lochan. The slope ahead is steep and rocky, so turn right, north, to slant

Northeast Ridge, Beinn a' Chreachain

Gleann Meurain is an old drovers' pass to Rannoch.

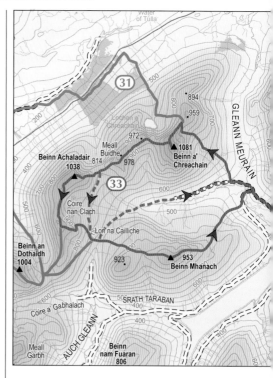

up grass onto the northeast ridge of Beinn a' Chreachain just above.

Follow a clear path up to the left, along the sharply defined ridgeline. On the stony plateau above turn left for 300 metres past a quartz outcrop to the **Beinn a' Chreachain** cairn, itself decorated with quartz chunks.

Return (just west of north) along the narrow stony plateau for 300 metres until the ground steepens ahead. Turn left, just south of west, and descend a grassy slope with steeper drops to your right. A sketchy path forms, and leads down to the col and the continuing lower ridge. There are steep drops to the north.

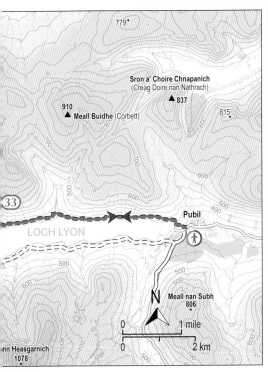

The path skirts left of a first ridge rise to the col just beyond. The more obvious path continues to skirt the left-hand slope, but it peters out, and it's better to head up this next rise to the toplet at **972m**. Now follow a path along the crest to the cairn (978m) at the far end of **Meall Buidhe**. The path continues down, with impressive drops on the right and views ahead to Beinn Achaladair, to the col Bealach an Aoghlain at **814m**. ▶

The first rise towards Beinn Achaladair is steep and broken. The path zigzags up confidently, weaving among the outcrops. Less steep ridgeline with formidable drops on the right leads up to **Beinn Achaladair** cairn.

From here it's possible to bypass Beinn Achaladair, slanting down left to Lon na Cailliche col leading to Beinn Mhanach – see Route 31.

From the lowest point, a descent left would be possible into Coire nan Clach; easier but less interesting than the route over the south top, and may be preferred by those using the hard-to-read Explorer map.

A well-defined ridge runs southwest, becoming a broad grassy plateau, with sheep and a small pool. Head gently down south, with no clear path. ◄ Keep on south, gently rising. The small path skirts to right of the low sprawling cairn on Achaladair's south top (1002m).

Head down southeast, on a fairly well-defined ridge with steep drops left into Coire nan Clach. At the 900m level the ridge forms a slight shoulder, with craggy drops below. From this shoulder, contour out to the left (north-west), on a small sheep path across steep grass. As the grass gets less steep, descend the short slope to the floor of **Coire nan Clach**.

A broken fence runs down to the right. Head down alongside it, to the broad col **Lon na Cailliche** (637m) leading to Beinn Mhanach. ◄

From this col you can cut down left, joining the Allt Cailliche and following its glen out to Loch Lyon.

At the col the fence runs through a peat swamp. Rejoin it beyond, following it uphill to its corner, then slanting up east to the broad col (849m) west of Beinn Mhanach. From a gateway at the top of the broken fence, a faint path runs up the broad rounded slope, fading in the stones around the summit cairn of **Beinn Mhanach**.

Head down east, on what will be a pleasantly angled, grassy and rapid descent. Right at the start there are some good drops on the left – the northern face of Mhanach is impressively rocky given its status as 'tedious lump' (see Summit Summary at the start of this part). At the 700m level the broad slope levels and becomes peaty. Head down left (northeast) in a wide stream hollow. Keep to left of the stream for gentler slopes. The stream runs down in a small gorge with a few rowan trees, to a corner of the track around **Loch Lyon**.

Ahead, cross the track ford over Allt Meran on stepping-stones, and follow the track up through a gate to rejoin the outward route.

PART FIVE
PERTH AND DUNKELD

Braan Falls, the
Hermitage at
Dunkeld (Route 35)

Shakespeare, renowned for never mentioning mountains, is reputed to have done a little light hillwalking at Birnam by Dunkeld. The small hills here, at the extreme edge of the Highlands, show how the noble schist stone, like Macbeth himself, can be corrupted on the blasted heath – one might use even stronger language for the heather of Craig Lochie.

But below those blasted heaths the woodlands are lovely, and these days they scarcely ever creep about the countryside to Dunsinane or anywhere else. Up on top, those who hunt down grouse and trout have left comfortable trackways across the high moors.

Before the harshness of the wild Highlands, there's one hillwalk in the fair city of Perth itself.

34 Perth and Kinnoull Hill

Start/finish	Quarrymill Woodland Park (NN 120 252)
Distance	12.5km/8 miles
Ascent	300m/1000ft
Approx time	3¾hr
Max altitude	Kinnoull Hill 222m
Terrain	Smooth paths, a bit more rugged on Kinnoull Hill ascent

Length

Difficulty

In this book, this is the one walk in the non-Highland part of Perthshire. But the county town has its own small hill, with impressive crags of black volcanic dolerite. The view is of the wide River Tay – but also of the equally impressive Friarton motorway viaduct. The walk's mix of hill and woodland is altogether Perthshire: the bonus is the attractive town centre.

Quarrymill car park is at the edge of the city on the A93 road towards Braemar. From the south or southwest, follow signs to Braemar up the east side of the River Tay. The car park fills up at dog-walk times of day. There's a coffee shop.

Kinnoull Tower

Start south down the main road's pavement to its junction with the A94. ▶

Keep ahead at this point to turn right over the bridge into the town.

▶ Once over the bridge, start by crossing half-left into George Street, passing the **Museum**; at once bear right to the oval Concert Hall. Here turn off left into the narrow Skinnergate, and its continuation Kirkgate, to St John's, the city's

If you don't like city centres, follow the signs south to Norrie Miller Park from here.

From here the route continues south through the older buildings to the railway before turning left to the viaduct.

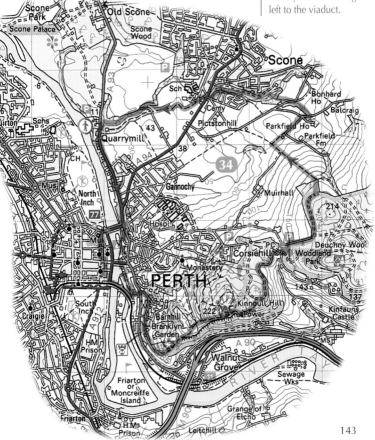

Perth from the railway viaduct over the River Tay

oldest church. Pass round to left of it into St John Street. At its end, turn left in South Street towards the river, then right past Speygate car park, to a gate into Greyfriars old graveyard. Exit through a gateway on the left, onto busy Tay Street alongside the river. Head downstream for 200 metres to the railway viaduct.

> **Perth** lost its city status in 1974, but regained it in 2012 as part of the UK's Diamond Jubilee upgrade. Among cities, why is Perth the world's smallest? Because it's entirely contained within two inches. The North Inch and South Inch are the town's two parks, with Inch meaning island, although neither of them actually is one.

Just south of the railway, on the city side, is the impressive rotunda of the Perth Waterworks.

Cross the viaduct on a walkway attached to the north (upstream) side. ◄ At the bridge end, keep ahead (with Perth Sculpture Park on your left) into a walled path, and up steps to the A85.

Cross this main road, and turn right for 50 metres, then bear left to an entrance to **Branklyn Garden**. Head left, uphill, signed for Kinnoull Hill. Take the first right along Fairmount Terrace. Bear left up a dirt track, which becomes a well-surfaced path, entering woods with a green-trail waymark post.

The path heads uphill along the tops of the crags. Pass a viewpoint bench at a levelling, then as the green trail bends left keep ahead up a small, steep path, staying near the cliff top. At another levelling, a wider path rejoins from the left; again it turns away left, but you can take a direct path uphill. The main trail rejoins once more, to an open area at the highest point of the cliff, featuring a graffiti-ised stone table. **Kinnoull Hill** trig point is found 100 metres in from the edge.

The wide smooth path continues along the cliff top, dropping left with views to **Kinnoull Tower**, then rising to the structure. The wide path continues along cliff tops, bending left (north) to run into a wider track. Here turn sharp right (blue marker). The track bends left, north, to run along the top of east-facing drops, then around the tops of fields to a lane.

Cross into Jubilee car park. At the top end of this, a signpost (blue marker, 'Coronation Road') points to the right, up the edge of woods, with open fields on the left. At

Friarton motorway bridge over the River Tay, from Kinoull Hill

the field top turn left. The earth track runs north along the edge of a pinewood, then bends northeast into the wood. A blue-top waymark post points down left to the wood foot. Head up to the right for 50 metres to a small gate exiting into Coronation Road, which is a hedged track.

Follow the track down through gorse and broom, to fields at the slope foot. Turn right in a farm track, northeast, to reach a road at the entrance to **Parkfield House**. Turn half-right on the public road for 100 metres. A signpost on the left ('Scone') marks a path crossing a stream. ◀

From this point the route just follows paths downstream to the walk start.

Follow the path to right of the stream, bending right to another lane. Turn left for 100 metres, then take a gate (signposted 'Perth Road') onto a broad earth path to right of the stream. A footbridge crosses the stream, then a longer one crosses the Annaty Burn to a track.

Turn downstream (signpost 'Scone') along the Den of Scone on what becomes a residential track. After 500 metres turn left over a footbridge to a field with a small football pitch. Take the tarred path uphill, turning right on a side-path that becomes a street leading to the A94 at the west end of **Scone**.

Turn right, over the stream, then left at Scone Arms Hotel (bar meals) on a street signed for Scone Parish Church and the David Douglas Memorial. At the church, keep left across the end of a car park (less busy than the one at Quarrymill) for a streamside path. After 300 metres it crosses a footbridge. A few steps later cross back again and turn right (green-top waymark post, 'Ridge Wood').

The path runs up the wood edge and turns left along its top. Cross a track by two kissing-gates, to descend to a footbridge, but don't cross it. Turn right, downstream (beige-top posts), on a path that rises above the stream in woods. With the A93 road ahead, the path bends down left to a footbridge and the **Quarrymill** car park.

Start/finish	Quarry car park under King's Seat (NO 042 404)
Distance	17.5km/11 miles
Ascent	500m/1600ft
Approx time	5½hr
Max altitude	King's Seat 404m
Terrain	Waymarked paths, mostly smooth, but rough and steep over King's Seat

Length

Difficulty

Side-trip to Pinecone Point, a striking viewpoint, adds about 30min.

Few roads make the entry into the Highlands as obvious as the A9 at Dunkeld. King's Seat rises steep and schisty, Craig a Barns looms over the town, and oak trees pile right up to the sky. The scene scarcely needs its embellishments of Victorian grottos and follies, ruined cathedral, and half-ruined ancient oak. But it's got them anyway, along with a totally unnecessary Shakespeare legend: a band of English players visited in the 1580s, and it must have been William S himself, or how else did he know to make great Birnam Wood to high Dunsinane come?

Quarry car park is 250 metres off the A9 up the B867 (signed to Bankfoot).

Start by following the signpost 'Birnam Hill Walk' on a track under the railway. In 50 metres turn off left (signpost) slanting up under trees roughly south. With clear-felled ground ahead the path turns more steeply uphill, then contours above a wall with the clear fell below.

A green path forks down left ('Stair Bridge Viewpoint') but keep up to the right. The good path climbs again, westwards, then at a fence corner turns uphill to the right (north), now through heather. In 500 metres it turns sharply up left, in zigzags then on wood-and-earth steps between outcrops. At the top of this steep bit, the path becomes informal peat and tree roots, over schist and under larch, to the rock knoll with large cairn at **King's Seat** summit.

Keep ahead on a rough path descending northwest then north. An outcrop on the right gives views down onto Dunkeld. After a way-mark post, the path is reconstructed in sweeping zigzags, down to a three-way signpost above **Inchewan Burn**. ◄

Turn left, 'Link path to Inchewan Path'. This soon joins the lower Inchewan Path to continue upstream to left of the burn for 1km, then cross a footbridge. The path joins a track where you turn left (yellowy-brown-topped waymark post), to a track junction where all three directions are marked 'Inchewan Path'.

Turn right, northwest. In 400 metres again turn right, signposted for Inver car park. At the next junction, take the main track half-left, downhill, still for Inver car park.

To the right here is the continuing 'Birnam Hill Path' which rounds the hill base above the railway line for a quicker return to Quarry car park.

Dunkeld from King's Seat, to Beinn a' Ghlo

At the **A822**, cross
to a wide grassy path
descending to a minor
road. Inver car park is just
below.

A gate at the bottom left corner
leads to the Braan Path to Hermitage
footbridge. In 2012 this path had a landslip
and was closed, that closure being enforced by a barrier
at Hermitage Bridge. The diversion takes the road downhill
from above the car park, turning left over Inver Bridge into
Inver. Don't turn left into caravans, but at a red phone box
keep round to the left. At the A9 follow a roadside path
alongside the river into **The Hermitage** car park.

Stay next to the River Braan through the car park and under the railway. Continue upstream, bearing left on the riverside path to the stone Hermitage Bridge. Just above is the fine Braan waterfall. Overlooking it on the right is the scenically contrived Ossian's Hall. You could also scramble the rocks above the river for a more intimate view of the falls – holds are good but the rock can be slippery.

Continue upstream to right of the river for 50 metres to a bench. Now don't take the upstream 'Braan Path' with its green arrow; instead move 20 metres to the right, away from the river, for the mauve-arrowed Inver Path. This passes a totem pole then turns right to a forest road.

Cross into the forest road ahead, soon entering a cleared area. After 250 metres, at the highest point of the track, a well-surfaced path turns back up to the left. Take this for the out-and-back excursion to **Pinecone Point**. The path zigzags up to a higher track. Turn sharp right, and follow the track contouring north to its end, and a smooth path to a viewpoint shelter looking up the Tay and across to Craig a Barns.

You must now return along the wide path and the higher track. Around 50 metres back along the track, a steep path down to the left is a mountain bike trail, so is better avoided. However, you can short cut down the wooded slope. Otherwise return down the zigzag path and turn left to continue along the lower track.

At once on the right is Torryvald, a modern folly on the site of a crumbled-away Victorian one. Follow the track for 1.2 km to meet a lower track. Turn down right (signpost 'Inver Path') for 100 metres, then turn left (another signpost) in a soft green track. It descends to join a track, where you turn right through a car park to a road.

From here you'll follow the north-bank branch of Fiddlers' Path (mint waymarks). Take the road out to the A9 and turn left to cross the Tay on the upstream pavement of the concrete Jubilee Bridge, with views to Ben Vrackie. Don't cross the busy A9 itself, but at the end of the bridge, turn down left over the crash barrier to a track. Follow this back under the road bridge and downstream, with the wide river on your right.

After about 300 metres look out for a small path on the right along the riverbank. After a rough half-kilometre, the path gets wider and smoother; 1.2km from the bridge you reach a riverside grotto, with spongy tufa rock in its pillars. Here you rejoin the track just above.

The River Tay and Craig a Barns from Pinecone Point

Pass the Dunkeld House Hotel, and again fork right on a smaller path beside the river. The Dunkeld Bridge appears ahead and you pass another grotto. Before you get to the bridge, the path swerves left to pass the end of the ruined **cathedral** and then along its side.

Just after the cathedral, leave the path to keep ahead under a monkey puzzle tree. A dirt path has a high wall on its right; soon turn through an arch into **Dunkeld**. Keep ahead to the Perth Arms and the main road, and turn right to cross Thomas Telford's Dunkeld Bridge.

At the end of the bridge, steps down left lead to a riverside path. Follow this downstream, now with the river on your left. After 800 metres, interpretation boards identify the historic **Birnam Oak**. The path continues downstream past two fields, to run into a track. Turn sharp right, signposted 'Birnam Path'. After 200 metres, turn left and scrabble up the steep banking by a fallen fence, to reach the A9 opposite the turn-off for Bankfoot.

36 Tracks to Loch Skiach

Length

Difficulty

Start/finish	Balmacneil (NN 976 507)
Distance	13.5km/8 miles
Ascent	350m/1200ft
Approx time	4hr
Max altitude	Loch Skiach 430m
Terrain	Tracks, mostly good but sometimes mere wheelmarks in the heather

Cut this one to length: the shortest walk is 6.5km with 200m of ascent (4 miles/700ft) – about 2hr. The medium walk is 10km with 350m of ascent (6 miles/1200ft) – about 3¼hr.

Fishermen's tracks wander up through woods to moorland above Strath Tay, with a lochside bothy for lunch – only slightly marred by the tops of the wind turbines planted on the slopes beyond.

Best parking is a lay-by on the uphill side of the road 400 metres northwest of Balmacneil. There is also some parking opposite the entrance of Kinnaird Estate Guest House, where the walk turns up off the road. Note that cars can cross the old railway bridge over the Tay at Logierait.

Loch Skiach and Craig Lochie

Start along the road down-valley for 1.2km. Just past the entrance to **Kinnaird Estate Guest House**, a track forks up right, marked 'Castle Peroch'. It bends right to pass below the small castle, then back left above it.

After a gate, it slants easily up the glen side, to turn southwest across moorland. In another 200 metres the main track bends right at the first junction. Take the lesser track ahead. It runs gently uphill for 1km to a second junction.

Shorter walk options

For the shortest walk, at the first junction follow the main track right, through a broad col, then down to the shore of a fishing lochan. Here it passes a tin hut with picnic table.

For the medium-length walk, at the second junction, take the smaller track up right. It is stony at first, but soon grassy. It passes through a high col, then through a gap in a wall, and drops towards the shallow valley of Bainamuir Burn.

For the **main walk**, take the track left, across the stream. It climbs quite steeply for 1.5km. As it reaches the upper moor, Little Loch Skiach and wind turbines beyond come into sight. At this point, look out for a faint track turning off right past a metal pole, as that's going to be the descent route. But for now, keep ahead on the track that crosses level ground to a stone bothy with picnic table on the shore of **Loch Skiach**. ◄

For a much harsher continuation over Craig Lochie, switch to Route 37.

Return along the track for 1km, to the point where it starts downhill towards the far-away Tay. Here turn left on a wheelmark track through heather, passing a metal pole. The track becomes clearer, running between Loch Skiach's northeast shore and a stone wall up on the right. At the loch's north corner the track bends right, downhill. ◄

Route 37, Craig Lochie, rejoins here.

Follow the wheelmarks down north, keeping just to right of a boggy valley floor with a fence running 200 metres to your left. The wheelmarks fade to a single path, contouring slightly right (northeast) to join a much clearer track. ◄

The medium-length route rejoins along this track.

Turn left. After 200 metres, the track bends right, out of the shallow valley of Balnamuir Burn. The rough track winds down northeast towards a nameless loch with a tin hut, but then wanders left to lose sight of it. At a duck pond the track bends right, to arrive alongside the nameless loch. ◄

The short alternative rejoins here, arriving from beyond the tin hut.

About 200 metres before the tin fishers' hut, turn sharp left on a faint green track (north). It slants down to a well-built stone sheep fank (pen). Go through a gate to right of the fank, and bear left through another gate with a stile. The track behind slants down through woodland, turning directly downhill and joining a bigger track that arrives from the right. The latter continues downhill to the road above the River Tay.

Turn right for 400 metres to the lay-by, or for 2km to **Kinnaird Estate Guest House**.

37 Craig Lochie

Start/finish	Balmacneil (NN 976 507)
Distance	15km/9½ miles
Ascent	450m/1500ft
Approx time	5hr
Max altitude	Craig Lochie 519m
Terrain	Tracks; rough deep heather for 2km

Length

Difficulty

Add just 1.5km to the previous walk – but also four squares'-worth of difficulty. For those who must have some summit, well, Craig Lochie is some summit. Deep heather, soggy grass, a boulder or two, and a fine cairn poised above Loch Skiach.

Follow Route 36 to the bothy at Loch Skiach.

Return for just 200 metres, then turn off sharp right on a faint wheelmark track through the heather. It becomes a bit clearer, with a small bridge across the loch outflow then a gateway in a fence. After crossing a low hump, the track dips into marshy ground and divides: take the one ahead, not the left fork.

The track climbs the low hump ahead, appears to bend left but in fact turns right just beyond the crest, now heading west of north towards Craig Lochie. The wheel-marks end at Black Moss Burn. Turn downstream towards the loch for 200 metres, then turn left over a fence and up a grassy stream strip to left of **Craig Lochie**'s rocky nose.

The track down to the nameless lochan, looking towards Ben Vrackie

At the stream top turn right through deep heather to the summit cairn perched on its rock. The trig point is just below.

Head down steep heather and grass northeast to the loch shore. Follow the shoreline to the loch's north corner. Turn left alongside a fence to a gate at the fence's high point. Go through, and cross the sunken trace of an old path to a wheelmark track beyond. Turn left, rejoining (possibly with some relief) Route 36 where noted above.

PART SIX
ABERFELDY

Kenmore and Loch Tay from the Rob Roy Way (Route 39)

Perhaps the only pop song to feature a Scottish hillwalker celebrates Tom Weir (of the Scottish Television series *Weir's Way*) and reached number 60 in the UK charts in 2005. The band was 'Aberfeldy'. Two centuries earlier, Robert Burns stopped off here and wrote *Birks of Aberfeldy*. Scotland's famous Black Watch regiment was raised at the riverside, and the footpath dedicated to cattle thief and hero Rob Roy runs through the town.

Aberfeldy wears its weight of cultural resonance lightly. Within sight of Scotland's 10th highest hill, but only 27km from the Highland Line, it has a booted foot in both Lowlands and mountains, with woodland walks and streamsides, some serious hills, and a handsome village centre with plenty of pubs.

38 Farragon Hill from Strathtay

Start/finish	Strath Tay, west of Strathtay village (NN 893 524)
Distance	19.5km/12 miles
Ascent	950m/3100ft
Approx time	7hr
Max altitude	Farragon Hill 783m
Terrain	Hill tracks, with 1.5km of rough heather tramping

Length

Difficulty

The tracks above Strathtay village offer wide green views of distant glens, while foreground sparkle is supplied by various fake lakes built for fishing. This is typical Perthshire gentleness, the track used on the descent being especially pleasant. On top, typical Perthshire harshness is a short stretch of heather-covered rocky knolls.

Parking on this narrow back road is very limited. Cars of normal size can park (with care) east of Edradynate track foot, for example at a disused gateway beside a small stream under the road (NN 893 524). There is some street parking in Strathtay, such as opposite the golf course. Don't use the customer parking at the village shop.

If parked at Edradynate, walk the back road to the edge of **Strathtay**. Start up the lane below Findynate: not the grand entrance with lodge, but the small lane 100 metres west, up alongside a stream.

Head up under trees to where the lane divides into two unsurfaced tracks. Turn right, passing below **Findynate** farm. Keep ahead, contouring through two gates, to meet a more used track.

Turn up left on this, to pass a small lake. As the slope becomes a moorland shelf around 400m, more lakes appear ahead. Ignore a side-track on your left, and keep ahead to pass to left of **Loch nan Eun**, then to right of a new loch (not marked on older maps) and a plantation, to **Loch na Ba** behind it. The smooth track ends at a waterside hut, but rough wheelmarks continue uphill through the heather roughly northwest, to end in a heathery hollow.

Follow the grassy banks of a small stream up north. Where the slope eases, you can continue northeast to Point **620m**, with views over Lochan Sgaradh Gobhair towards Beinn a' Ghlo. Then return across the top of the stream valley and continue southwest along the knobby ridgeline.

There is a mixture of grass and heather up here. If you do become exasperated, slant down northwest to join the track on the slope below. Otherwise continue over three or four rough hillocks, the last being Tom an

Farragon Hill across Loch na Ba

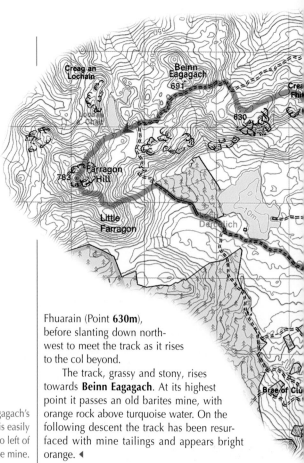

Fhuarain (Point **630m**),
before slanting down northwest to meet the track as it rises
to the col beyond.

The track, grassy and stony, rises
towards **Beinn Eagagach**. At its highest
point it passes an old barites mine, with
orange rock above turquoise water. On the
following descent the track has been resur-
faced with mine tailings and appears bright
orange. ◀

Beinn Eagagach's
summit is easily
reached up to left of
the mine.

> **Barites** is the mineral yielding the element barium,
> familiar from the 'barium meal' that allows your
> stomach to show up on X-rays. Barium was an
> essential stiffener for the rubber of bicycle tyres;
> today its important use is in the mud used in drill-
> ing for North Sea oil. Barite is a flaky-looking
> white mineral; you may find fragments of it in the
> mine tailings.

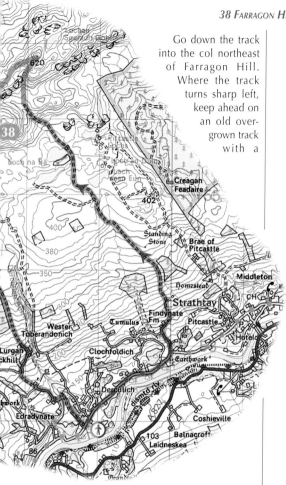

Go down the track into the col northeast of Farragon Hill. Where the track turns sharp left, keep ahead on an old overgrown track with a

faint path, to pass just south of **Lochan a' Chait**. The path fades as the slope becomes go-anywhere grassy. Head straight uphill. The final steep slope is boulders of a landslip. Slant right from the top of the boulders to the summit of **Farragon Hill**.

Descend southeast. There's a steep descent immediately below the summit. Avoid it on the right, to a small shoulder (730m). From here you could descend rather steeply north of east; more comfortable in clear conditions is to descend via Little Farragon. Again, the direct descent is steep and slightly rocky, so slant down roughly east, to left of steep ground, then slant back to the right to the peaty col before **Little Farragon**. Descend east, to meet a track near the top corner of a plantation.

After 300 metres down the track, at the 420m contour, there's a gate where a flag is flown on stalking/shooting days. Below the plantation foot, fork left over a stile on a grassy track running to south of **Loch Derculich**. The track runs down southeast, past a felled plantation. Above **Lurgan**, fork right on the main downhill track, which soon becomes a tarmac private road. At a house on the left, the map marks an old disused track contouring left, northeast, which could take you down via Ballinduin. The main lane continues downhill, past **Edradynate** Steading. It makes a big zigzag down through woods, to descend to the woodland north of the River Tay.

Turn left, back towards **Strathtay** village.

39 Aberfeldy: Rob and Rabbie

Length

Difficulty

Start/finish	Aberfeldy 'Birks of Aberfeldy' car park above A826 (Crieff Road) at south entrance to town (NN 856 486)
Distance	21km/13 miles
Ascent	500m/1700ft
Approx time	6hr
Max altitude	490m, joining hill road
Terrain	Tracks, stony and grassy; a few waymarks but routefinding on return leg needs care

Rabbie is Rabbie Burns, who visited Moness Burn, sat in the small cave, and wrote *Birks o' Aberfeldy*. (Rabbie was adapting an existing folk song *Birks o' Abergeldie*; and Abergeldie, on Deeside, has woods that actually are mostly birch trees.) Rob is Rob Roy, whose Way has two variants into Aberfeldy, used for the outward and return halves of this walk.

The wooded gorge with its waterfall is a delight. The stony track by Urlar Burn is a bit bleak. The return, on grassy tracks in and out of woodland above Strath Tay, is the kind of easy walking that we wish Scotland had rather more of.

Route 40, **Aberfeldy to Kenmore along the River Tay**, can be followed to give a quite different first half to Route 39. You could also use a bus to Kenmore before a return along the slopes above Strath Tay.

About half those buses to Kenmore make the short diversion to Acharn. This allows you to enjoy a linear walk from Acharn to Aberfeldy, with the Acharn Falls as an entrée, then the return half of Route 39. It's 15.5km with 500m of ascent (10 miles/1700ft) – about 5hr.

Start up alongside Acharn Burn (see map for Route 42) – possibly best to the right of the falls, on the stony track rather than the wooded path, but with the Hermit's Cave and view of the falls. Cross above the falls and follow Rob Roy Way to the minor road above Kenmore, joining it above its steep uphill. Turn right up it for 800 metres to a stream bridge at Tombuie, joining the main route below.

Starting from the lower car park, head on up the track to the upper car park. A wide path continues upstream. After 50 metres, turn left over a wide footbridge and continue on the path now to left of the stream, passing a bronze Burns on a bench.

The path zigzags up steps to a higher level, and reaches a viewpoint with a view across to the **Falls of Moness**. Then it crosses the footbridge above the waterfall. At the junction beyond, turn left ('Aberfeldy by Urlar Road'). The main path passes under birches to a tarred road (Urlar Road).

Turn left. About 100 metres before **Urlar** farm, a gate on the left is signed as the path for walkers. Pass along the

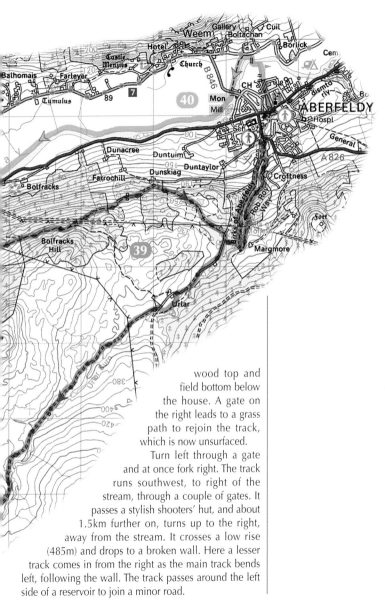

wood top and field bottom below the house. A gate on the right leads to a grass path to rejoin the track, which is now unsurfaced.

Turn left through a gate and at once fork right. The track runs southwest, to right of the stream, through a couple of gates. It passes a stylish shooters' hut, and about 1.5km further on, turns up to the right, away from the stream. It crosses a low rise (485m) and drops to a broken wall. Here a lesser track comes in from the right as the main track bends left, following the wall. The track passes around the left side of a reservoir to join a minor road.

Birks of Aberfeldy

Routes arriving from Kenmore and Acharn arrive from down the road at this point.

Turn right and descend quite steeply towards Loch Tay. After 1.2km the road bends left into pine forest with a stream and waterfall down on the left. After a right bend and another 400 metres, the road is about to cross the stream.

Here turn right on a track passing just below **Tombuie Cottage**. ◀ This is the Rob Roy Way, but you won't see more than a couple of waymarks. After 400 metres gently downhill, the track bends left, straight downhill, passing to left of a new house.

Don't go through a gate into a plantation but follow a sign to fork off right, just above it, on a rough path that soon becomes a track again. This passes into the plantation for 800 metres then emerges into a field. Here the green track slants slightly downhill, with views across to Schiehallion and back to Loch Tay.

The track re-enters plantation, and after 1km, a larger track joins from below. In another 400 metres the track runs under power lines, then bends uphill through an open field. Where it forks, take the left fork, only gently uphill, to pass back under the power lines before re-entering plantations.

After 800 metres there's a fork in the rutted earth track. Fork left, downhill, passing below a different set of power lines. The track exits through a gate into an open field. Follow it ahead, faint at first, then turning downhill to **Upper Farrochill** house.

Pass above this house onto its gravelled access track. This runs gently downhill under birch trees, to approach **Dunskiag**. ▸ Don't double back left to the house, but take the green track ahead, slanting uphill between birch groves. The track passes above a reservoir, to meet the tarred lane Urlar Road.

Turn up right for 100 metres, then left (white waymark) into the path under birch trees used on the outward walk. Just before the bridge over the **Falls of Moness**, turn left, signed Nature Trail. The earth path, quite steep in places, descends to left of the gorge, to the upper car park.

The Dunskiag access track is the short way back to Aberfeldy but the wide smooth track soon turns to tarmac, so it's nicer to go back via the Birks.

On to Aberfeldy

The centre of Aberfeldy, with cafés and tourist information, is only 500 metres away. From the lower car park, cross the A826 at traffic lights to a gate and steps down to a path. This runs to right of the road, then drops to the stream. (Take the branch path up to the right to view poetry extracts.)

The main path crosses a footbridge, then runs beside the stream and through a public park to emerge under a war memorial arch onto the corner of the town square, opposite Breadalbane Arms Hotel.

The River Tay from Wade's Bridge, Aberfeldy

40 Aberfeldy and the Tay

Length
■ □ □ □ □

Difficulty
■ □ □ □ □

Start	Aberfeldy, the Square (NN 856 490)
Finish	Kenmore, loch side (NN 774 454)
Distance	14km/9 miles
Ascent	None
Approx time	3½hr
Max altitude	Maxwell's Temple 120m
Terrain	Level paths

This route can be combined with **a return to Aberfeldy high above the Tay** by the final half of Route 39. The circuit totals 26.5km with 500m of ascent (16½ miles/1600ft) – about 7½hr.

A gentle walk beside the big river, on good paths.

For the return journey frequent buses start from Kenmore, opposite the car park at the loch side, at the south edge of the village. They arrive at Aberfeldy's main square at the top end of Chapel Street. Just before that, they pass the Black Watch Monument beside Wade's Bridge over the Tay, where there's convenient car parking.

About half the buses divert past the Crannog Centre to Acharn. So if you miss the bus at Kenmore, head to the junction at the corner of Loch Tay to pick it up 10min later.

Start at the Square, **Aberfeldy**. Head all the way down Chapel Street to its end, and go through a metal kissing-gate onto Aberfeldy golf course. Just to the left, follow Moness Burn downstream, ignoring two footbridges, to take the third one alongside the **River Tay**.

At once turn right over a giant footbridge: it's made of fibreglass, is grossly over-engineered and accordingly has won a design award. Turn left, upstream. Cross a small footbridge on the left, and follow the main river to the end of General Wade's bridge.

Wade's Bridge, Aberfeldy

If leaving a car at Aberfeldy there's convenient street parking at the Black Watch Monument, just across the bridge. In which case you'll do this first mile of the walk at the end of your day after the bus journey back from Kenmore.

Cross the main road, and descend onto a riverside footpath signposted 'Kenmore 8 miles'. You'll keep to right of the river and alongside it all the way to Comrie Bridge. About 1km from Wade's bridge the path forks. Bear left; or else bear right past the corner of a power line to a footpath signpost, and turn left back to the riverside.

Passing a fishermen's hut, the path widens to an earth track. Soon you pass the confluence of the Tay and Lyon, continuing beside the Lyon along a field edge. Don't join the B846 road straight away, but stay on a narrow riverside path below it, rising to join the road at a small lay-by just short of Comrie Bridge (the bridge near **Comrie Castle**).

Turn left over this bridge (signpost 'Kenmore 3'). Follow the minor road, passing one establishment offering café and gold panning, another with woodburning stoves, retail and café (Karelia House). After 800 metres reach forestry plantations, and a 'rustic lodge' with pine-trunk porch. Around 400 metres later, a forest track on the right is Peeler Gate. Opposite this, pass through a wall gap on the left for a footpath alongside the lane, to join a track heading off left towards the **River Tay**.

In about 400 metres, approaching the river, fork right at a waymark post onto a less-used track. This runs muddy under rhododendrons, to exit at an ornamental fortification above the river (the Star Fort). The wide, smooth track continues above the river. After 750 metres, a track on the right would lead to the nearby lane at Rock Lodge (an ornamental ruin), and down left is the Chinese Bridge to **Taymouth Castle**. ◄

The wide track continues under beech trees, with a smaller riverside path down on the left. Pass the tall stone spire under the taller trees: Maxwell's Temple isn't really a temple, just a pointless ornament. The path drops to the riverside, and follows it past a chalet estate to the Tay Bridge at **Kenmore**.

Turn left over the bridge, then fork right for a lane around the loch headland, passing a café and the piers, to a car park with a decorative roofed gateway.

To return to Aberfeldy

For the return along the high south side of Strath Tay, follow the main road (direction Aberfeldy) until it bends left at the corner of Loch Tay. Here take a minor road steeply uphill, marked 'Weak Bridge 4 miles'. After a steep zigzag ascent, the road has open ground on its left. In another 700 metres, cross a small bridge to a track on the left at **Tombuie Cottage**. This is the Rob Roy Way, where you pick up and continue on the second half of Route 39.

Taymouth Castle, mostly Georgian, is on the other side but the Chinese Bridge was under repair and unusable during 2012 and again in 2020.

Start/finish	Kenmore, loch side (NN 774 454)
Distance	10km/6 miles
Ascent	100m/300ft
Approx time	2½hr
Max altitude	Drummond Hill woods 230m
Terrain	Level paths

Length

Difficulty

Where is Taymouth Castle? Not at the mouth of the Tay – but at its very start, emerging from Loch Tay. This short walk takes in the loch, the river, and the handsome village of Kenmore.

Start to left out of the car park on a lane along the loch side. When it rejoins the main A827, turn left over Kenmore Bridge.

From the north end of the bridge, head up the road for 50 metres, then turn into the entrance for the Waterfront Restaurant. Keep on past it and along the front of houses protected by a monster gateway. A path, in places peaty, leads in under laurel trees. A giant redwood indicates that this is a former arboretum.

After 600 metres the path emerges to the A827 opposite Rustic Lodge, a cottage in overworked stone. To its right is a grassy forest track, signed 'Short walk to Kenmore'.

It returns above the main road, joining the side road opposite the entrance to **Mains of Taymouth**. Turn left around a right-hand bend, and take a wide path forking up left to a car park in the forest.

Turn sharp left, up a forest track, for 200 metres; then turn right at a red-banded waymarker. The wide earth path contours northeast through dense woodland. After almost 2km, emerge past two red-top posts onto a wide earth path.

Short cut to Chinese Bridge

Turn down to the right here to a road beside Rock Lodge, an ornamental grotto. Cross into the middle of three tracks opposite, to reach the North Terrace track immediately above the Chinese Bridge.

The **main route** turns up left to a forest road immediately above. Keep ahead along this. After two side-tracks on the left, the track zigzags down to join the road below at Peeler Gate.

Cross the road diagonally, and pass through a wall gap on the left. A footpath alongside the lane soon joins a track heading off left towards the River Tay.

In about 400 metres, approaching the river, fork right at a waymark post onto a less-used track. This runs muddy under rhododendrons, to exit at an ornamental fortification above the river (the Star Fort). The wide, smooth track continues above the river. After 750 metres, a track on the right is signed 'Drummond Hill Walks'; down left, probably not visible, is the Chinese Bridge to Taymouth Castle. ◀

The short-cut route rejoins here.

The wide track continues under beech trees, and would take you to Kenmore. For a prettier path, however, after just 50 metres turn sharp left down a shrubbery path to Chinese Bridge, under slow renovation, including in

*Looking across
Loch Tay to Kenmore*

2020. (Another option is to cross, examine **Taymouth Castle**, and then take the south bank back to Kenmore.) Before the bridge, turn sharp right on a narrow and somewhat overgrown riverside path. It runs in a rhododendron tunnel, then is joined by a wider path from up right.

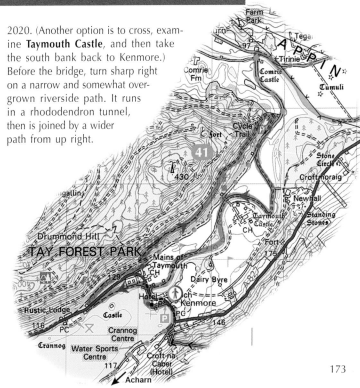

173

Finally it runs into the main North Terrace track (west of Maxwell's Temple) at the corner of a chalet village.

This wide path follows the riverside to Kenmore Bridge, bearing up right to join the road at the bridge end. Turn left through the village to the lochside car park.

42 Falls of Acharn

Length

Difficulty

Start/finish	Acharn: parking around village square or at track foot on south side of bridge (NN 756 438)
Distance	8.5km/5 miles
Ascent	450m/1500ft
Approx time	3hr
Max altitude	Above Acharn Burn 500m
Terrain	Paths and tracks

Strath Tay marks the path of a pretty grand glacier. When it melted, streams on either side found themselves dropping off from the former ice-top level to the present-day level of the loch. Result: waterfalls. The one at Acharn is viewed through a romantic 'Hermit's Cave' – actually a man-made tunnel so that you emerge to the waterfall, blinking, out of darkness.

Signs 'Acharn Circular Walks' point up the track to right (west) of stream, but ignore them for now and start on the Kenmore side of the river. At the back corner of the village square a street leads upstream, becoming a track then a path with a yellow warning sign about precipices.

Down right now leads to the Hermit's Cave, seen at the very end of this route, and straight back to Acharn, for a very short walk.

The path runs up to left of the stream, through woods above the gorge. It passes above a waterfall, then a branch path runs down to the right. It crosses a foot-bridge, then rises to meet a track. ◀

Turn left, uphill, and follow the track across the Upper Bridge. The track turns uphill, going up to left of the stream for 200 metres, then bending left across the hillside. It passes along the foot of a plantation, to a bridge over the next stream. Don't cross, but turn uphill on a smaller track. This becomes very faint as it runs up a grass field. It's found again at the field top, where it exits up through a gate. Just to right of the track here is a **stone circle**, one of the most scenically sited in Perthshire.

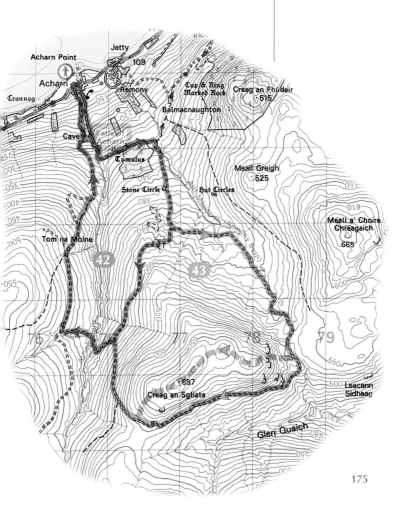

Falls of Acharn

The track is now stony through heather moor. After 1.2km of widening views back across Loch Tay, arrive at a junction with pine clumps to right and above. ▶ Keep ahead, uphill. The track bends right, passes through a pine clump, and contours west. In 200 metres, a cairn 100 metres below the track, Creagan Odhar, is a fine viewpoint and lunch spot. The track bends left around the hillside, rising for a while then descending to a junction high on the side of the stream valley of Acharn Burn. ▶

Here the longer Route 43 turns off left.

Turn down right, on a track slanting downhill (but up-valley) to ford the **Acharn Burn**. It now climbs 60m vertical height to a crossing track. Turn right, gently downhill, past a shooters' hut (often open). After 1km the track bends right and starts descending more steeply. Here ignore a grassy side-track on the left. In another 300 metres the track bends slightly left, while directly ahead is a faint old track, just a green trough. Head down this old track, but where it becomes a strip of mossy swamp follow grass to its right. The old track heads directly downhill to a gate, where it rejoins the stony track.

Here the longer Route 43 rejoins this route.

Down through the gate the track is faint on firm grass to another gate directly below. After another gate, the track bends down left, then back right at a ruin, to join the track alongside Acharn gorge.

Turn left down this steep stony track. In about 50 metres, look out for a stone hobbit entrance on the right. The tunnel leads to a balcony (the Hermit's Cave) looking across the gorge to the **Falls of Acharn**. Take the other tunnel to rejoin the track, and follow it down to **Acharn**.

43 Falls of Acharn to Creag an Sgliata

Length

Difficulty

Start/finish	Acharn: parking around village square or at track foot on south side of bridge (NN 756 438)
Distance	13km/8 miles
Ascent	650m/2200ft
Approx time	5hr
Max altitude	Creag an Sgliata 697m
Terrain	Path and tracks; on the harsher alternative, rough heathery grassland and peat

Extend Route 42 for a few more miles of high-level trackway above Loch Tay. You can take the track high above the remote Glen Quaich; a more rugged alternative crosses an unvisited moorland viewpoint called Creag an Sgliata (same distance and time as the main route). With luck the extra walking will delay you until 7pm, the hour when the evening sun strikes the Acharn waterfall.

Follow Route 42 to the junction near the pine clumps.

Here the tougher route over Creag an Sgliata turns off – see below.

Here turn left on the track that runs around the hill-side, descending slightly. After 800 metres it turns uphill to right of **Allt Mhucaidh** (Remony Burn). It's rather rough and stony before it reaches a high point at the col Moine Bhuidhe. There's a single fence post to left of the track. ◄

Keep on along the track above Glen Quaich, which descends briefly, then curves around the back of **Creag an Sgliata**, gently uphill and grassy green. About 1.5km from the pass it passes below an old shieling, a former summer residence, with more ruined ones below. It then levels off for 1km, to a shooters' hut (open when I passed it). Now the track turns around the end of Creag an Sgliata. Still grassy green, it slants quite steeply down north towards Loch Tay.

Creag an Sgliata option

The harsher alternative over Creag an Sgliata has heather which is at worst ankle deep. At the col Moine Bhuidhe turn right, and head up the rough spur, on grassy patches among the heather. A small cairn greets the arrival on the summit plateau.

Head northwest at first. There's a narrow band of hags to make your way through in the col before Point 678m. Here turn southwest, with another haggy col before Point 694m. Pleasanter going leads to the small quartz cairn on Creag an Sgliata.

Keep on along the crest, with another hag moment, to the slight rise Sron na h-Iolaire. Now the end slope is grassy – you can head southwest to meet the track below at its highest point near the shooters' hut, or descend west on steepish short grass to meet it lower down.

With the two routes now rejoined continue down the track to a junction on the valley wall: the junction above **Acharn Burn**. Continue as Route 42. Alternatively, to avoid the uphill section beyond Acharn Burn, you could continue along the track ahead, rising slightly around the north spur of Creag an Sgliata, then descending gently to the junction near the pine clumps and follow Route 42 in reverse back to **Acharn**.

The track west of Acharn Burn, to Loch Tay, Kenmore and Farragon Hill

44 Creagan na Beinne and Ardtalnaig

Length

Difficulty

Start/finish	Ardtalnaig phone box (NN 702 393)
Distance	17.5km/11 miles
Ascent	1150m/3800ft
Approx time	7hr
Max altitude	Creagan na Beinne 888m
Terrain	Grassy track, then rough grassy ridges

Various permutations of **Routes 44 and 45** can be made in order to take in the two Corbetts and Shee of Ardtalnaig.

- Creagan na Beinne to Dunan and down by Gleann a' Chilleine track: 17.5km and 800m of ascent (11 miles/2700ft) – about 6hr
- A short day over just Shee of Ardtalnaig uses the start of Route 45 before switching back into Route 44: 13.5km and 650m of ascent (9 miles/2100ft) – about 4½hr
- For a thoroughgoing two-Corbett day, strenuous but satisfying, you can combine Creagan na Beinne and Creag Uchdag. Tighten your rucksack straps for 23km and 1350m of ascent (14 miles/4500ft) – about 9hr

Creagan na Beinne is a Corbett (2500-footer) of grassy peat: Shee of Ardtalnaig (Ciste Buidhe a' Chlaidheimh) is too low, by just 10ft, to even make that 2500ft eminence. Two features make this one more than just another meander above Loch Tay. Firstly, there's the delightful grassy track that lifts you from Ardtalnaig high onto the flank of Creagan na Beinne. Second, there's the steep-sided and (by Perthshire standards) narrow crest of Shee of Ardtalnaig.

Parking is at Ardtalnaig, to south of the stream bridge, below a red phone box.

Start by crossing to the north side of the river – there's a small waterfall underneath the road bridge.

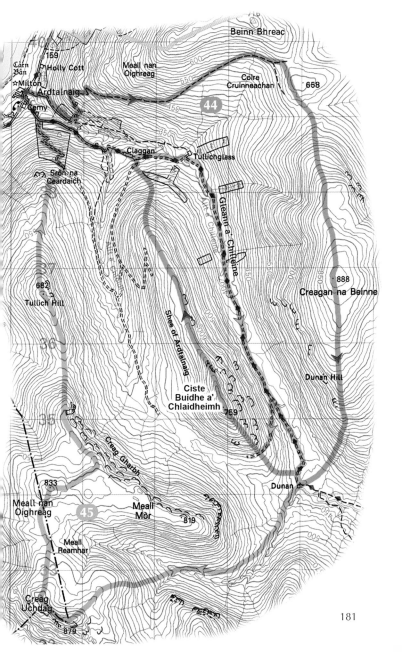

Landslip, Bual a' Chaidheimh, on Ciste Buidhe a' Chlaidheimh

At the north end of the bridge take a gate on the uphill side of the road – marked 'No Dogs' in lambing time. A green track runs up to left of the stream, then after 200 metres bears uphill away from it, through a couple of gates, onto open slopes. The track continues to slant uphill, to the edge of scrubby hazels. It zigzags uphill until it emerges through a gate onto heather slopes.

The track contours southeast, then rises gently around the hill in rather deep heather. After a final gate the track emerges onto grassland. Now it is visible as a green shelf slanting uphill. It gently rises to a point not far below the ridgeline, southeast of **Beinn Bhreac**.

Here the track turns directly uphill, but abandon it, to contour around the west slope of Point **658m** to avoid the top of it, which is peat hags. Soon you join a fence down towards the col north of Creagan na Beinne.

This col again is peat-hagged, but the fence passes just below and to the right, around the edge of the hags, before slanting left and then running straight up the ridge-line above the col. At the plateau the fence turns away, but a few old fence posts run south over short crowberry heath to the slight rise and cairn at the top of **Creagan na Beinne**.

Head south down the gentle ridge with some shallowly excised peaty bits and spongy dry moss. The grassy ridge below is **Dunan Hill** and develops a quad-bike path. This runs down southwards, then turns right to run down to right of a stream (marked Coir Reidh on Explorer maps). It crosses the valley floor to **Dunan**. The hut is shuttered and locked but its gable offers some shelter.

A track, serving the hut, runs north through a gateway. ▶ At its highest point turn up left through a nearby gate. Head up slopes mostly grassy, cross a fence and then a grass track contouring across. Head up the steep spur of **Ciste Buidhe a' Chlaidheimh**, on short vegetation, mostly grass.

To bypass Shee of Ardtalnaig, just follow this track down Gleann a' Chilleine back to Ardtalnaig.

A small path starts at the summit cairn and runs down the ridgeline. After 600 metres, near the foot of the first descent, keep right to see the striking landslip feature Bual a' Claidheimh. ▶ The near-level ridgeline below, **Shee of Ardtalnaig**, is defaced on top by peat hags. The path threads along the crest on the stony basement level, avoiding peat steps. As the ridge starts to descend, keep directly down it, roughly north towards Claggan farm. A sunken peat alleyway leads downhill. At the foot of the peat the alley emerges onto grass – a quartz boulder is not far below.

The name means 'sword-slash'. It's at NN 727 356, not marked on Landranger. Shee means 'fairy hill'.

As the grass steepens with bilberry and heather, turn half-right, to descend less steep slopes of grass northeast. When the slope eases, strike down left to join a track just above **Claggan**. Turn right down to the farm.

Down through the farmyard is the start of a tarred lane, which leads steeply down into **Ardtalnaig**.

The old path above Ardtalnaig

45 Creag Uchdag

Length

Difficulty

Start/finish	Ardtalnaig phone box (NN 702 393)
Distance	19.5km/12 miles
Ascent	900m/2900ft
Approx time	6½hr
Max altitude	Creag Uchdag 879m
Terrain	Track and path, grassy slopes, 400 metres of peat hag

With its long but easy approach walk, the hidden eastern valley, and the grassy descent above Loch Tay, this is a surprisingly good day out on what ought, objectively speaking, to be a dull hill. The peat-hag section merely injects a quarter-hour of proper Perthshire plateau – or you can swerve round most of it.

Parking is at Ardtalnaig, to south of the stream bridge, below a red phone box.

Start up the lane signposted as a footpath to Glenalmond. At the top of the lane, wiggle right and left between the buildings of **Claggan** farm, following signs. Just above the farm, take the left track, with a footpath signpost for Comrie. It runs through between Shee of Ardtalnaig and Creagan na Beinne.

Short walk option
At the track top, ignore the green track forking up to the right. But for the short walk over just Shee of Ardtalnaig, follow this track for 800 metres until below the steep southeast nose of Shee of Ardtalnaig. Go straight up the nose, switching back to Route 44.

But for those following the **main route**, after 5km along the track, you arrive at the closed-up bothy **Dunan**. Pass to left of the hut to a wheelmark path up to right of the

stream, soon crossing a sidestream with a little bridge. The track is sometimes peaty and wet, but is a help anyway through the heather zone. It rises away from the stream around the grassy base of the eastern spur of Meall nan Oighreag.

Passing the rocky spur opposite (**Creag nan Eun**), the path drops towards the stream again. After a stream junction (NN 723 329), shielings are beside the stream and a fenced enclosure is ahead. Drop left to cross the stream upstream from the junction, and head up grassy slopes southwest. Once the slope eases, it's a grassy stroll across the plateau to **Creag Uchdag**'s trig point (879m).

The stony ridgeline rises just above the peat. Follow it northwest, with an occasional old metal fence post. Just before the ridge end (863m on Harvey) the fence posts turn down right and head north. Follow them down into the broad peaty col. On the slope of Meall nan Oighreag is a wide, wet peat hag. The fence posts head confidently straight through, but most of the peaty mess can be avoided by swinging well to the left. Beyond the peat, Oighreag's upper slope has an abandoned mine, marked by a spoil heap with white vein quartz.

Creag Uchdag from Lawers Burn, evening

The path started at the old mine, and was apparently used for transporting ore to the brink of Gleann a' Chloidh and tipping it over for collection at the bottom.

Meall nan Oighreag summit is crossed by a fence. Follow this to the right, east. Where it bends down north, keep ahead into the following dip, and turn half-left down the line of an old green path. ◀ At the cliff brink, turn left and follow a long grassy ridge down north. You rejoin the fence (which has been dipping its posts in some deep peat).

The grassy ridgeline descends over **Tullich Hill**, with some great views of Loch Tay and Ben Lawers. Descend north until the fence divides at the 550m contour. Between the two fences, continue down east of north, to see a young wood on the slope below. Head to a gate at the top right corner (NN 707 383). Through this, an old green pony path descends in zigzags through recently planted rowan, willow and birch. At the wood foot emerge through a deer fence gate, and zigzag down a field with briar rose bushes to a gate onto the lane above **Ardtalnaig**.

*Queens' View:
Loch Tummel and
Schiehallion*

PART SEVEN
TUMMEL AND LOCH RANNOCH

Long Leachas (Route 56)

If Perthshire is, as it claims, the heart of Scotland, then Schiehallion is the centre of Perthshire. The tall, stony cone rises into a thousand scenic calendars from the birch-tree shoreline of Loch Tummel. But lurking in the back of the Queen's View are the dark pines of Loch Rannoch and big Ben Alder. And behind that, the wild Rannoch Moor itself.

46 Schiehallion end to end

Length

■ ■ □ □ □

Difficulty

■ ■ ■ ■ □

Start/finish	Braes of Foss car park at west edge of plantations, Strath Fionan (NN 753 557)
Distance	12km/7½ miles
Ascent	750m/2500ft
Approx time	4½hr
Max altitude	Schiehallion 1083m
Terrain	Minor road, rough grassy slopes with a bit of heather, stony ridges, and good path to descend on

The straight-up-and-down from the car park carries 20,000 walkers a year, according to the John Muir Trust. The walk of 9.5km and 750m of ascent (6 miles/2500ft) takes about 4hr. From the end of the car park, the well-built path runs south near a stream, then bends southwest onto the end of the mountain. At a tall slender cairn it ends. The awkwardly stony ridgeline leads up west to a sprawling cairn, then more gently to the rocky summit.

Schiehallion's high cone is the crown, as it were, of the Queen's View along Loch Tummel. It is the 'Fairy Hill of the Caledonians' and as anyone with an accordion can tell you, 'Schiehallion stands high, almost touching the sky' (the song is *Kinlochrannoch Lullaby*, recorded by The Jacobites).

Celebrated in scenery, in song – but also in science. Because of its simple, symmetrical shape, astronomer Nevil Maskelyne in 1774 used Schiehallion as a counterweight to measure the mass of the Earth. Suspend a plumb line, and see how much it's dragged sideways by Schiehallion. Or rather, point a telescope straight upwards; and find that 'straight up' points to a slightly different part of the sky. The deflection measured, of 0.0015 degrees, put the Earth's weight at around 12 billion Schiehallions.

Is such science altogether useless? To determine the weight of Schiehallion, they had to measure its shape. To measure its shape, they invented the contour line.

Schiehallion's shape, as appreciated by the astronomers, makes for a straightforward ascent route: the very good path built by the John Muir Trust up the eastern end, for the 2km of stony ridgeline and the bare rock at its top. Its isolated position, as also appreciated by the astronomers, makes for great views. So Schiehallion is a busy hill. Here I've preferred a roundabout approach, to the wilder western end. This leaves the stony ridgeline, and the JMT's good path, as treats for the downward journey.

Start along the minor road westwards around the base of Schiehallion's northern slope. After 1km you can bear off left beside a small quarry. Cross a stile onto a faint old track, just a wide groove in the heather, running just above the road. Don't bear up left following modern wheelmarks, but keep ahead on the older, fainter track, passing below a cairn into an open plantation. The track emerges at the plantation corner above the road, which you rejoin through a gate.

Up Schiehallion west ridge

About 3km from the
car park, the road rises slightly over its **358m** high
point. In another 50 metres, a track branches off to the
left, passing up to left of a small waterfall with birch
trees. Leave the track (it bends up south) and cross the
burn, **Allt Leathan**. Head up to right of the burn, or on

the spurline further up to the right, mostly on rough grass but with occasional sections of heather to bash through.

Near the top of the stream's small valley, keep up right onto the hummock Tom na Fuine (534m). Follow a broken wall up south, past a cairn on the small hummock at 570m. You are now at the base of Schiehallion's steep upper slopes.

Slant up to the right, around the mountain, following a slight terrace for about 250 metres. This brings you to the western extremity of the hill. Now turn directly uphill. The ground is steep to start with, but after about 50m of height gain it becomes a gentler stony spur, with a very small path.

The going gets gradually less steep, but at the same time stonier, as you ascend the spur to the bare rock of **Schiehallion**'s summit. This you may find as busy as the Lake District, with people strung all along the main eastern ridgeline below.

Descend east, on the broad, gentle ridge of quartzite boulders. Once off the stony ground of the summit, a path forms. It runs past a large cairn as the slope steepens downwards, and not far below this a small pointed cairn marks the top of the rebuilt path.

This path sets off down the right, southern, flank but soon bends round to descend the eastern end of the hill. At the hill base it swings northeast, and crosses a track beside a small ruin. Then it runs down to left (west) of the boggy Allt an t-Socaich to a gate into the car park.

47 Schiehallion Foot:
Limestone and McGregor's Cave

Length

■ □ □ □ □

Difficulty

■ ■ ■ ■ ■

Start/finish	South end of Lochan an Daim (NN 719 571)
Distance	8.5km/5½ miles
Ascent	400m/1300ft
Approx time	3½hr
Max altitude	Speirean Ruadh 492m
Terrain	Grassland and path, then bracken and knee-deep heather

A little rocky summerhouse, a glimpse of Dunalastair's turrets, and a grandstand view of Schiehallion; the shore of Dunalastair Water. But the real feature of this walk is Schiehallion's small limestone pavement: a feature commoner in Yorkshire and the west of Ireland. This particular limestone is Precambrian, from long before the dawn of life. It is chemical in origin, deposited by precipitation – so don't bother looking for fossils. Like other limestone pavements, the rock has been smoothed off by a glacier and then sculpted and selectively dissolved by rain.

With all this going for it, it's a shame that the walk's return leg is rather harsh, on heather moorland with outcrops of rock. When the struggle gets too much, there are fine views to stop and look at.

A small pull-in is just south of **Lochan an Daim**. Start along the road northwest beside the lochan, then fork off left onto the grassy knoll above the lochan foot (362m, mislabelled **339m** on Landranger). Even from the road-side you can glimpse the limestone pavement.

Descend towards Dunalastair Water, rejoining the road at a small limestone quarry (rainwater runnels are in its rock). Cross and go down an open birchwood along-side the road, rejoining it where it becomes enclosed.

The road bends downhill through woods, to a drive-way on the right marked 'Pedestrians and authorised vehicles'. Follow it round to left of **Crossmount** house and down to **Dunalastair Water**.

Just before Bridge Cottage, turn right up a wide path, with a small crag up on its right. After a gateway the path contours east under spruce trees, below a deer fence. It then winds its way uphill, roughly southeast, through open woods of birch and ash, then oaks.

A stream is heard down on the left. The path contours in to meet it and crosses it, with a narrow exit under a rockface. The grassy path contours north, with glimpses of the turrets of Dunalastair Castle across the River Tummel. As the path bends east at the point of the spur, **McGregor's Cave** is on the right; a rock cleft adapted into a rough stone howff (shelter).

From here the route becomes very rough, crossing country reminiscent of a Macgregor on the run. Continue on the path, southeast, until it peters out. Make your way up through bracken to the spur crest above, and follow it up southeast. A deer fence crosses the ridgeline, with a convenient ladder stile. Behind this, **An Catachan** rises steeply – take a rough path out left, then work back up to

Limestone pavement, to Loch Rannoch and Dunalastair Water

the right to regain the crest. Keep to the right-hand edge for some grass among the heather, and occasional bits of bare rock.

The going becomes slightly easier as height is gained. A stone wall arrives from the left, and is followed eastwards over burned-off heather. The wall turns right, towards a small but steep hump 487m (above Clac Chairn). But before visiting this, the high point of this bit of moor, **Speirean Ruadh** (492m) is 400 metres ahead through the heather, reached via small deer paths.

From Speirean Ruadh retrace your steps to the 487m hump. The drop ahead to the road is also steep, so turn left, descending west at first. Then slant back to the right down grassy patches, past two circular stonepiles that are prehistoric hut circles, to join the road at its highest point. Turn right for 1km to the walk start.

48 Craig Varr and Kinloch Rannoch

Length
■ □ □ □ □

Difficulty
■ ■ □ □ □

Start/finish	Kinloch Rannoch village square (NN 662 587)
Distance	7.5km/5 miles
Ascent	350m/1200ft
Approx time	2½hr
Max altitude	Ceann Caol na Creige 540m
Terrain	Hill paths and tracks

Fancy an **evening stroll**? Without the village ramble 6km, 350m ascent, 2¼hr.

Rocks, lochs, waterfalls, and a grandstand view of Schiehallion. If you want more, there's the impressive concrete works of Loch Rannoch's dam.

Start north (Tummel/Pitlochry direction) up the village street, then turn off right towards the school, signposted

'Craig Varr Path'. Before the school, turn right onto a similarly signposted tarmac path, which crosses a footbridge. Where it bends left towards houses, keep ahead on a grass 'Riverside Path'. It runs near the River Tummel, through woods to a car parking area. Pass along this to a continuing path, which emerges after 60 metres at the road.

Cross to a gate, marked 'Craig Varr Path'. ▸ After 40 metres is a waymark post where the earth track of the 'Craig Varr Path' turns back left – but keep ahead, with

Kinloch Rannoch Walks 'Craig Varr Path' goes along the foot of Craig Varr above the road; Route 48 goes to the top.

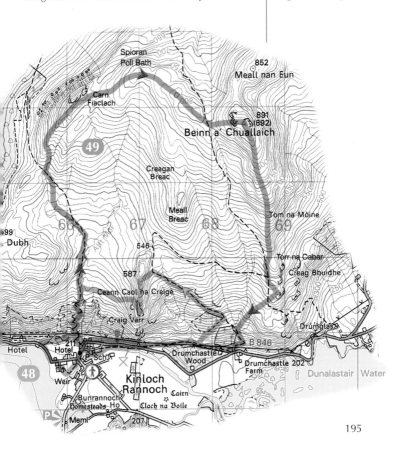

Allt Mor at Kinloch Rannoch

a deer fence on your right, heading down-valley above the road.

Ford a stream and go through a field gate to left of a pylon, onto a continuing track. In a few metres bear up left to join a green track. This runs up the right-hand side of a wood to a gate onto open hill.

Continue uphill through a broken wall. Running back to the left about 50 metres above the wall is an old green path. Follow this up until it passes through a sidewall at the 450m contour. The path fades away; but continue above the original wall, as it contours around the hillside towards Ceann Caol na Creige, the hilltop above Craig Varr. ◀

Ceann Caol na Creige: the head of the narrows of the crag.

196

The wall turns uphill past a larch tree, then ends. Here take a sheep path contouring left around the steep slope, onto the ridge crest of **Ceann Caol na Creige**. Turn downhill through scattered larch trees. At the lowest tree, emerge to steep drops below, and a view of Schiehallion, Dunalastair Water and Kinloch Rannoch.

Turn back uphill for 50 metres to a well-built cairn, one of several on this hilltop area. Bear down left, north-west, past a smaller cairn, to find a path slanting down to the moorland. Here join a broken wall, contouring west. Join a fence, which then joins a track running west to a footbridge.

At a track junction beyond the footbridge turn down left, to a gate and stile into a wood. Just inside the wood, bear left on an older, greener track passing a slender cairn. Where it bends right near the stream, you can either continue down it, rejoining the main track which zigzags down through the wood; or simply head down through the wood next to the stream. This is steeper but prettier, with waterfall glimpses and a path forming lower down.

Either way, you come down to a kissing-gate at the slope foot. Down left through this leads to the pool below a zigzag waterfall, and the end of **Kinloch Rannoch**'s main street. But for the ramble round the village turn right, signed 'Loch Rannoch'. The rough path follows the hill foot, above a wall, passing a cistern of stone slabs with roof, no longer holding water. The path emerges on road alongside Loch Rannoch at the Macdonald Hotel timeshare complex.

Turn left along the road. It bends sharp left to enter the village. At once turn off right at a footpath signpost for the village square. Take the left-hand of two gates, for a path to the huge concrete weir at the foot of Loch Rannoch. The path follows the river through woods and under the road bridge. Turn up left past a defunct toilet block to the village square.

Beinn a' Chuallaich from Craig Varr

49 Beinn a' Chuallaich

Length

Difficulty

Start/finish	Kinloch Rannoch village square (NN 662 587)
Distance	12.5km/8 miles
Ascent	750m/2500ft
Approx time	5hr
Max altitude	Beinn a' Chuallaich 892m
Terrain	Rough grassy slopes, grassy tracks

Beinn a' Chuallaich has a fine cairn, and its isolated position gives it very wide views. But the treats on this trip are at lower levels. There are the fine waterfalls on the edge of Kinloch Rannoch, and the steep woodland track alongside them. There's the surprising sub-summit Carn Fiaclach, with its little ridge. And there are the evening views of two lochs and Schiehallion from the low shoulder of Torr na Cabar.

Start at the north end of the village, just before the bridge, where a signpost points left, 'Meall Dhub Path'. The path runs up to the pool below the fine fall of **Allt Mor**, then through a kissing-gate. Here it divides. Take the grassy track (signed Craig Varr) zigzagging up through woods – or head up through the wood to right of the track for glimpses of the narrow upper falls of Allt Mor.

The track divides: the right-hand branch is grassier. At the wood top the two tracks rejoin above a tall cairn, and slant up to a gate onto the open hill. The track runs up to left of Allt Mor. ▶ At old shielings, the track bends left near a tall cairn, crosses a sidestream and heads up northwest beside it.

The right fork track crossing the stream is for Craig Varr, Route 48.

The wheelmark track fades away at a stream junction (NN 658 606). Turn right, uphill, crossing the first stream and joining the second, more westerly one. It runs up a grassy hollow, letting you avoid heather to either side. Just up to the left of it is the heathery southwest spur of Carn Fiaclach, with a broken wall running up it. Join this spur, for a pleasant narrowing ridge with new views to Ben Alder. A small path runs up the crest to **Carn Fiaclach**'s medium-sized summit cairn. ▶

Carn Fiaclach: the toothed stonepile.

Continue down the small northeast ridge for 100 metres or so. It becomes mildly rocky, but at this point double back right to cross the peaty col to the east. Head north of east, up rough grass and heather, to the levelling with a small cairn at **Spioran Poll Bath**. Easy plateau with a small path runs east, then south of east. Cross the path marked on OS maps, which is visible on the ground as a wheelmark track; beyond it is the steeper rise to **Beinn a' Chuallaich** summit. It has a large cairn and a trig point.

Head down east of south, on a well-defined spurline. At 550m is a levelling before the heathery **Torr na Cabar**. Here head down right to join a wheelmark Landrover track. This is the western one of the two paths marked on Explorer maps, the one path marked on Landranger. The track runs down through a broken wall, then slants left to join another broken wall that runs down the spurline below Torr na Cabar. Follow this wall down to a shoulder just below, with views up Loch Rannoch and across to Schiehallion.

Just below, a deer fence crosses. Head down to the right above this fence. It leads to a corner where two streams join and enter a plantation. Here a gate on the left leads out through the deer fence, to an old green track zigzagging down to the road opposite **Drumchastle Farm**.

Turn right, and at once bear right on a track towards Wester Drumchastle. Keep ahead on a smaller track, heading along the foot of the hillside, with a gate through a deer fence. Where the track ends, keep ahead through the gate to right of a pylon. Ford a stream and find an old grass track. It runs roughly underneath the power lines, and just above the top edge of a wood. At a waymark 40 metres before rejoining the road, the old track enters woodland. ◄

Slightly quicker but less pretty: keep ahead to rejoin the road, continue 50 metres to a car park (left), and take the riverside path to the back of the village.

Here fork up right on an earth track, which runs above the road and below the crags of **Craig Varr**. Where the track bends uphill at the village edge, bear left on a small path through a gate. It runs above the road, dropping to join it just before Kinloch Rannoch Outdoor Centre. Turn left into the village.

50 Black Wood of Rannoch

Length

Difficulty

Start/finish	Carie forest car park (NN 617 571)
Distance	12km/7½ miles
Ascent	450m/1500ft
Approx time	4hr
Max altitude	Gloomy reservoir 350m
Terrain	Good paths, with a short section of rough soggy woodland (avoidable, adds 1.5km)

Footbridge Airigh nan Cuileag

Shorter version, which is the yellow-marked Allt na Bogair Trail, is 8km and 350m of ascent (5 miles/1200ft) – about 2¾hr.

This wood is 'black' because of pines, rather than more cheerful-coloured oak or birch. Most of the walk is through semi-natural Caledonian forest, Scots pine and some birch, allowed to reseed itself and run wild. In another century or two it will be truly magnificent... In the meantime it's a pleasant, sheltered walk, with a couple of lively streams. The best of the woodland, and the most atmospheric path, is on the longer version, beside Dall Burn. That also involves a 300-metre stretch of truly wild woodland, pathless and soggy, at the back of the abandoned Rannoch School. The bushwhacking can be bypassed, adding another 1.5km to the measured distance.

The car park has toilets, closed in winter. Start on the wide path upstream. Don't cross a fancy footbridge on the left (blue trail), but keep ahead along a path to a covered shelter and past it to join the red trail. This wide, smooth path leads along the riverside, above a small waterfall, then turns up away from the river to join the stony-surfaced yellow-trail track.

Turn left, and follow this pleasant track for 3km. After the first 1km it wanders south then runs along the steep slope above the **Allt na Bogair**, with wild pine and birch on the opposite side. It then gradually drops to join the river. In another 800 metres is first a footbridge on the left, which you ignore, then the track meets a wide, smooth forest road. Here left is signed 'Right of Way to Glen Lyon'. But turn right, down the forest road, crossing the dam of a gloomy reservoir. In another 200 metres, the track bends left.

Shorter walk option

Here a wide path with yellow-top poles continues ahead, gently downhill. After a couple of swampy moments where its drainage has broken down, it crosses the outflow stream of the reservoir above, and reaches another wide forest road (see below).

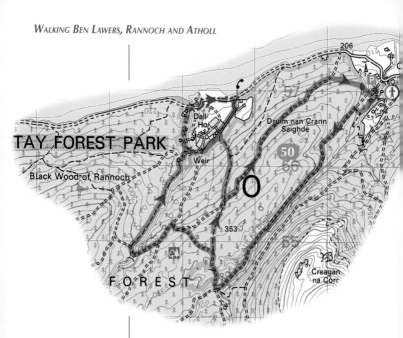

The longer **main route** keeps on down the wide forest
road, below some middle-aged natural pines. Ignore
two side turnings down right (which combine to form a
smaller track). Reach a T-junction, with clear-fell below it
giving views to Loch Rannoch. Here turn left on another
wide, smooth track for 300 metres. As the main track
bends slightly left and uphill, keep ahead in a much
smaller grassy track, contouring then descending to cross
a river (Dall Burn).

In another 100 metres, as the track bends up left
away from the river, keep ahead on a path along an
overgrown old track below pines. Heather and cowberry
encroach on the path, which leads down with Dall Burn
on its right splashing over some small waterfalls. After
1.2km, it runs onto a rough track. Turn down right to a
gate and a gravel-surfaced track at the outbuildings of
Dall House, former Rannoch School.

Diversion north of Dall House

Ahead is the stretch of bushwhacking, 300 metres that feels like a mile… to avoid this, turn left down this track, past houses to the south Rannoch road. Turn right for 800 metres, crossing the river then passing below the crumbling baronial mansion. Turn right up a tarred lane, with SRWS sign to Glen Lyon. After 500 metres the lane is about to enter the school grounds with 'No access' signs, but another signpost for Glen Lyon marks a path up to the left.

If you can face a spot of **bushwhacking** turn right, across the river. At a track junction among houses, bear right to pass to left of 'Tigh na Fraoch' on a rough track. At once turn off right through a decomposing fence, and turn left through untrammelled woodland. Keep northeast, with houses on your left, through soggy birchwood that gives an idea of the walkability of the original wildwood. Cross a stream, and arrive at the corner of a tarmac lane. ▶

Here the diversion north of Dall House rejoins the route.

At the lane corner turn uphill on a path signposted for Glen Lyon. As it enters plantation it becomes a stony track. Ignore a side-path left. The main path ahead is being used during further clear-felling hereabouts, so it may become a rutted track. For now it continues gently uphill, alternately swampy and firm, with clear-fell above and left of it. About 1km from its start it reaches a wide, smooth forest road. ▶

Here the shorter option arrives from the opposite side of the forest road.

Turn left (or if arriving by the shortened route, turn right), down the forest road. There are occasional yellow-top posts. Clear-felling below the road is opening views to Loch Rannoch. After 1km, below the road is a granite boulder carved into a very rough seat (the boulder must be a glacier-carried erratic, as the quarry above the road shows schist). Continue down the forest road for another 1.5km. As the road enters scattered oaks, a path turns off on the right between two cairns. Follow it among the oaks, then uphill past a bench with a line of what presents itself as poetry, and down to meet a narrow track. Here multicoloured posts mark the paths to right and ahead. Keep ahead, bearing left near the covered shelter to the car park.

SUMMARY: BEN ALDER

Ben Alder, Bealach Dubh, Lancet Edge and Geal-charn from the path to Culra Bothy

Dalwhinnie, Kinloch Laggan, Kings House of Glen Coe, Loch Rannoch and Fort William: they're well scattered around central Scotland, but every one of them is a start point for Ben Alder. All true mountain lovers love the 'Long Walk In': accordingly, Ben Alder should be the busiest hill in Scotland. Oddly enough, I've usually had it to myself.

Ben Alder is rather different from the soaring ridges, great rockfaces and clean, sharp scrambles of Glen Nevis or the Mamores. Ben Alder is a plateau, 3500ft up from an awful lot of moorland bog, where plovers make plaintive little squeaks and ptarmigan nest among the heather.

But what you could get at the end of your long walk in is a Long Leachas (or possibly a Short one). The two little scrambles are easier than such classics as the Ledge Route on Ben Nevis or the Ring of Steall. You'd have to be pretty clever to fall off them, although mossy rock and unstable rockpiles do make it possible. The thing is, if you do manage to fall off, it's a very very long way to carry out the body.

BEN ALDER ROUTES

51 Walk in to Benalder Cottage (from Rannoch Lodge)
52 Ben Alder from Benalder Cottage
53 Benalder Cottage to Culra Bothy via Beinn Bheoil
54 Benalder Cottage to Culra Bothy via Bealach Beithe (and in reverse)
55 Walk/ride in to Culra Bothy (from Dalwhinnie)
56 Long Leachas from Culra Bothy
57 Short Leachas from Culra Bothy
58 Descent from Ben Alder to Bealach Breabag

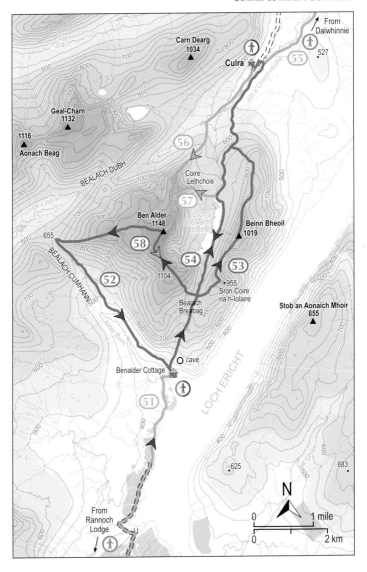

51 Walk in to Benalder Cottage

Length

Difficulty

Start	Loch Rannoch head, Rannoch Lodge (NN 506 576)
Finish	Benalder Cottage (NN 498 680)
Distance	13km/8 miles
Ascent	250m/800ft
Approx time	3½hr (one way)
Max altitude	Benalder Cottage 380m
Terrain	Tracks and paths
Note	Bicycle to track end, 2km from bothy, saves 2hr

This is the easiest way in to Ben Alder from any direction. The footpath section alleviates the forest trudge, and then Loch Ericht opens up splendidly. As a base for the mountain, Benalder Cottage is less busy than Culra, and prettier.

Parking for a couple of cars is at the foot of a forest track; also at informal campgrounds where the road runs alongside Loch Rannoch 300 metres east.

Start up the track through a gate (pedestrian gaps either side). After 1.2km it emerges to moorland, but in 1km enters another plantation by an awkward ladder stile (very tricky with a loaded bicycle) beside a locked gate.

The track passes a small quarry. Just before it enters mature trees through a deer fence, turn up right on a faint track, to a gate just above with another awkward stile. ◄ A green track runs up the edge of the plantation, becoming a faint path. At the plantation's top corner, contour forward, with the path very faint, to rejoin the main track at its highest point.

This path diversion saves 0.6km, and is pleasanter on the feet; cyclists just stay on the main track.

The track dips briefly, then runs across the moor and through another plantation. Then it drops to **Loch Ericht**, where it runs to an ugly hut.

The hut is locked up, but has a veranda with bench and loch view. Follow a new track left (west) to a bridge at the reservoir corner, then north along the reservoir

side for about 2km. When it ends, keep along the shore. Cross a wooden bridge and turn right, on a small path with marker post, to remain on the loch shore outside the deer-fenced regeneration area.

After 1km you pass the corner of the fence, with a ladder stile that you don't cross. Turn north, following marker posts away from the loch across boggy ground. At the last post bear slightly right to a path on firm ground under larches. It emerges between two clumps, to run down to an interestingly engineered footbridge across **Alder Burn**. Keep ahead to the loch side and **Benalder Cottage**. ▶

The **bothy** is panelled and cosy, but has two disadvantages. Firstly, it is haunted by the ghost of a former gamekeeper. According to legend, this man hanged himself from a hook above the doorway and in the night you can hear his heels drumming against the wood. McCook died of natural causes in a hospital bed in Pitlochry, and the legend was invented as a discouragement to hillwalkers.

The second 'disadvantage' is that the cottage is on quite the wrong side of the hill for the Leachas corrie, which means that if you're after either of the fine scrambles (Routes 56 and 57) you'll have to bag Beinn Bheoil on the way over.

Alder Burn bridge to Benalder Cottage

The bothy can also be reached by boat or canoe from Dalwhinnie, but Loch Ericht can be a wind tunnel.

52 Ben Alder from Benalder Cottage

Length

Difficulty

Start/finish	Benalder Cottage (NN 498 680)
Distance	14km/8½ miles
Ascent	800m/2700ft
Approx time	5hr
Max altitude	Ben Alder 1148m
Terrain	Rough path, tough ascent from Bealach Breabag, gentle plateau, steep descent to Bealach Cumhann, and long, easy path to finish

The well-built stalkers' path from Bealach Cumhann is the long way back that shows both the steep side and the gentle plateau of Ben Alder. Even so, this makes for a short day out from Benalder Cottage. Time for a swim in the loch, or to hunt down Prince Charlie's Cave.

See Route 51 for directions to **Benalder Cottage**. Behind the bothy start uphill past a tree, to find the rough path running uphill to right of the stream. It remains to right of the stream right up to where the angle eases at 750m

level, where it fades away. Continue up to the wide saddle, **Bealach Breabag**.

> **Prince Charlie's Cave** is marked on OS maps (NN499684) above Benalder Cottage. An isolated rowan stands at the entrance. It's a cramped and uncomfortable hole below a boulder, and not midge-proof. But there's a nice view as well as the historical resonance.

The slope to Ben Alder is fairly steep, with small outcrops. It is wide, and there is no specific path. A good bearing from the col is 290° (magnetic 2012), eventually following the topmost waters of the Allt a' Bhealaich Bheithe. As the slope eases, continue uphill, northwest, to reach the edge of steep drops near Point **1104m**.

Follow the rim of the plateau northwest to cross a small lochan's outflow, then northeast to **Ben Alder** trig point and large cairn.

Descend due west, stony at first then over gentle meadow. Still west, descend a steepening spurline with sharp drops on the left, right down to the 655m peaty col **Bealach Cumhann**. A well-made stalkers' path runs through the col. Follow it down to the left, along the length of the **Alder Burn**, to **Benalder Cottage**.

Ben Alder plateau above Garbh Choire

53 Benalder Cottage to Culra Bothy
via Beinn Bheoil

Length

■ ■ ☐ ☐ ☐

Difficulty

■ ■ ■ ☐ ☐

Start	Benalder Cottage (NN 498 680)
Finish	Culra Bothy (NN 523 762)
Distance	10.5km/6½ miles
Ascent	750m/2400ft
Approx time	4hr
Max altitude	Beinn Bheoil 1019m
Terrain	Paths, stony ridge, heathery descent

A bothy-to-bothy crossing over the hill ridge of Ben Alder's outlying Munro, with great views of Ben Alder itself and Loch Ericht.

Start as Route 52 to Bealach Breabag. Turn right, to find a small path up east. It fades on the stony plateau above. The outlying **Sron Coire na h-Iolaire** is over on the right. It has a cairn but no path. Its Gaelic name suggests eagle viewing; there's a fine view of Ericht and Beinn Bheoil anyway.

Cross the stony plateau north to the continuing ridge, which is pleasingly narrow, with a steep descent to the neck leading on up Beinn Bheoil. The path is slightly to right of the crest. After an ornamental knob for false summit, you reach the cairn on **Beinn Bheoil**. ◀

'Ben Vee-al', meaning Mouth Hill – traditional Gaelic 'mouth music' is puirt a beul. The 'mouth' here may be the gaping gap between it and Ben Alder.

Head down northeast, with a slight rise onto a grassy plateau. Follow this northeast to a gentler drop to a lower ridge plateau. Here start slanting down to the left (the ridge end ahead would be very steep). Head down northwest, over ground becoming increasingly heathery, until you strike (with relief) a very-well-made stalkers' path. Modern reconstruction has been in the traditional style, well done in environmental and in engineering terms.

Follow the path around to the right, then straight downhill, north, to **Allt a' Chaoil-reidhe**. This is not usually crossable with dry feet, so continue down the good path to right of the river, keeping on past the bothy for 300 metres. A side-path left is signed 'To bridge', and the low bridge is visible from the junction. Follow the side-path to a track, and turn left back to **Culra Bothy**.

54 Benalder Cottage to Culra Bothy via Bealach Beithe (and in reverse)

Start	Benalder Cottage (NN 498 680)
Finish	Culra Bothy (NN 523 762)
Distance	10km/6 miles
Ascent	500m/1600ft
Approx time	3½hr
Max altitude	Bealach Breabag 833m
Terrain	Mostly paths, pathless across the top of the pass

Length

Difficulty

Good (but still wild) paths most of the way and spectacular surroundings at Loch a' Bhealaich Bheithe make this one of Scotland's finest high passes.

Loch a' Bhealaich Bheithe and Ben Alder

Start as Route 52 to **Bealach Breabag**. From the middle of the saddle, head down towards **Loch a' Bhealaich Bheithe**. As the stream forms, keep to left of it, to find the old stalkers' path which runs down to the loch's inflow.

Pass round to right of the loch, on a rough path but grassy ground. At the loch outflow there starts a well-made stalkers' path. It leads around the flank of Beinn Bheoil and down to **Allt a' Chaoil-reidhe**. If the river is low, cross it at any convenient point. Otherwise continue past the bothy for 300 metres. A side-path leads left to a low bridge: turn upstream on a track to the bothy.

In reverse, Culra to Benalder Cottage
The route has only 400m (1300ft) of ascent in this direction, so is 15min shorter.

If you can't cross opposite the bothy, **Allt a' Chaoil-reidhe** is not usually crossable at all, so turn down the track to the bridge 300 metres downstream. Take an excellent stalkers' path upstream to left of the river. After 1.5km it turns uphill, slanting round to the right and up again to **Loch a' Bhealaich Bheithe**. ◂

The path fades, but the going is easy along the left-hand shore of the loch. Cross the inlet stream, to find an older but still well-made stretch of the stalkers' path heading uphill beyond. This stays to right of the stream up to the 800m contour, where it fades just below the wide saddle **Bealach Breabag**.

Through the pass, head down southwest into a wide bowl. The path is found just to left of the drainage stream, leading down to **Benalder Cottage**.

Pass of the birch trees – none hereabouts now.

Start	Dalwhinnie (NN 635 849)
Finish	Culra Bothy (NN 523 762)
Distance	16km/10 miles
Ascent	100m/400ft
Approx time	4hr
Max altitude	Loch Pattack col 460m
Terrain	Track and path
Note	Bicycle all the way saves 2½–3hr

Length

Difficulty

Culra Bothy, northeast of Ben Alder, is the obvious attack-point for the Leachas ridges. It is an ugly refuge but cosy inside. Given the easy bike access and convenience for six Munros, it tends to be overcrowded, especially on summer weekends with good weather forecasts. The track walk in along Loch Ericht is dreary, and even drearier when you walk it out again. The solution is a bicycle, or the high grass ridge of the Fara that runs above.

The **Fara** is just 6m lower than Geal-charn across the loch. But those 6m are the crucial difference between 2990ft and 3008ft; and Geal-charn receives 100 visitors to every one on the Fara. Its ridgeline is 5km almost level above Loch Ericht. Deer fences and plantations have changed since I walked it, and it's several miles outside Perthshire, so it's left here as an exercise in exploration.

Beinn Bheoil, Ben Alder and Lancet Edge, approaching Culra Bothy

Start from Dalwhinnie, where the level crossing south of the station leads onto the long, smooth track along **Loch Ericht**'s western shore. After 1.5km you pass a fantasy granite gatehouse. In another 6km, near the full-blown fantasy castle to which the gatehouse was a teaser, the track slants up to the right, climbing to a gentle pass.

Loch Pattack appears ahead. About 400 metres before the track reaches it, turn off left on a well-made stalkers' path, smooth enough to be cycled along. It joins the **Allt a' Chaoil-reidhe**. With the bothy in sight 300 metres ahead, a path turns off right, signed 'To bridge'. Once across, turn left along the track to the bothy.

56 Long Leachas from Culra Bothy

Length

Difficulty

Start/finish	Culra Bothy (NN 523 762)
Distance	16km/10 miles
Ascent	950m/3100ft
Approx time	6hr
Max altitude	Ben Alder 1148m
Terrain	Heather, scrambly ridge (serious difficulties avoidable), exposed plateau

Distance and time are for the **classic circuit** descending to Bealach Breabag and continuing over Beinn Bheoil back to Culra. Returning from the Bealach by Loch a' Bhealaich Bheithe is 15.5km with 700m ascent (9½ miles/2300ft) – about 5¼hr.

The Long Leachas and the Short Leachas are not named on the Landranger map. They are the bounding ridges of Coire na Lethchois, at the northeast corner of Ben Alder's plateau. 'Half-hollow corrie' – Leachas is just an anglicised spelling of the corrie name.

The Long Leachas is the northern (right-hand) rim of the corrie, running up northwest to the very corner of the plateau. It is the longer and slightly more interesting of the two (Scramble Grade 1).

For directions to **Culra Bothy** see Route 55. Start along the path upstream to right (north) of **Allt a' Chaoil-reidhe** for about 2km. Once above the confluence with the outflow stream from Loch a' Bhealaich Bheithe, cross the stream. Now there's a slog through heather to reach the ridge foot (NN 507 741).

The Long Leachas ridge rises in a couple of short walls. You can scramble up these on good holds or avoid them on a path round to the right. Now the ridge gets narrower, with drops on either side and loose, scrappy rock along the top. The small path shows the easiest way.

Some rock-towers decorate the ridgeline above. The towers are Gothic and tottering. Going over them involves loose rock and exposure, but they are easily avoided. Not far above, the ridge arrives suddenly on the plateau.

Coire na Lethchois (Short Leachas left, Long Leachas right skyline) from Bealach Beithe path

It's a stony wander south up to the summit of **Ben Alder**. On the way, you peer over the edge into the corrie, and examine the top of the Short Leachas.

See Route 58 to descend.

57 Short Leachas from Culra Bothy

Length

Difficulty

Start/finish	Culra Bothy (NN 523 762)
Distance	18km/11 miles
Ascent	950m/3100ft
Approx time	6½hr
Max altitude	Ben Alder 1148m
Terrain	Heather, scrambly ridge (serious difficulties avoidable), exposed plateau

Distance and time are for the **classic circuit** descending to Bealach Breabag and continuing over Beinn Bheoil back to Culra. Returning from the Bealach by Loch a' Bhealaich Bheithe is 17.5km with 700m ascent (11 miles/2300ft) – about 6hr.

The Short Leachas is Coire na Lethchois' left-hand rim. It's very like the Long Leachas but shorter (Scramble Grade 1). Its advantage is that you can reach it without fraying your bootlaces in the heather.

For directions to **Culra Bothy** see Route 55. Start by crossing **Allt a' Chaoil-reidhe** opposite the bothy, if possible: otherwise head downstream 300 metres to the bridge. Take the excellent stalkers' path which runs to left of the river, turns uphill, and slants round to the right and up again to **Loch a' Bhealaich Bheithe**.

Cross the outflow stream. Immediately above rises the ridge of the Short Leachas, heading straight up west.

Short Leachas

It's a stroll of a few minutes on short vegetation to the ridge foot (NN 507 727).

Broken rocks leading up to the ridge can be scrambled or avoided by a grass slope on the left. Above rises a spur of jammed boulders. Again, a small path winds around seeking the easiest way where everywhere is without real difficulty.

The ridge narrows into a sharp arête that looks good in the photographs but can be walked without use of handholds. A notable tower ends the narrow section, with a couple of moves of exposed climbing on not altogether helpful footholds. Again, this can be avoided. Not far above, the ridge arrives on the summit plateau of Ben Alder.

Head south along the rim of the great corrie, crossing stony ground to **Ben Alder** summit with its stone shelter and trig point.

See Route 58 to descend.

Length

■ ■ ■ ▨ ▢

Difficulty

■ ■ ■ ■ ▨

58 Ben Alder to Bealach Breabag (descent)

Start/finish	Ben Alder summit (NN 496 718)
Finish	Bealach Breabag (NN 505 701)
Distance	2.5km/1½ miles (as part of longer routes)
Ascent	300m/1000ft
Approx time	1hr (as part of longer routes)
Max altitude	Ben Alder 1148m
Terrain	Stony plateau and steepish descent among outcrops

This descent forms part of any west-east or north-south crossing of Ben Alder. The high plateau along the corrie rim is magnificent. In mist the descent to Bealach Breabag is not straightforward, and it's possible to stray onto Sron Bealach Beithe with further descent requiring a parachute. Taking care not to do that, one may stray onto the southwest ridge, which is tiresome if you weren't actually heading for Benalder Cottage.

Starting from **Ben Alder** summit, head south to the plateau rim with big drops to Garbh Choire on the left – in full winter conditions this plateau edge can carry dangerous cornices. Head southwest along the plateau rim for 200 metres, to cross the outflow of the tiny Lochan a' Garbh Choire.

Keep following the plateau edge, briefly south and then southeast. You'll drop to a slight col, ascend again just 21m of vertical height, and exactly 1km from the lochan reach Point **1104m**.

Warning If you find yourself heading along what's more a ridge than a plateau edge, and heading east or northeast, then you're en route for Sron Bealach Beithe and a dead end above crags (or an even deader end at their foot...). Return to Point 1104m.

Descend southeast, bearing away from the plateau edge down a stony slope. Soon the ground steepens, becoming grass and outcrops. Continue southeast, which

Ben Alder plateau: Sron Bealach Beithe to Beinn Bheoil (the two tiny figures, right, have overshot the turn-off for Bealach Breabag and are heading for cliff tops)

should be directly downhill. Fortunately, the col below is a wide target to aim for.

If descending to Benalder Cottage in clear weather, you can avoid the **steep slopes above Bealach Breabag**. From Point 1104m take the ridgeline descending gently southwest for 20mins, to a slight rise at 900m altitude. Now head down the grass slope on the left, slanting back in an easterly direction.

From **Bealach Breabag**, continue easily to **Culra** by Bealach Beithe (Route 54), or more excitingly over **Beinn Bheoil** (Route 53). Another option is to reverse the outward part of Route 54 and descend to Benalder Cottage.

BEN ALDER ALTERNATIVES

The one way in to Ben Alder that doesn't involve dreary trackwork is from the west, where lonely Corrour Station and romantic Loch Ossian youth hostel are specks of habitation at the edge of Rannoch Moor. Corrour has a railway but no road, or the path (Route 59) from Rannoch Station.

After the track either side of Loch Ossian, the Uisge Labhair has a good path, with wild campsites in a country where almost everywhere is a wild camp. A short heather slog leads to Bealach Cumhann and the back ridge onto Ben Alder. Corrour to Culra by Ben Alder and Beinn Bheoil is 27km with 1050m ascent (17 miles/3500ft) – about 9hr.

On a good day, the crossing of Carn Dearg and Sgor Gaibhre to Bealach Cumhann is a splendid mountain walk to Ben Alder. In foul weather, the path through Bealach Dubh to Culra makes a dramatic walk in its own right.

PART EIGHT

RANNOCH MOOR

Rannoch Moor from Rannoch Station (Route 59)

Scotland has hundreds of mountains, so it's odd that the centre of it all should be neither Ben Nevis nor the noble Cairngorms, nor the jagged black mountains of Skye away on their island. The centre of it all is 23km of peat bog and lochan, heather and granite boulder, and the lonely cry of the curlew.

Rannoch Moor is better to see than to be in. Look down on the great, grey-green emptiness from the hill track called the Road to the Isles; from Meall Bhuidhe and Beinn Pharlagain. And you're gazing, if not over the edge of the world, at least over the edge of Perthshire.

59 The Road to the Isles

Length
■ ■ □ □ □

Difficulty
■ □ □ □ □

Start	Rannoch Station (NN 422 578)
Finish	Corrour Station (NN 356 664)
Distance	18.5km/11½ miles
Ascent	350m/1200ft
Approx time	4½hr
Max altitude	Carn Dearg flank 550m
Terrain	Good tracks

Variant over Meall na Lice (584m) adds 1km and 100m of rough hillside (difficulty = 3) for a grand viewpoint over Loch Ossian and Rannoch Moor – about 30min extra.

'Oh by Tummel and Loch Rannoch and Lochaber I will go' – that's a long way, so this is just the linky bit between Rannoch and Lochaber. Look out across the great Moor of Rannoch, but at the same time keep your feet dry. The walk also allows you to travel along, and then look back across at, the rail line used by H Potter and chums on their thrice-yearly school trip from Platform 9¾ at King's Cross. The film *Harry Potter and the Prisoner of Azkaban* has exactly this view of the West Highland Line and a graphically enhanced Rannoch Moor.

Southbound is sensible: start with the train ride and there's no need to worry about the timetable along the walk. But the song takes the reverse direction, and it's more romantic to walk the walk and then ride home again in reminiscence. Between walk and ride you could take your evening meal at the remotest restaurant, at Corrour Station Lodge.

The route is described northbound, which also allows a diversion over a fine small viewpoint; then in summary southbound (there's 100m less ascent in that direction).

Walk down the road for 2km to Loch Eigheach, and turn left at the Scotways signpost on the north side of the road.

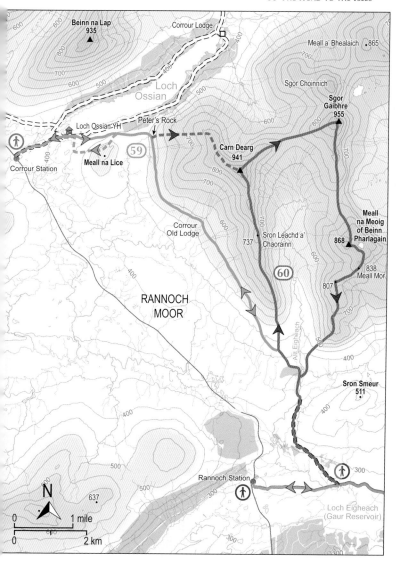

Road to the Isles

(Alternative parking here.) The stony and grassy track rises across the shoulder of Sron Smeur, then dips towards **Allt Eigheach** river. Ignore a track forking off to the right, ford a sidestream, and reach the riverside.

The track crosses a new bridge and runs upstream, passing an underground bunker suitable for some future Bond villain. Okay, it's a half-buried turbine station, with a useful sheltering wall for donning waterproofs. The track then rises past a small plantation and bends left.

After 500 metres the main track bends uphill. Here a smaller and narrower track keeps ahead, rising northwest then contouring to pass below the ruins of Corrour Old Lodge. After another 3km, above Loch Ossian, the track bends down left at **Peter's Rock**. ◄

The name is carved on the downhill side of the small outcrop.

Follow the track down to the loch side to join a wider track near the youth hostel. Turn left, then keep ahead, south of west, on the wide track up to Corrour Station.

Variant
For a fine wee hill to finish, from **Peter's Rock** head down the track for just 1km, then turn up left onto the slopes of **Meall na Lice** (Mell na Leaka, the hump of slabs).

This will give great views across Rannoch Moor and down onto Loch Ossian, but the going's pathless and quite rough. Head up heathery grass to the hill's north-east spur and up it to the first summit above the crags that drop towards Loch Ossian. Walk round the head of a grassy gully dividing the crag, to the cairned main summit.

Descend west, to a wide grass path (quad-bike track) across the moor. Follow it north; it soon upgrades to a firm surfaced mini-track. It rejoins the Peter's Rock track just above the youth hostel. At the bigger track below, turn left to Corrour Station.

Southbound

Southbound it may be convenient to leave a car at Loch Eigheach track end and walk up the road to Rannoch Station before taking the train north. From Corrour Station, take the track beyond the station house gently downhill, east, to the head of **Loch Ossian**. Keep right, onto the track around the south side of the loch. Just past the youth hostel take a smooth track forking up to the right.

Loch Ossian youth hostel

Track below Peter's Rock

After 2km of steady climb, this bends right, south, at **Peter's Rock**. The track contours around the side of Carn Dearg, bending southeast and passing below the ruins of **Corrour Old Lodge**. After another 4km you arrive on the southern end of the ridge and join a descending track. It passes above a plantation then turns down alongside it to **Allt Eigheach** river.

Cross the river and continue downstream. The track rises very slightly around the end of Sron Smeur then descends to the roadside at **Loch Eigheach**. Turn right to Rannoch Station.

Start/finish	Parking pull-in at Loch Eigheach, at foot of 'Road to the Isles' track (NN 446 578)
Distance	24.5km/14 miles
Ascent	1200m/3900ft
Approx time	8½hr
Max altitude	Sgor Gaibhre 955m
Terrain	Grassy ridges

Length

Difficulty

To walk just the **Carn Dearg ridge** with its Moor of Rannoch views, take the train to Corrour Station, and follow Route 59 (reverse direction) to Peter's Rock. Head uphill, east, on grassy slopes. A more definite ridgeline leads up southeast to the tall summit cairn. Follow the ridgeline southeast for 300 metres, when it turns south, with a small path, over several humps.

Finally, descend east of south to pick up the rough Landrover track at about 500m level. It runs down south to rejoin the Road to the Isles track, Route 59. The walk is 19.5km with 650m of ascent (12 miles/2200ft) – about 6hr.

If hill ridges have a spectrum from pleasant (but unexciting) to exciting (but perhaps unpleasant), these ones are firmly at the pleasant end. The going is grassy and, once up on the high ground, surprisingly gentle. Take the circuit clockwise: morning light is good for the views over Rannoch Moor, evening light is best for Rannoch and Schiehallion from Beinn Pharlagain.

This circuit isn't the quickest way to grab the two Munros, and incorporates a mere Corbett, but it's so natural and satisfactory that it is starting to develop its own small path.

Loch Ossian area is awash with Carn Deargs, and Sgor Gaibhre is another hard-to-remember Munro, so this circuit takes its name from the lowest of the three summits. Pharlagain is also the least featureless of the three, sporting granite chunks and several lochans.

Carn Dearg summit, to Ben Nevis (middle of the picture)

Here a smaller and narrower track keeps ahead: the Road to the Isles, Route 59.

Start at the Scotways signpost on the north side of the road. The stony and grassy track rises across the shoulder of Sron Smeur then dips towards **Allt Eigheach** river. Ignore a track forking off to the right, ford a sidestream, and reach the riverside.

The track crosses a new bridge and runs upstream then rises past a small plantation and bends left. After 500 metres the main track bends uphill. ◄

Follow the main track north up the rounded ridgeline to the base of steeper ground (below 500m level). It then starts to contour round to the right – to become the rough track/path to west of Allt Eigheach up into Coire Eigheach. But leave it as it levels off, and head north up grassy slopes onto **Sron Leachd a' Chaorainn**.

The grassy ridgeline runs north, with a small path. After several humps, the ground becomes granite and a longer rise leads to the cylindrical summit cairn of **Carn Dearg**.

Head down northeast, with a clearer path as this is now the standard baggers' ridgeline between the two Munros. The path runs down across the wide, peaty col Mam Ban, then up onto **Sgor Gaibhre**.

The next ridge runs south from Sgor Gaibhre, with a small, intermittent path. The final drop to the col has glacier-smoothed granite boilerplates. A small lochan lies across the front of **Meall na Meoig**. ▶ Head southeast to Point **838m (Meall Mor)**, which is layered schist. Now head southwest to Point **807m**, which is also schist, but whose summit is formed by a knee-high granite boulder.

In mist, geology can aid topography: Meall na Meoig is made of rough, rounded granite.

Head down east of south over another slight rise. From its end drop rather steeply to a lower ridgeline (700m level). Follow this south to its end, then drop southwest towards the river. As the slope eases, faint quad-bike wheelmarks lead to the left, down-valley. Eventually they reach the track at its bridge over **Allt Eigheach**.

Follow the 'Road to the Isles' track ahead, retracing the outward walk, to **Loch Eigheach**.

61 Meall Buidhe and Cam Chreag

Start/finish	Bridge of Gaur (NN 504 565)
Distance	25km/15½ miles
Ascent	1150m/3800ft
Approx time	8½hr
Max altitude	Meall Buidhe 931m
Terrain	Rough tracks, grassy slopes and ridges with rough ground between the two peaks and on the descent from Cross Craigs

Length

■ ■ ■ ■ ▨

Difficulty

■ ■ ■ ■ ▨

Meall Buidhe is not actively unpleasant, provided you don't mind a bit of mud. But unexciting it is. Taken by its standard up-and-down from Loch an Daimh, it's a nominee for the most dull Munro. The standard Munro-bagger can, it's true, combine it with a straight up-and-down of Stuchd an Lochain from the same parking place, thus achieving two dull Munros in a day...

Combine it instead with the Corbett Cam Chreag, for a day that adds a long track wander through deer-haunted bogs, a fragment of Caledonian pine, and some attractive rocky moorland. And to show you're not any sad bagger, you could even add in the small evening hill of Leagag, from Route 63.

There's parking and picnic tables at the tin shed that's the village hall, just west of the bridge over Allt an Fheadain.

Start by ignoring a wide, smooth hill track just to the west, but crossing the bridge and climbing a locked gate onto the small grass-middle track running south, with the river on its right.

> The manning of the **small church at Bridge of Gaur** was sufficiently undemanding to allow its minister, Aeneas E Robertson, plenty of weekday hillwalking. He became in 1901 the first person to ascend all the Munros of Scotland.

The path turning off left here will be your return route.

After 2.5km, the track rises to the gap at the west end of Leagag. ◄ Continue ahead on the track, still slightly uphill. In another 1.5km, the main track turns left over a bridge. Keep ahead, through a gate, with a ladder stile alongside, onto a little-used track through plantations. After 1.2km it emerges from the scattered, open plantation via another locked gate and ladder stile. In another 400 metres the track ends. (The continuing up-valley path marked on Landranger maps is not visible on the ground.)

Here bear down left to a stream junction. Cross the main stream and head up alongside the sidestream, southeast, using grass beside the stream to bypass the first, densest heather. As the slope steepens, head up to the right, onto the spur south of the stream. It steepens to a levelling at 700m. Continue up grassy slopes to the cairn of **Meall Buidhe**.

A small Munro-baggers' path leads south along the rounded ridge, around the rim of the quite impressive Glas Choire. From Meall Buidhe's south summit, the path leads down steepish grass east. Keep east across a wide

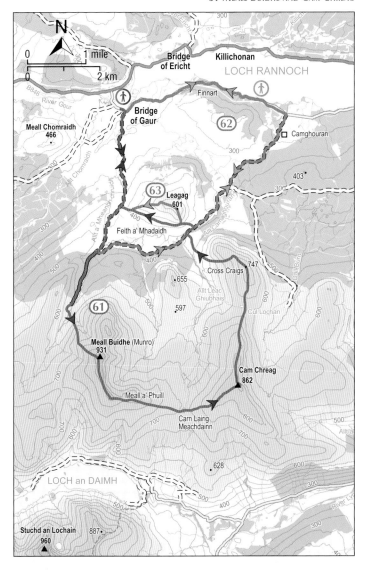

Meall a' Phuill is hump of the pool. Gaelic 'puill' becomes phuill, pronounced 'fool'.

grassy col with a small pool, and head up past a well-built cairn to the summit of **Meall a' Phuill**. ◄ From here Cam Chreag appears as a wide sprawl across rather a lot of peat. It's a bit better than it looks.

A few old cairns now mark the watershed, probably built as boundary markers between estates. They are too far apart to act as guides but do mark the best line. Descend east, grassy at first, and swing very slightly north past two cairns to avoid dissected peat ground on the south flank. Keep east down into the wide peaty col. A few moraine humps (with old low cairns on) are the best way across. **Carn Lairig Meachdainn** is too grand a name for a 5m hump rising out of the peat.

Up the slope opposite, peat gives way to rough grassland. The west top is a glacier-scoured summit with many perched boulders. Continue to **Cam Chreag**'s main top, with a large cairn, and cliff drops not far beyond.

Down the north ridge of Cam Chreag; Leagag is to the left of the walker

Head north, along a ridge with low rocky knolls and enjoyable walking. There's a quad-bike wheelmark line just left of the crest, but the rock knolls are worth visiting. The wheelmarks trail away down left but keep north down the heathery ridge. (The stones are granite rather than schist, and if the bedrock is indeed granite that

Cam Chreag from Meall Ghaordaidh

would explain why this down-slope is especially heath-ery.) Pass to right of small **Cul Lochan** (the 'back lochan') and up the slope opposite. A small cairn marks the sum-mit of **Cross Craigs**.

Continue northwest down the rather rocky crest for about 400 metres, to where it levels. ▶ Here turn down left, southwest, then bending round to the right below the steep ground. Aim for the foot of the glen of Allt Leac Ghiubhais.

Below the nose of Cross Craigs, deer fences converge into a corner near the stream confluence. Cross the foot of **Allt Leac Ghiubhais** above the deer fence, then cross two ladder stiles to reach a grassy track. Turn right on its bridge over the **Allt Camaghouran** and continue uphill for 200 metres. At the top of the rise, just before a perma-nently open gate, turn left on a well-marked peaty path.

The path slants up the south flank of **Leagag**, to pass above a solitary alder tree. ▶ After this the path becomes quite indistinct. Keep at exactly the same level along the flank of the hill, with the path becoming clear again as it passes from bracken to rough grassland. The path passes below the final hump of Meall Dubh, then drops around the western end of the hill to rejoin the track of the out-ward route.

It would be possible to continue northwest down the steep nose: steep, and seriously heathery unless you sought out rocky scrambling.

To cross Leagag, switch to Route 63 here.

62 Tracks to the Foxes Bog

Start/finish	Bridge of Gaur (NN 504 565)
Distance	15km/9½ miles or 17.5km/11 miles
Ascent	250m/800ft
Approx time	4–5hr
Max altitude	Leagag side 400m
Terrain	Grassy tracks, with a rougher option on the Leagag flank path; quiet lochside road

Length

Difficulty

The shorter, rougher route by Leagag side is easier in this anticlockwise direction, as the path along Leagag side is easier to follow eastbound. The longer route, on tracks all the way, is straightforward in either direction. If you might be tempted onto Leagag itself, then take the route clockwise – Route 63 following.

Feith a' Mhadaidh is the Foxes Bog, a quiet moorland hollow at the back of Leagag that's favoured by large herds of deer as well as the foxes. The tracks are of the pleasant sort with rough grass in the middle. The descent track is through ancient natural woodland. The 5km of road are rather longer than you'd want, but the south Rannoch road is very quiet and the loch is lovely.

There's parking and picnic tables at the tin shed that's the village hall, just west of the bridge over Allt an Fheadain.

The Leagag flank path – see below

Start by ignoring a wide, smooth hill track just to the west, but crossing the bridge and climbing a locked gate onto the small grass-middle track running south, with the river on its right. After 2.5km, the track rises to the gap at the west end of **Leagag**. ◄

Continue ahead on the track, still slightly uphill. In another 1.5km, the main track turns

234

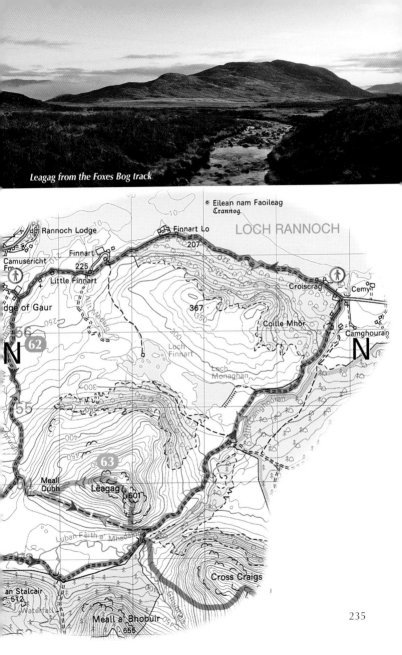

Leagag from the Foxes Bog track

left over a bridge. After 1.2km it crosses a second bridge, and runs northeast to a bridge over the main river, Luban Feith a' Mhadaidh.

The track rises to a gateway then runs downhill, northeast, with the river nearby on its right. Old pines are across the river, then the track reaches the edge of the Coille Mhor. Soon it enters the wood at a gate with ladder stile. Very pleasant track now runs under wild pine and birch, the river with cataracts down on the right. Exit at another gate and ladder stile and pass to left of a house, joining its driveway to emerge at the south Rannoch road.

Turn left for 5km to **Bridge of Gaur**.

Leagag flank option

At the west end of Leagag, a cairn marks a path which sets off on the left. It crosses swampy ground where a stream has an ancient slab culvert, now partly bypassed. After its first 10 metres the path becomes clearer, slanting up the south flank of **Leagag**. Below Leagag's western end, Meall Dubh, the path levels off and contours across the south flank.

As the path enters bracken it passes two fragments of stonework, remains of a small settlement. Here the path becomes indistinct. Keep contouring at the same level. Around the final curve of the hill you'll spot a solitary alder tree, at the site of another former enclosure or hut: the path passes just above this. Now clear, it slants down the shoulder of the hill, to join the track below, 200 metres up from its bridge over Luban Feith a' Mhadaidh.

Continue left (away from the bridge) along the track of the main route, down northeast to **Loch Rannoch** and left along the road to **Bridge of Gaur**.

Start/finish	Croiscrag Bridge (NN 649 564)
Distance	10km/6 miles
Ascent	400m/1300ft
Approx time	3½hr
Max altitude	Leagag 601m
Terrain	Rough tracks, quiet back road, and rough, steep hillside

Length

Difficulty

Leagag fails by 9m to achieve even the lowly designation of Graham, so your motives for ascending it are utterly pure. It is small but entertaining, with only a moderate amount of heather. Its isolated position gives it fine views, of Loch Rannoch and Ben Alder, the shapely northern bumps of Meall Buidhe, and the top bit of Schiehallion. In clear weather there's also a sight line right across Rannoch Moor into the slot of Glen Coe.

It's easier to take the steep southeast end of Leagag uphill, so this route is clockwise. The most convenient parking is at any of the lochside pull-offs between Croiscrag and Finnart Lodge, then walk east along the road to the start point.

Start at a triangle junction just west of the bridge over **Allt Camghouran**. Take the track south, the river on your left – there's a small parking pull-off 50 metres along the track. As it reaches a house, bear right on a rougher track.

Follow the track up through Coille Mhor woodland reserve. Leaving the wood, the track runs up open moorland to a high point below the craggy south end of Leagag. ▶

The adventurous could make a direct attempt on this steep face, on heather between the various small crags.

Just before the track turns downhill towards the bridge over Luban Feith a' Mhadaidh 200 metres away, turn off to the right on a peaty path. This slants up and leftwards around the hill flank, with the steep rocky end of Leagag up to the right. Follow the path up and around the hill flank until it levels at a solitary alder tree.

To bypass Leagag

At the alder tree keep ahead on the path. It becomes unclear, but keep on around the hill at the same level to rediscover the path as the slope changes from bracken to grass and heather.

To continue **over Leagag**, at the alder tree turn uphill, on grass. When the slope above becomes unavoidable heather, slant out to the right to the rim of the craggy drop, and head up to the small cairn on **Leagag** summit.

The alder tree on Leagag, and the steep north end of Cross Craigs

Head along the peaty, rocky plateau to the cairn at the plateau's west end. Head west down low heather and grass, and cross a peaty col to the low-rise Meall Dubh. Drop southwest to the Leagag flank path not far below, and follow it down around the hill's western end to meet a track.

Turn right down the track, which runs north for 3.5km to **Bridge of Gaur**. Turn right on the south Rannoch road for 5km – or less if you used one of the loch-side car parks.

The River Tilt at the foot of An Lochain sidestream (the crossing point used on Routes 71 and 73)

Pitlochry is where your woodland walk will be interrupted by waterfalls, by the mighty River Tummel – but also by a tartan tearoom. No town in Scotland has a better selection. That said, the café at House of Bruar is also entitled to a listing in the Tables of Substantially-Sized Tea Cakes.

A fine place for riverside and forest, Pitlochry offers just one hill: the small but shapely Ben Vrackie. Blair Atholl, by contrast, is the jump-off for Beinn a' Ghlo, the big stony hills of Atholl Forest and for Part Ten's long routes northwards to the Cairngorms.

Length

■ □ □ □ □

Difficulty

■ □ □ □ □

64 Pitlochry and its loch

Start/finish	Black Spout car park, Pitlochry (NN 951 576)
Distance	7.5km/4½ miles
Ascent	150m/500ft
Approx time	2½hr
Max altitude	Golf course 195m
Terrain	Paths and tracks

The special feature of this walk is waterworks: man-made ones at Pitlochry Dam, and equally impressive natural ones at Black Spout waterfall. Other points of interest include a plague pit, a 'Crusader' grave, a distillery, a brewery, and a fake lake.

The route uses four different Pitlochry Paths and linking paths. While the written description is complicated, the route can be followed more simply using the inexpensive Pitlochry Paths Network leaflet from Pitlochry Tourist Information, in tandem with a compass.

Black Spout car park is 200 metres up a signed lane at the east end of Pitlochry; or use car parks in town.

Start from the car park entrance, up the track signed 'Black Spout'. It runs under sessile oaks (the open-woodland sort). At a three-way signpost turn right, 'Black Spout', up a path, but in 100 metres turn right again on a smaller path, with the burn down on its right. It leads up to the viewing platform opposite **Black Spout** waterfall.

The path continues up to another signpost. Turn right, uphill (Edradour Path), but in 50 metres bear left at a waymark post with yellow-on-green arrow. The path runs gently downhill, below the top of Black Spout Wood. At a downhill track, cross to the path ahead signed 'Moulin', gently downhill.

After a footbridge over a stream, the path crosses an open field, then drops to another stream. Cross it to the field path ahead, still signed for Moulin. It runs to the top

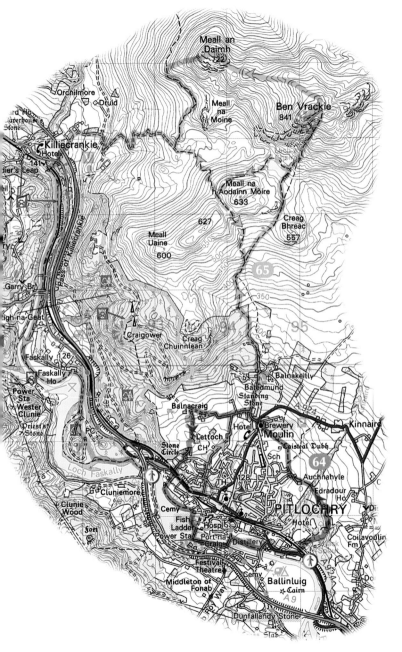

edge of a housing estate. Follow back streets and signs for Moulin, to leave the houses by an overgrown path to left of a field ditch.

The four-cornered spire of Moulin Church is a way-mark ahead. Ignore 'Moulin Path' turning right over the ditch – it's a roundabout way to Moulin – but keep ahead to left of the ditch. To your left stand the ruins of **Caisteal Dubh**, the Black Castle. ◀

An important stronghold in the Scottish Wars of Independence, but later burned down in an attempt to sterilise the mass grave of plague victims within its walls.

At the field end cross a stile on the right, then take a gate on the left to pass Moulin Hall to Moulin church, now a heritage centre.

> **Moulin** is the original settlement, away from the river's bogs and floods; Pitlochry is a mere sub-urb housing estate of the 19th century. Round left behind the church is the 'Crusader's Grave', marked with a white sign. It shows the Claymore or two-handed Scots broadsword.

Above Moulin Hotel take Baledmund Road, passing the **Moulin Brewery**. Bend round left where the lane for Ben Vrackie continues ahead, and pass below Dane's Stone (standing stone) in a field on your right.

Where the road turns down left, keep ahead in a tarred lane marked 'Craigower'. Bear right past **Balnacraig** farm, then turn down left at a signpost 'Pitlochry via Golf Course'. A path runs down the edge of the golf course. At the next signpost, keep ahead ('Loch Faskally') across the golf course. The wide path bends right to a signpost in the middle of the course, where you turn downhill to a gate.

The track below winds down behind houses, to join Cuilc Brae. Turn down right, to a level crossing and the main road.

Cross into a lane with path signpost 'to Dam'. Where it bends left, keep ahead on a path to the shore of **Loch Faskally**. Turn left to the huge concrete dam at the loch foot.

Cross the high walkway, and turn left alongside the **Fish Ladder**'s square concrete pools.

Take steps down left to the **fish viewer**; from May to August, during opening hours of the adjacent visitor centre, you can watch some of the 5000 salmon that pass up each year.

Pitlochry Dam

Continue downstream, passing below Pitlochry Festival Theatre and the riverside Fisherman's Bar, to turn left over a dangly footbridge towards the town centre.

At the northern riverbank, pass under the footbridge to a rough riverside path, at once fording a stony stream (there's a more formal crossing further up). A track leads downstream past a rugby ground; then bear right on an overgrown riverside path. At its end steps lead up onto a road bridge. Turn left, away from the river, to the main A924 at the Bell's **Distillery** – named Blair Athol (yes, Atholl does usually have two 'll's) Distillery. Turn right for 500 metres for the lane to **Black Spout** car park.

65 Ben Vrackie and the River Garry

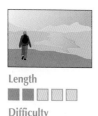

Length

Difficulty

Start/finish	Pitlochry waterside at north edge of town (NN 928 587, or Pitlochry town centre, or Killiecrankie Visitor Centre NN 917 626)
Distance	17km/10½ miles
Ascent	550m/1800ft
Approx time	5½hr
Max altitude	Ben Vrackie 841m
Terrain	Paths, mostly good, but small and rough over Meall an Daimh

Ben Vrackie from Moulin above Pitlochry The well-built Ben Vrackie path takes you from the high car park above Moulin (NN 943 597) up through a wood, over open moorland, past a reedy grey lochan to the rocky summit slope. The straight up-and-down can be varied by a return around the head of Loch a' Choire.

For a wilder version of Vrackie use the route below over the side summit of Meall an Daimh, but then turn back to Moulin via the Bealach na Searmoin. From the Moulin car park, this gives a Vrackie (but not Killiecrankie) day of 12km with 850m ascent (7½ miles/2800ft) – about 4½hr.

Ben Vrackie fails to make Munro height, but is reasonably rocky on top and looks out southwards over the Lowlands and downwards onto the fine River Tummel. It's a justly popular peak.

Killiecrankie is where an army of Scots who didn't support King James VII (James II of England) was defeated by a smaller army of Scots who did, in the year 1688. It's also where one of Scotland's great rivers flows below oaks in a gorge that's more like the French Jura or Vosges than anywhere in the UK.

Most of the walk is on wide, well-drained paths. So this is an outing that could be called comfortable – provided nobody leaps out and ambushes you in the gorge of Killiecrankie. Tarry by the Garry and take a crack at Vrackie, and answer the old, old question: 'Cam' ye by Killiecrankie O?'

From the waterside start back along the lane that leads up onto the main road into **Pitlochry**. Head into the town, crossing the railway, to take the next street uphill to the left, Larchwood Road. It doglegs left and right, leaves Pitlochry past a pool, and then bends right, to the hamlet of **Moulin**.

A **standing stone**, the Dane's Stone, is in a field on the left; just past it, an SRWS signpost for Ben-y-Vrackie marks a track climbing to the left. Head uphill, forking right through a car park onto a path at its back corner. ▸

This car park above Moulin is the start point for the 'just Vrackie' walk: see box above.

The path heads up the Moulin Burn, switching from one side of the stream to the other, to emerge from trees at the 340m contour. The wide path, to right of the stream, rises up heather moorland for another 400 metres to a junction.

Bad weather option

If there's nasty weather high up, you can turn up left here, signed 'Bealach Path', to pass through a col (Bealach an Searmoin); then head down a widening path to rejoin the main route on its descent from Meall an Daimh.

The **main route** bears right on the wide main path, signed for Ben Vrackie. It runs up through the little col to left of **Creag Bhreac**, and then bends right to cross the dam on **Loch a' Choire**. Ben Vrackie rises rocky behind the loch.

Shorter walk option

From here you can skip the high tops by turning left along the far side of Loch a' Choire. The path runs around the loch head, then climbs gently southwest to join the Bealach Path at a signpost (NN 938 622). Here turning left would take you back to Pitlochry, while the track down right, signed 'Killiecrankie', continues as the main route below. You've eliminated 2.5km and 300m of ascent – about 1hr – and all the walk's rough ground.

The **main route** climbs on up the steep path, rebuilt in places, with the craggy slope of Ben Vrackie on your left. Above the crags, the path contours left and climbs to a

Ben Vrackie summit

point just past the summit, returning southwest for the last 150 metres to **Ben Vrackie**'s trig point and cairn.

Leave the summit northeast, which is confusingly almost the direction you arrived in. Cross level ground for 200 metres to a cairn. Now turn down left, northwest, for 600 metres, to find a gentle grassy ridge running down westwards. There's a very small path.

After a col, the path leads through heather up the short rise to **Meall an Daimh**. There are sheltered grass hollows, then a heather plateau without summit cairn.

Descend briefly west, to the corner of a falling stone wall. Follow this down left, with deep heather and a small peat path. At an easing of the slope the wall bends slightly left. The descent steepens again, past a small stonefield. Immediately below this, look out for the groove of an old path crossing the slope. (If you miss this, the wall leads down to a crossing fence, and you can turn left along that.)

For Pitlochry turn left, up this green track and over Bealach an Searmoin.

Follow the old path to the left. It runs downhill for a few steps, contours, then gradually rises to meet a more visible track. Bear right down this, as it slants down to the green track of the Bealach Path. ◄

The track gets wider and smoother as it zigzags down the steeper slopes below. At a T-junction turn down left, soon reaching a tarmac lane. Here turn right, to pass under the A9 and reach the B8079 (old A9) opposite the **Killiecrankie Visitor Centre**.

From the back corner of the visitor centre, a signed path heads down steps into the wooded gorge. At the first junction, turn down left, signed for the Soldier's Leap. At the next one, the side-path for the **Soldier's Leap** is on the right.

> A few metres lead to a **viewpoint** looking down on the narrows of the river where a redcoat fleeing from his kilted, sword-slashing opponents cleared a gap of 7m. The actual battle took place in open ground near Blair Castle; displays at the visitor centre describe it.

On the main path, head down shallow steps to the riverside. The broad path heads downstream below a railway viaduct. A stone in the path marks where one of the generals from the losing side was caught up with by those chaps in kilts.

After 1.5km of riverside, the path reaches the end of a long footbridge. Don't cross, but keep ahead ('Pitlochry') under a high road bridge **Garry Bridge**. ▶ In 400 metres the riverside path diverts left to a footbridge over a side-stream then rejoins the main river. Soon it curves around the edge of a very wide pool, actually an end of Loch Faskally, and reaches a lane. Turn right, along the waterside. Ignore a forest track with barrier on the right but take the second one, which has a signpost. At once turn left to pass along the right-hand side of the lily-infested Loch Dunmore.

Follow red waymarks alongside the water to where a footbridge crosses a narrows of the lochan. Don't cross this footbridge either, but bear right, away from the water, on a small path that soon joins a wide waymarked trail. Turn left for 200 metres, until white markers indicate a smaller path on the right. This returns to **Loch Faskally**,

Bungee jumpers fling themselves off this bridge occasionally.

and follows its shore to the end of the very long Clunie Footbridge, with the A9 road bridge just beyond.

This footbridge is really tempting, but by now we've got used to ignoring footbridges. So pass under the high concrete bridge of the A9 and down to the waterside parking.

66 Blair Castle to Glen Tilt

Length

■ ■ □ □ □

Difficulty

■ □ □ □ □

Start/finish	Old Bridge of Tilt car park (NN 875 663)
Distance	17km/10½ miles
Ascent	250m/800ft
Approx time	4½hr
Max altitude	Lane at end of walk 280m
Terrain	Tracks and paths

Turning back across Gilbert's Bridge shortens the walk to 11.5km with 250m ascent (7 miles/800ft) – about 3hr.

A sign at the car park indicates when the track past the Jubilee Rifle Range is closed: some summer weekends but not most of them. In that case, stay on the riverside track to arrive at Gilbert's Bridge along the east bank of the Tilt.

When it's grey and rainy in the 21st century, the answer is to head back into the 1780s. Retrace the steps of James Hutton, the first geologist, who rode from one side of Scotland to the other suffering a badly blistered behind working out where it all comes from. Some rocks – such as sandstone – are made out of other, earlier rocks. Chunky crystalline granite, on the other hand, seems to be where it starts. The theory was that granite had crystallised out of the Universal Ocean in the time of Noah. James Hutton hoped, by going up Glen Tilt, to show that the granite had actually arrived, red hot, from underneath.

But there are plenty of other reasons for heading up Glen Tilt. There's the river itself, big and full between its rocky banks, with a silly ornamental grotto above. There's the ramble past the gardens, Blair Castle shining white between tall trees. There are a couple of slightly sexy statues, even, on the way round to Old Blair.

And then there's the long straight glen itself, green below its high heather walls, with the big river leading into the heart of the hills.

Start under trees (yellow arrows) to the River Tilt. Take the path downstream for 300 metres, through a grotto, to steps on the right. These lead up past the edge of a caravan site. Head directly away from the river into a beech avenue towards Blair Castle. At a statue of Hercules (large club, casual lionskin look) bear left to reach the car park at the front of **Blair Castle**.

Turn right (north) to a path junction, where you bear right into Diana's Grove. Keep ahead – under tall ornamental conifers there are various paths, one passing the Diana statue herself. At the north edge of the grove, don't exit to a lane, but turn right to cross Banvie Burn on a

The River Tilt, below Old Bridge of Tilt

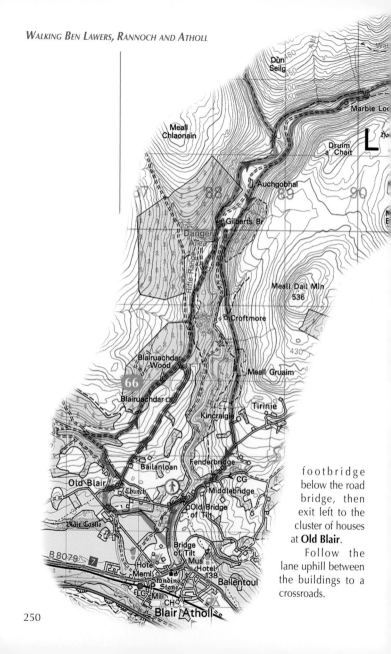

footbridge below the road bridge, then exit left to the cluster of houses at **Old Blair**.

Follow the lane uphill between the buildings to a crossroads.

Lambing variant

The route ahead passes through a field used for lambing. From April to early June, those with dogs should short cut to avoid this. At the crossroads above Old Blair keep ahead on the lane rising northeast. Soon it becomes a smooth dirt track, which bends left to a T-junction in forest as the main route rejoins from the left.

Meanwhile, the **main route** turns left up a track for 100 metres, then takes a path on the left (black waymark arrow) along the high riverbank. Soon it rejoins the track, which you follow up to a junction.

Turn back sharp right. The track rises gradually through the woods, then emerges to cross an open field, with wide views. The track then enters another plantation, where it passes above a small reservoir. Soon it joins a better-surfaced track arriving from down on the right.

With the dog and non-dog routes rejoined, in another 400 metres keep ahead as a smaller track forks up left. In a few yards a grassy track back down to the right has a green waymark – it's your bypass route if the firing range ahead should be preventing further progress. ▶ The main track emerges from the trees at a gate into the range. Red flags fly when it is in use, but this doesn't always mean that the track ahead is out of bounds. If you didn't check the one at Old Bridge of Tilt, check the notice beside the gate here.

From here on, yellow arrows guide you around the rest of the walk: whether on the shorter or the full-length version. The track slants gently downhill – ignore two side-tracks on the left up into the rifle range. A track junction is just before **Gilbert's Bridge**. Here the shorter and longer variants diverge.

To avoid the firing range, head back down this grassy path to a riverside track, and turn back left, upstream, crossing the river in 1.5km, to recross at Gilbert's Bridge.

Shorter walk option

For the shorter route back, keep ahead to cross Gilbert's Bridge, then take the track downstream. In 300 metres, a waymark post 'short cut' marks a path up to the left, under spruce trees, to reach a green track. Turn right on this, rejoining the longer route on its return to Old Bridge of Tilt.

For the **full-length** route to Marble Lodge, don't cross Gilbert's Bridge, but take the rougher, gated track forking left and keeping to left of the river. When it emerges from the plantation, a waymark indicates a green track through fields below. After the main track is rejoined, it rises slightly above the river, shrinks to a path, and crosses Allt Mhairc on an old stone bridge, with a small gorge below.

A waymark suggests a diversion left to a viewpoint – the view isn't any better than you're about to receive anyway. The main path continues along the grassy north banks of the River Tilt for 1.5km to Marble Lodge. As you

In Glen Tilt, to Marble Lodge

approach Marble Lodge, pale off-white marble blocks are in the riverbed.

> Stop 200 metres short of Marble Lodge if you want to examine the **geology**. There are cracks in the riverbank, and into them the granite has squeezed itself, pushing apart the grey schist rocks. Or, as James Hutton (a great geologist but one of the world's worst writers) put it 'breaking and displacing the strata in every conceivable manner, including the fragments of the broken strata, and interjected in every possible direction among the strata which appear'. Either way, the granite has to be younger than the surrounding rocks.

Cross the River Tilt by the bridge above **Marble Lodge**, and take the smooth gravel track downstream. Around 400 metres past the house, a waymark post suggests a green path above the main track; after 400 metres it rejoins the track below. In another 400 metres, another waymark post again suggests the green path forking up left. This runs above the house at **Auchgobhal**, then above a small plantation just above the main valley track. ▶

Shorter walk option rejoins here.

The green track contours south, down-valley, getting higher above the river over the next 2km. After a gate into a birch wood, fork left on the main, upper track. It continues level or slightly uphill for another 1.5km, to join a lane above **Fenderbridge**.

Turn down to the right, keeping downhill at the next junction, to turn right over **Old Bridge of Tilt** to the car park.

67 Glen Tilt and Carn a' Chlamain

Length

Difficulty

Start/finish	Old Bridge of Tilt car park (NN 875 663)
Distance	29km/18 miles
Ascent	950m/3100ft
Approx time	8½hr
Max altitude	Carn a' Chlamain 963m
Terrain	Tracks and an old zigzag path

Carn a' Chlamain can be combined with the lower hill **Beinn Mheadhonach**, to descend Mheadhonach's pleasant south ridge. The link to Beinn Mheadhonach is shown on the map below; switch into Route 68 for the descent. That covers 32km with 1200m of ascent (20 miles/3900ft) – about 10½hr.

A stonking long route combines Beinn Dearg, Beinn Mheadhonach and Carn a' Chlamain; use Route 68, then the same link line to Carn a' Chlamain, then down the Landrover track to Marble Lodge, giving 38km with 1500m of ascent (24 miles/5000ft) – about 12½hr.

Carn a' Chlamain is a huge and shapely hill when seen as part of the western wall of Glen Tilt. But look at it the other way, across the moors of Atholl, and it's nothing but a hump. It's notable as one of just nine Munros bagged by Queen Victoria. She went up it on her pony Fyvie – and you could just about manage it by bicycle as well, with the Landrover track up its southern spur from Marble Lodge.

But given the contrast between the steep, dramatic Glen Tilt and the bleak bare moorlands above, let's have a bit more of both. Let's have fully 12km of Tilt, right up to Forest Lodge. The old stalkers' path zigzags up the steep slope at pony gradients. The modern Landrover track on the south ridge makes for a convenient descent.

For the route start see the map for Route 66. Start from the back left corner of the car park, following yellow arrow posts to the River Tilt. Turn upstream, on the path that crosses a bridge over the roadway to join a smooth track upstream to left of the river. After rising slightly through open fields and descending under trees, the track crosses the river.

Continue upstream now to right of the river. Just before **Gilbert's Bridge**, at the end of a plantation, turn right at a waymark post in a cairn. Earth steps lead up to a green track along the top of the narrow plantation.

This gentle track runs above **Auchgobhal**, to rejoin the valley floor track below. After 400 metres, again you can divert onto a green track just up on the right. The tracks combine again to **Marble Lodge**.

Cross the track's bridge beyond the lodge. In another 800 metres, the track crosses a military-built bridge with the slogan 'Ubique' (meaning 'Everywhere') on a nearby plaque. ▶

The valley floor track continues upstream; or walk the grassy riverside. After Clachghlas there's also an old green track on the left just above the valley floor. It rejoins the main track before Forest Lodge.

To ascend Chlamain's south ridge track, immediately after the Ubique bridge head up the spur to right of the stream on a small zigzag path to join the track corner at the 400m contour.

Carn a' Chlamain summit track

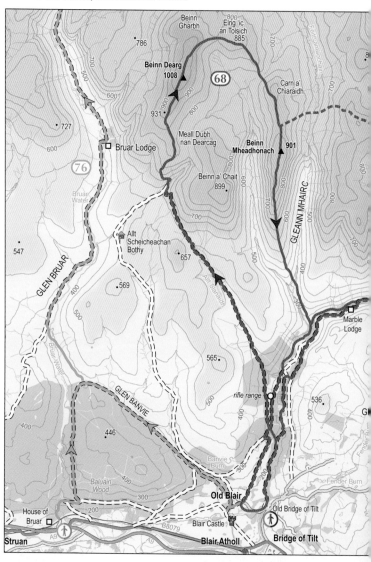

The track passes **Forest Lodge** in its pinewood. At the end of the wood, turn left through a field gate, to a small gate in a muddy corner. Head up the top edge of the plantation to a fence. Turn uphill alongside this to a stile at its top corner.

Just above, the old path starts its first long zig out to the left. After 400 metres it embarks on an even longer zag back to the right. Follow it up, clear all the way, to arrive suddenly on the plateau. The path continues west across a wide, peaty col, and up onto a ridge of stony ground. Here it joins the track up the shoulder of Carn a' Chlamain.

Keep ahead up the stony track. At its high point there's a cairn on the right. This is a good point to strike left up the stony slope to **Carn a' Chlamain**'s summit.

Return down the track, ignoring the fork-off to the path you arrived by. The track heads southeast to a corner of the plateau above **Glen Tilt**. It then bends right, southwest, to descend the long ridge towards the valley floor. ▶

You don't have to follow it quite all the way. At the 400m contour,

Atholl Estate managers have apologised for this intrusive motor track, build by their predecessors.

257

just above where the track bends down left towards Clachghlas, a fainter track turns off sharp right and at the same point a small, faint path runs down ahead. Follow this path down the spur to arrive at the 'Ubique' bridge.

You can vary the route for the return without adding extra distance. At the bridge upstream of **Marble Lodge**, stay on the right bank, on a grassy path. It rises slightly to a stone bridge over Allt Mhairc. Descending again, it widens to a track, which undulates through a plantation to reach **Gilbert's Bridge**.

If the range track is closed, cross Gilbert's Bridge back onto the outward route.

Consult the firing range notice here. ◀ Unless the range track is closed, continue ahead up it. Beyond the range it enters trees again, levels, and descends as a tarmac lane to **Old Blair**. Cross a crossroads down into the village, and where the lane bends right, keep ahead along a yew avenue to the ruined chapel.

Beinn Mheadhonach and Carn a' Chlamain, seen from Blair Atholl

Turn left behind the chapel to a gate and a fenced field path. At its end a stile leads onto a track, which joins the lane to **Old Bridge of Tilt**.

Start/finish	Old Bridge of Tilt car park (NN 875 663)
Distance	32km/20 miles
Ascent	1200m/3900ft
Approx time	10½hr
Max altitude	Beinn Dearg 1008m
Terrain	Tracks, rough moorland grass and some heather

Length

Difficulty

The usual way to do Dearg is by a long, long Landrover track, and an ascent of 500m up a heathery slope. It's true that you can then use a different Landrover track (via Allt Slanaidh) for the return. However, having slogged up onto the high plateau, you might fancy spending some time there, as well as bagging the Corbett Beinn Mheadhonach. If you do, prepare for a strenuous Atholl outing.

For the route start see the map for Route 66. Yellow waymarks will guide you for the first 3km of this walk. Start by following one of them to the River Tilt. Take the path upstream, over a high bridge above the roadway. The path crosses a steep bank above the River Tilt to join a smooth track. Follow it north for 200 metres. A yellow arrow points to a short path diversion along the high riverbank, rejoining the track.

After 1.2km the track runs into woods and starts to descend. In 300 metres, a grass track forks up left through the wood, crossing a bridge below a field corner. It runs up with a deer fence on its right to join an upper track high in **Blairuachdar Wood**.

Stop following yellow arrows here. Turn sharp left for 50 metres, then sharp right up a less-used track. It runs along the top edge of the rifle range (this upper track is not in the range's danger area). Another gate leads into

Above the old bridge over Allt Mhairc, descending from Beinn Mheadhonach

regenerating birch woods. The track emerges onto open moor, with **Allt Slanaidh** down on the right.

After 2km the track fords the stream, and runs north-west, to right of it. At the valley head it passes across the base of Beinn a' Chait along the 650m contour, then drops to Allt Scheicheachan stream.

An old terraced path sets off to the right. It slants up-valley above the stream, then turns back left, to zigzag northeast up the nose of **Meall Dubh nan Dearcag**. (A much smaller path contouring away ahead here is easily ignored; it leads to Bruar Lodge.)

At the slope top the path runs northeast through heather, then turns left at a small cairn and heads north-west across a wide neck of land. Here the path to Beinn Dearg divides. The left-hand fork passes to right of a cairn at the slope top (931m, Sliabh na Cloiche Moire), then gently uphill to the trig point of **Beinn Dearg**. ◀ Head north, to the wide saddle before the north top. As the ground rises again, fork off right on a small path along the base of the stonefields. It slants down the flank of the stony north top. Where it fades, head down east across the col below. Cross **Elrig 'ic an Toisich**, to descend the wide rounded ridge southeast, keeping to the highest ground for shorter heather.

A steep and slightly rocky descent leads to a low col, best crossed slightly to the left for fewer peat hags. Ascend **Carn a' Chiaraidh** slanting to the right below its

Beinn Dearg is Red Mountain; the summit is rounded boulders and stones of pinkish granite.

stony top, to the ridgeline running south beyond. Keep left of the peat hags guarding the saddle itself, for a pleasant grassy slope onto **Beinn Mheadhonach**. From either of the 900m contour rings the other looks higher. But you'll cross both, to head on down the south ridge.

This ridge is narrow, at least by Atholl standards, with low heather and peat and a small path. By the ridge foot the heather has deepened to calf height – and here the small path separates into several and may get lost. Across the stream hollow on the left, paths can be seen emerging beyond the bridge, and then the bridge itself appears. An eroded path leads down to it.

Cross the handsome stone bridge and take the path along the brink of the birch-branched river hollow. The path crosses green grassland with old shielings above the river, then drops to join the Glen Tilt path at a waymark post.

Here you turn right to a stone bridge over Allt Mhairc. Descending again, the path widens to a track, which undulates through a plantation to **Gilbert's Bridge**.

Consult the firing range notice here. If the range track is closed, turn left over Gilbert's Bridge. Otherwise continue up the track ahead. Beyond the range it enters trees, and descends as a tarmac lane to **Old Blair**. Keep ahead into the village, and where the lane bends right, keep ahead along a yew avenue to the ruined chapel.

Turn left behind the chapel to a gate and a fenced field path. At its end a stile leads onto a track, which joins the lane to **Old Bridge of Tilt**.

Stony summit of Beinn Dearg

69 Bruar Falls and Glen Banvie

Start/finish	House of Bruar (NN 822 659), or Old Bridge of Tilt car park (NN 875 663)
Distance	16km/10 miles
Ascent	300m/1000ft
Approx time	4¼hr
Max altitude	Glen Banvie Wood 390m
Terrain	Path and tracks

Length

Difficulty

The point of this walk is the Falls of Bruar. Starting at House of Bruar itself (plenty of parking) means you get the falls at both ends of the walk. Starting from Old Bridge of Tilt the walk is a little longer, but includes the small gorge of Banvie Burn and the back of Blair Castle. Just slot yourself into the route description at the appropriate point. However you work it, you get the silly structure at the Whim, and a taste of high moorland at the top of Banvie Burn.

Start from the commercial courtyard, and go through a gap at its back right corner to the riverside; here turn left, upstream (or head round to right of the shopping complex, and take the signed path up to left of the river). The path heads under the railway by a damp stone arch, and to the Lower Bridge, which you don't cross.

If starting from Old Bridge of Tilt, this point is reached across the Lower Bridge, to the west bank of the stream, then followed by a complete circuit of the gorge walk.

Follow the path upstream to left of the gorge, to the Upper Bridge. Across the bridge, the wide path zigs to the left then back right, to return downstream. It meets a bend in a forest track.

Turn left onto the left-hand, upper branch of the forest track, running level. Ignore a green old track running back left, but 400 metres from the **falls**, take a gravel track up left (orange waymark).

After 600 metres uphill, fork left at a waymark post onto an older track. This runs level, north, with Bruar River far below. You may notice a milestone 5/4: this is the Nine Mile carriage drive from Blair Castle, with 5 miles ahead and 4 miles back the other way.

After 2.5km the track passes through a deer fence into open pinewood. It bends round right to run along the northern edge of the wood. Soon it emerges from the wood, to run southeast down **Glen Banvie**, above Banvie Burn.

The Lower Bridge and rock arch, Falls of Bruar

263

As the track re-enters woodland, ignore a track down left to a bridge. After 800 metres ignore another bridge on your left. Another 300 metres later, an earth track up right, with a black arrow marker, would be for the Whim; head up there and return if you want. Otherwise keep ahead, with what's now a fine river down to left of the track, to reach a tarmac lane just west of **Old Blair**. Here you will turn right. ◄

To return to the Old Bridge of Tilt start point, go left here.

Old Bridge of Tilt start point

From the car park, turn left along the lane for 1km to a junction above Old Blair. Turn down left, bending right among the houses, and keep ahead towards a T-junction to pick up the main route description below. Follow it in a clockwise direction back to this point.

For the most interesting route back to the Old Bridge of Tilt start point cross the tarred lane to a gate in a wall into Diana's Grove woodland garden. Immediately turn left to cross Banvie Burn on a lower bridge attached to the road bridge.

The path climbs above the road. Take the second side-path on the right, to the ruins of St Bride's Church. Bend left behind it on a grass track. Through a kissing-gate, the track slants down above a field to houses. Cross a stile ahead onto a track, which runs above the houses and joins a tarred lane. Keep ahead on this to the **Old Bridge of Tilt** car park.

Follow the tarred track west to a T-junction, with **Blair Castle** left beyond a 'No entry' sign. Turn right on a field track, with the Whim dead ahead on its hill. The track soon bends left up the main valley, through parkland and past a small ornamental pond. When it re-enters plantations, keep ahead at a five-way junction, then cross the railway. Emerge through a stone gateway at West Lodge to the B8079.

Follow the road ahead for 300 metres, round a bend to the right, to take a gravel track (the second one on the right) which passes under the railway. Rooks sometimes nest under the arch. The track runs just above the railway; after the second house keep ahead on an old green path, which joins a newer track. This carries on above the railway, then slants uphill to arrive above River Bruar (it's the lower branch of the track you earlier took the upper branch of).

Turn left down the riverside path to cross the Lower Bridge. Those who started from Old Bridge of Tilt turn uphill here and leap all the way back to the start of the route description. Those who started at **Bruar** turn left to enjoy jolly big cream cakes at House of Bruar.

70 Bruar Falls and Blair

Length

■ ■ ■ ■ ■

Difficulty

■ ■ ■ ■ ■

Start/finish	House of Bruar (NN 822 659)
Distance	12.5km/8 miles
Ascent	200m/700ft
Approx time	3½hr
Max altitude	Upper Bridge 250m
Terrain	Path and tracks

This is the previous walk, without the wild moorland section. It's one of the less serious walks in this book, not least because it takes you to the silly structure called the Whim, designed to be viewed from Blair Castle.
There is plenty of parking space at the House of Bruar.

Start from the shopping precinct, where you go through a gap at the back right corner to the riverside. Turn left, upstream. The path passes a cairn dispensing nature leaflets, then heads under the railway by a damp stone arch, and up to the Lower Bridge, which you don't cross.

> The trees here were planted after an appeal in verse by **Rabbie Burns** in 1787. 'Let lofty firs, and ashes cool, My lowly banks o'er spread.' The Fourth Duke of Atholl duly obliged.

Follow the path upstream to left of the gorge, to the Upper Bridge. Across it, the wide path zigs to the left then back right, to return downstream. It meets a bend in a forest track.

Turn left onto the left-hand, upper branch of the forest track, running level under pine and larch to a junction. Keep ahead, level, with clear-felling offering views, before the track runs gently downhill to another junction. Follow the blue arrow bearing left and uphill. After a turning circle, the track becomes grassier and levels. As

it turns north, a wide grass path turns down right. Follow this down to the forest foot, where it bends left and in 100 metres reaches the Whim. This is a strange stonework with views of Blair Castle and Ben Vrackie.

Keep ahead down an earth track to a junction above **Banvie Burn**. Take the track down to the right, above the river, to a junction west of **Old Blair**.

Turn right, and follow the tarred track west to a T-junction with **Blair Castle** down left beyond a 'No entry' sign. Continue as on Route 69. After the Lower Bridge, you could circle the gorge again in the evening light; or just turn down left to enjoy tea and slab of short-bread at the House of Bruar.

The Nine Mile Drive above Glen Banvie (Route 69)

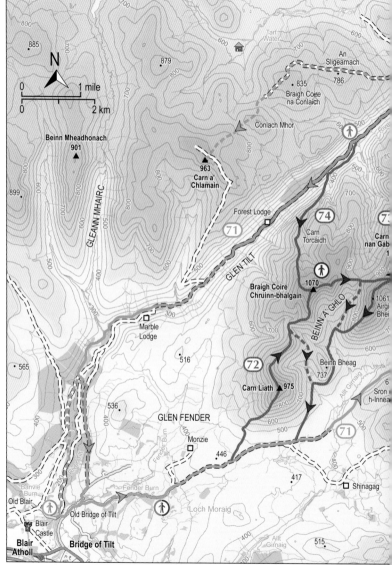

SUMMIT SUMMARY: BEINN A' GHLO

Beinn a' Ghlo is Scotland's number 30, and is Perthshire's second highest, after Ben Lawers. It's also big sideways – 6km of summit ridge, three Munros, with a dozen humpy side-ridges which, according to the story, enclose 18 corries, in each of which you can fire a rifle without being heard in the other 17.

That ridgeline lacks crags, but its stony and sculptural curves make it one of Scotland's most satisfying. Even the Gaelic names encapsulate a progress in Perthshire peak-bagging: they translate as 'grey stone-pile', 'place of small blisters', and 'acting the goat'.

The high car park at Loch Moraig means you can capture the 6km of ridge and the three Munros in a strenuous daywalk. But the standard southward descent off Carn nan Gabhar is somewhat nasty – whereas a long and tempting ridgeline runs down northwards, ever deeper into the wilds of Atholl.

BEINN A' GHLO ROUTES
71 Around Beinn a' Ghlo (from Loch Moraig)
72 Beinn a' Ghlo from Loch Moraig
73 Carn nan Gabhar north ridge to Glen Tilt (descent)
74 Glen Tilt to Braigh Core Chruinn-bhalgain by Carn Torcaidh

einn a' Ghlo from the path to Loch Loch

71 Around Beinn a' Ghlo
(with optional ascent of Ben Vuirich)

Start/finish	Loch Moraig parking (NN 905 670)
Distance	39km/24 miles
Ascent	600m/2000ft
Approx time	11hr
Max altitude	Pass to Glen Loch 590m; or Ben Vuirich 903m
Terrain	Tracks, paths, grassy riverbank

Length

Difficulty

Ben Vuirich adds 2.5km and 300m of ascent and some rough heather – about 1½hr extra.

The walk around the back of Beinn a' Ghlo is a good one, with an old path that's still usable and no heather tramping at all (unless you boldly decide to divert over Ben Vuirich). The return along Glen Tilt is by a smooth Landrover track. After heavy rain there can, however, be problems crossing the Tilt.

From **Old Bridge of Tilt** (alternative parking and start point), take the uphill lane for Monzie. Keep uphill to moorland pasture, and park alongside Loch Moraig.

Start along the track continuing towards **Monzie**, but turn right through a gate onto another track. After 1.5km, it bends left to pass a hut on your left (here the path sets off up Carn Liath). Keep on the track ahead, fording a stream, then rising gently around the base of **Carn Liath**.

Around 2km after the hut, the main track bends right, downhill; here keep ahead on a fainter track, contouring. After 1km the track dips to ford the **Allt Girnaig**.

The continuing path is obscure. It runs straight up towards **Sron na h-Innearach**, the small summit ahead, but halfway up the slope, it turns left and contours around onto the steep northwest slope above the stream.

As it passes below a tiny rock outcrop, the path is terraced, and clear to see from above or below: make sure you regain it here if it was lost.

The path continues, well used, through heather above the stream, to a high point 300 metres up right from the col leading over to Glen Loch. By this point the path has become a rough wheelmarked track.

Ben Vuirich variant

The Corbett Ben Vuirich fails by just 11m to reach Munro height – but it's typically Corbett, a heathery hump with none of the elegance of Beinn a' Ghlo's three summits. It does have fine views, and can be reached from the pass to Glen Loch with only a couple of kilometres of heather harshness. Surprisingly, the descent of the north flank is pleasantly grassy.

At the high point of the path through the pass, turn up right along a small stream onto heathery moorland. The best way is to cross **Stac nam Bodach**, then turn southeast, keeping down to left of the peat hags in the flat col. Cross the head of two streams, to gain the west

Loch Loch, looking back to Beinn Vuirich

slope of Ben Vuirich. The green strip of a peat stream gives a way up through the heather, and above that the heather is short and walkable. Keep uphill to **Ben Vuirich** trig point.

Descend just west of north, passing a granite cairn as the slope steepens. Head down grass, all the way to the slope foot. Bear left across a stream to join the track through the pass at a fallen enclosure (NN 994 717, Bothan Ruigh-chuilein).

Bypassing Ben Vuirich, from the pass the track runs gently down into a hollow with a stream, then rises slightly, before dropping towards **Glen Loch**. It passes a fallen enclosure (Bothan Ruigh-chuilein). Follow the main track east, across another stream. About 150 metres later, turn back left on a fainter track. This runs to the head of **Loch Loch**. ◄

A loch called Loch? Well, it's the only loch in Atholl, so that's all the name it needs.

The map marks a path running along the loch's east shore. It could be any of several usable sheep paths along the grassland. From the outflow, follow the grassy banks of **An Lochain** river. The going is reasonable all the way down-valley to the **River Tilt**. ◄

See photo at the beginning of this part.

Crossing the River Tilt can be a problem. Around 150 metres upstream from the confluence, the river bottom has slabs of pale marble, which give better footing. If the river is just slightly too full for comfort, you can make your way upstream on grassy slopes for 1.5km, to a point opposite the Bedford Bridge. Upstream from the Tarf confluence, the Tilt is less than half the volume.

There is also a two-wire bridge 500 metres downstream from An Lochan confluence (NN 976 781). However, the attachment bracket on the west bank is bent and should not be trusted.

Fortunately a narrow but good path runs downstream on the east side, across steep slopes but followable all the way to the bridge (NN 956 763) 3.5km downstream.

Across the River Tilt, turn downstream on a clear riverside track. This is fairly popular with walkers and cyclists, unsurprisingly given the dramatic deep glen and its big river. After 7km you pass **Forest Lodge**, and now grassy riverbanks can be used instead of the track.

In another 3km, the track crosses a bridge north of **Marble Lodge**, but stay on the east bank. A grassy path leads downstream, after 1km rising slightly to a stone bridge over Allt Mhairc. Drop back to the River Tilt, to a track running to Gilbert's Bridge. ▶

See Route 66 (Blair Castle to Glen Tilt) for valley routes back to Old Bridge of Tilt.

Cross the river, and take the downstream track for just 200 metres. At a cairn with a post in it, turn up left under trees to a higher track. Follow this grassy track down-valley, rising above the river. After 2km ignore a lesser track forking down right into woods. The main track, running roughly level, reaches the Glenfender lane.

Turn right, steeply downhill. At a junction above **Old Bridge of Tilt**, turn up left for the stiff climb to **Loch Moraig**.

72 Beinn a' Ghlo from Loch Moraig

Start/finish	Loch Moraig parking (NN 905 670)
Distance	21.5km/13½ miles
Ascent	1250m/4200ft
Approx time	8hr
Max altitude	Carn nan Gabhar 1121m
Terrain	Hill paths, sometimes very rough

Length

Difficulty

The steep nose of Carn Liath used for the ascent is heather on quartzite scree, and the resulting eroded path used to be visible along much of Glen Garry. This was handsomely repaired in 2019. Please stay on the built path to avoid further erosion.

This is the standard route on Beinn a' Ghlo. From the high car park, reach the ridge the quickest way. Enjoy the three fine summits. And come down again the quickest way, even if that is a nasty peat path.

Main ridge of Beinn a' Ghlo: Braigh Coire Chruinn-bhalgain and Carn nan Gabhar from Carn Liath

From **Loch Moraig** start along the track continuing past a plantation, and as the main track bends left for Monzie turn right through a gate and up a stony track. After 1.5km, turn off left over a stile to pass a shuttered-up hut.

The path is not very clear as it heads north across a peaty swamp. Find it again as it heads uphill beside a fallen wall, with a small stream to its right. The newly rebuilt path is obvious as it ascends the steeper heathery end of Carn Liath.

The steep path used to be horribly stony and loose both below and above the slight shoulder at the 600m level. Eventually the slope relents, to reach a cairn at the plateau edge. Just ahead is the trig point on **Carn Liath**.

The ridge is of stones and low vegetation, with a clear path. Gently descending, it runs northwest then bends northeast, before running north down to a col. There's a spring just down to the right, a useful water source.

Escape route option

There is a **convenient escape route** from the ridge here. A few steps short of this col, a small stony path descends to the right, just above the spring and its stream. It

passes through the col northwest of Beinn Bheag, and slants down the slope of Carn Liath, eventually to join the track below.

The big **main path** continues ahead out of the col, and up the twisting ridge to **Braigh Coire Chruinn-bhalgain**.

From the summit cairn, a path descends east, to vanish at a wide plateau col just below. Keep east onto a slight rise. Follow the crest of this northeast for 300 metres, until it starts to dip. Now the descent line is eastwards: the path soon reappears as you start to descend to the major col (Bealach an Fhiodha on Explorer maps) below. ▸

From this col there's another escape path; see the alternative descent below.

The path out of the col slants up to the left, east, past a very small spring, to reach the ridge north of Airgiod Bheinn. Head on up the rounded ridge, northeast. The going is stony, tiresome to the tired, as you pass a first cairn, and a second one with a trig point on it, before the large cairn at **Carn nan Gabhar**'s true summit.

Returning, pass to right of the trig on its stonepile, to left of the southwest cairn on its stonepile. Return down the rough path to the ridge levelling before Airgiod Bheinn.

275

Alternative descent option

A wetter but gentler descent route involves retracing your steps down the slanty path to the main col Bealach an Fhiodha below Braigh Coire Chruinn-bhalgain. Just above the col, a smaller path forks left, down into the top of the little V-valley heading down south (Allt Bealach an Fhiodha).

The small, peaty path runs to left of the stream, crosses it, and then recrosses near the foot of the V-valley. At the valley exit it crosses the stream yet again (NN 952 712), now joined by the main route from Airgiod Bheinn, to contour around the flank of Beinn Bheag.

For the **more rugged** (but drier) **descent** from the ridge levelling, just keep ahead along the broad ridgeline, with a slight rise to **Airgiod Bheinn**.

Now the spur descends southwest, a stonepile with occasional rock, getting gradually steeper. At about 850m level the crest of the spur is split by a grassy hollow. Take the path down to right of this, then turn down right (west), the path now steep and stony. At the foot of the stones the path turns left and contours, with no real reason; just carry on down grassy patches to the valley floor, to meet the soggy alternative path above the stream Allt Bealach an Fhiodha.

At the V-valley's exit the path crosses the stream (NN 952 712) and contours around the flank of **Beinn Bheag**. Where it's on peat rather than stony moraine, the path is wide and blackly soggy. It drops to cross another stream, Allt Coire na Saobhaidh, at the base of the steeper slope. It then works its way around the flank of **Carn Liath**, gradually descending to join the old path to Glen Loch. Thus the going gets slightly firmer for the last 500 metres, to join the track from Shinagag.

Follow the track west to the hut at the foot of the Carn Liath path, and on down to **Loch Moraig**.

Down the north ridge of Carn nan Gabhar

73 Carn nan Gabhar
north ridge to Glen Tilt (descent)

Start	Carn nan Gabhar (NN 972 733)
Finish	River Tilt at An Lochain (NN 980 783)
Distance	5.5km/3 miles (as part of longer routes)
Descent	800m/2700ft
Approx time	1½hr (as part of longer routes)
Terrain	Pathless ridge of grass and short heather

Length
◼◼◼◼◻

Difficulty
◼◼◼◻◻

Ghlo, and keep going... before setting off down this **tempting ridgeline**, it's best to think about what to do next. First there's the crossing of the Tilt: see Route 71, which also describes the return via Glen Tilt. Assuming you arrived via Carn Liath and Braigh Coire Chruinn-bhalgain (Route 72), that's 36.5km and 1550m of ascent (23 miles/5200ft) – a long day of about 14hr, or two with a camp by the Tilt.

The north ridge is a long gentle descent mostly on grass, with the occasional heather no more than ankle deep. It's a delight, except that it deposits you in the middle of nowhere and in front of a dubious river crossing.

From **Carn nan Gabhar** the ridge runs down northeast, then down north to a slight rise (**947m**) – a small path bypasses this rise just down to the left. Don't head left to Meall a' Mhuirich, but keep down north, to the level section over Meall Gharran. Off the end of this the going is mildly heathery in parts. The final descent is on steep grass to the **River Tilt**.

ONWARD ROUTES FROM GLEN TILT

Just 1km down Glen Tilt there's a back track towards Carn a' Chlamain. From the track end, skirt north of Conlach Mhor to avoid getting bogged down in the hags behind it. Route 68 (in reverse) returns to Blair Atholl over Beinn Mheadhonach and Beinn Dearg. Two days, a good handful of Munros, and the heart of Atholl.

But having set off northwards, it's even more inviting to keep going. Just up Glen Tilt there's a right turn to Fealar Lodge, to continue through the obscure Iutharn Munros to Glen Shee. Or steer straight ahead, with the top of Tilt (Route 75) leading inexorably into the jaws of the Lairig Ghru...

Blair Castle to Beinn a' Ghlo

74 Glen Tilt to Braigh Coire Chruinn-bhalgain
by Carn Torcaidh

Start	Footbridge over Glen Tilt 3km past Forest Lodge (NN 956 763)
Finish	Braigh Coire Chruinn-bhalgain (NN 945 723)
Distance	5km/3 miles (as part of longer routes)
Ascent	750m/2500ft
Approx time	2¾hr (as part of longer routes)
Max altitude	Braigh Coire Chruinn-bhalgain 1070m
Terrain	Grassy ridge and low tundra-type crowberry

Length

Difficulty

Route 66 gives the approach **up Glen Tilt from Old Bridge of Tilt**. At normal summer levels, the River Tilt can be forded opposite the ridge foot. Otherwise, continue 1km to the stout footbridge at NN 956 763.

This could be the pleasantest little ridge in Perthshire. A waterfall ravine on the left, deep Glen Tilt on the right, and a grassy crest to walk up. There are two reasons why the world walks elsewhere. It lands you at the middle of the three-Munro ridge, with no way of including both Carn Liath and Carn nan Gabhar in any onward walk. And more importantly, it starts an absurdly long way up Glen Tilt.

But Glen Tilt's a nice place. A 14km walk in up it ought to be a bonus...

Start over the footbridge, then downstream on grassy riverbank for 1.2km, to cross a stream, Allt air Chul, aptly translated 'Stream at the Back'.

Turn uphill on the narrow ridgeline to right of the stream. The foot of the ridge has a few metres of old grass path, then rises quite steeply. The stream gorge alongside has birches and waterfalls. The ridgeline rises gently between the stream ravine and the hole of

Carn Torcaidh ridge, Beinn a' Ghlo

'Torc' means wild boar.

Glen Tilt, becoming a grass crest before the steeper rise to **Carn Torcaidh**. ◄

There's a cairn at the false summit, then a short ridge-line south to the smaller cairn at the true summit. The ridge runs briefly down to a wide col. Keep ahead up slopes of low tundra vegetation and moss, gently rising to the summit of **Braigh Coire Chruinn-bhalgain**.

For a return route over Carn nan Gabhar and down to Loch Moraig (for Old Bridge of Tilt) see Route 72.

OTHER ROUTES ON BEINN A' GHLO

The issue is to find heather-free routes up to the 600m contour. Above this, the vegetation is tundra-like, and gives comfortable going anywhere.

At the east side of Carn nan Gabhar, there is a fallen enclosure at the track bend in Glen Loch, NN 994 717, **Bothan Ruigh-chuilein**. Opposite the enclosure, a wheelmark track sets off towards Carn nan Gabhar, appearing to run right up to the 650m contour, above the deep heather and just below the stony upper part of the hill.

Braigh Coire Chruinn-bhalgain has been ascended from **Creag-choinnich Lodge** ruin (NN 918 704). The track to the lodge is reported as followable, and the ground above is ankle-deep heather, with going getting easier as you go up.

From Glen Tilt, the ridge **Luib Mhor** directly above the footbridge forms the true north ridge of Braigh Coire Chruinn-bhalgain. Its crest is grass rather than heather, but it looks less attractive than Carn Torcaidh alongside.

PART TEN

DRUMOCHTER

North down Gaick Pass, alongside Allt Loch an Duin (Route 78)

Drumochter Pass: the long smooth sweeps of the dual carriageway correspond with the featureless heather slopes above, the grey-green bogs below. The A9 is quick and convenient, through to the whole of the northern Highlands. And so, alongside the busy A9 run the Inverness railway, the Sustrans No 7 bike route, and even the Beauly–Denny power line and its gravel access track.

But underneath the A9 lies the old road of General Wade, built through the bleakness and the bog to link Perthshire with the Spey. The big emptiness goes quickly by at 70mph – but to the east, the other old passes through Atholl give you the long hill paths, the drovers' routes southwards to the Lowlands. Gaick is green hollows and three blue lochs, on easy tracks that can be cycled if you like. Minigaig is sterner, with a little path that goes up and up through the heather, until it bursts into Badenoch at an altitude of 850m. Finest of all, Glen Tilt and its silver river go like a steel arrow through the stony heart of the hills.

THE ATHOLL PASSES

75 Glen Tilt

Length

Difficulty

Start	Blair Atholl station (NN 870 653)
Finish	Linn of Dee (NO 062 897)
Distance	33.5km/21 miles
Ascent	400m/1300ft
Approx time	9hr
Max altitude	Tilt watershed 520m
Terrain	Tracks and path, one dodgy ford north of Bynack Lodge

From White Bridge towards the end of the route you can turn left for a very long walk out by Glen Feshie to the Spey. More natural is to keep on north through the Lairig Ghru for Aviemore: a through route as lovely as Glen Tilt but considerably tougher, with the advantage of ending on a coach and rail route back to Blair Atholl.

Atholl hills are rounded, heathery, and hard work. But like the yin nestled in the heart of the yang, Glen Tilt is altogether opposite: grassy-green, an easy Landrover track, and for 10km almost arrow-straight. The big river gleams like the big salmon that swim in it. Overhead, steep slopes rise to little crags and the windswept moors.

At White Bridge you're well outside Perthshire, but still not near anywhere else. Linn of Dee is 5km east, with Braemar 11km after that.

On-street parking may be found in Blair Atholl village.

From **Blair Atholl** station, start east (towards Pitlochry) along B8079. Across the River Tilt, turn left to **Old Bridge of Tilt** and cross that old bridge (see also maps for Routes 66 and 67).

Now the track up-valley would be to the right, but perversely you should turn left and left again into the car park. Here you can check the noticeboard for live firing at the Jubilee Rifle Range up-valley. You can also find the path to the riverside, turning upstream and crossing over the approach road on a high stone bridge. The path continues high above the river to join the track up the valley.

The track runs through fields to left of the River Tilt, and into a wood. After 500 metres, a broad path leads up left. Follow it up to a higher track, which runs down through the rifle range with fine views up-valley, to reach **Gilbert's Bridge**. ▶

Don't cross, but take the track up the western bank. It becomes a grassy path, moving up from the river to cross Allt Mhairc by a small stone bridge, then returning to the Tilt. Just north of **Marble Lodge**, join the track arriving from the other bank. Instead of the track, you can use the grassy riverbank until **Forest Lodge**.

About 7km after Forest Lodge, the riverside track becomes a well-used footpath. In another 400 metres you cross Bedford Bridge, named after a young man who drowned trying to ford the **Tarf**. Here Queen Victoria forded the river on a pony with bagpiper marching waist-deep ahead.

If the rifle range track is closed, follow the main riverside track, which crosses the River Tilt to the east end of Gilbert's Bridge; recross the river for the track up the western bank.

Heading down Glen Tilt

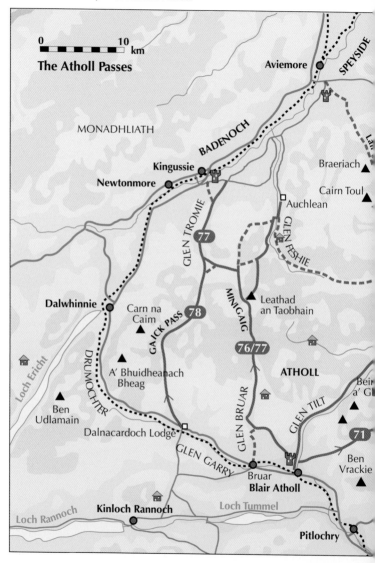

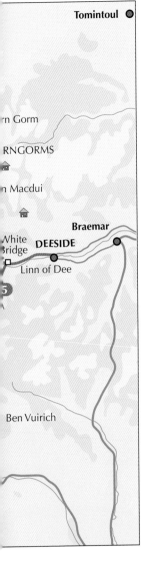

Tomintoul

rn Gorm

RNGORMS

n Macdui

Braemar

White
Bridge   DEESIDE

Linn of Dee

Ben Vuirich

Soon the Allt a' Ghlinne Mhoir arrives from the right: above this the Tilt becomes a mere stream, the **Allt Garbh Buidhe**. ▸ The path continues along the left sidewall of the stream's V-slot. After 2.5km the valley opens out a little, and the path crosses a sidestream, the outflow from hidden Loch Tilt.

Short but squelchy diversion to Loch Tilt

Turn up left, to right of the stream, finding a small deer path. Pass round to right of the loch, a big peat pool. On a settled summer night, my bivvy site was on the hump alongside, **Cnapan Loch Tilt**.

Go through the wide soggy col at its head, and drop down the hollow beyond, on grassier patches among heather, to find the path on the near side of the main valley.

Just past the Loch Tilt stream, the Tilt itself arrives from the right. Now the valley widens through the watershed, with a flat boggy bottom. The path is rebuilt here, on the left-side wall.

Immediately north of the Allt Ghlinne Mhoir, a path crosses the now very small River Tilt for Fealar Lodge. It can be used for through routes via the Iutharn group of hills to Glen Shee.

Looking back, the cairn on Cnapan Loch Tilt can be seen.

About 1.5km into Invernessshire, the path widens into a rough track. On joining the **Allt an t-Seilich**, the track runs into the stream. Keep ahead on rough path on the left bank. Soon a track runs left to **Bynack Lodge** ruin. ◄

A sign marks 'dangerous building' – well, it was known to be haunted when it still stood.

The boggy old path from Bynack Lodge marked on OS maps does exist, more or less, and avoids two small fords on the track route. Simpler though is to ignore the lodge track and stay on the stream bank. Soon a new track rejoins from the Bynack Lodge ruin. After 400 metres it fords the stream, and 400 metres later it fords back again. Around 300 metres later comes the serious ford, over the **Geldie Burn**. This can be impossible after heavy rain.

To the left is a tin shack alongside the track towards Glen Feshie. But keep ahead, rejoining the main river, on the track to right of a plantation (partly felled). The track and river bend right, to cross **White Bridge** over the River Dee.

For **Linn of Dee** turn right on the wide, smooth track for 5km.

76 Minigaig Pass to Glen Feshie

Length

Difficulty

Start	Blair Atholl station (NN 870 653)
Finish	Auchlean, Glen Feshie (NN 853 975)
Distance	41km/25½ miles
Ascent	900m/3000ft
Approx time	12hr
Max altitude	Leathad an Taobhain 912m
Terrain	Tracks, a good hill path, comfortable tundra-type hilltop

Starting from House of Bruar is slightly shorter, and almost as attractive – use Route 69.

Today we don't travel from Atholl to Badenoch: we go up Munros. Old paths and passes go one of two ways. They get overlain by an easy Landrover track – or else they fade into the heather. But an accident of soil structure (thin peat overlying pale gravelly subsoil) and of geology (quartz lumps lying about for marker cairns) means that, for five fine kilometres from Glen Bruar up to the watershed, the old path remains, visible and usable.

The Minigaig is the highest and wildest of the old through routes. That relict path sneaks up a grassy stream hollow, 10 metres of green in a wasteland of peat and brown heather stretching forever in every direction.

The other 35km, however, require use of the brain as well as the feet. The long approach track is uninteresting, at least until Bruar Lodge where the hills close in. So start at Blair Atholl (or House of Bruar) for gentler estate tracks, woodland, and a white castle. And after the pass, the proper path has not survived in the same way. The original Minigaig, scented with the cowpats of the old drovers, is described in Route 77. But here, we head for lovely Glen Feshie by an easier path. And yes, the almost-Munro summit of Leathad an Taobhain does turn out to be the natural route through.

On-street parking may be found in Blair Atholl village.

From **Blair Atholl** station, start east of the River Tilt, on the side road to Old Bridge of Tilt (see also maps for Routes 66 and 67). Cross this bridge, and take the lane ahead to **Old Blair**. Turn down left between the buildings, on a lane that bends right and crosses Banvie Burn. At once turn right up an estate track. ▸

The track runs gently uphill for 5km, first through woodland, then along moorland edge and under the edge of open pine forest. When the track bends west along the wood top, turn down right on a grassier side-track. It contours around the moor, past the abandoned house at Ruichlachrie, to a ford of Bruar Water south of **Cuilltemhuc**.

The water here is usually low, due to the intake dam upstream. If the river is too full to cross, make a way up the riverbank for 1.5km to that intake, which has a con-crete footbridge. Otherwise cross Bruar Water to join the wide, stony track up **Glen Bruar**.

In reverse: during Blair Castle opening hours you can take the little gate opposite the track foot into Diana's Grove, and head out to Blair Atholl past the castle.

The River Feshie at Achleum Bridge

After 6km, the track crosses the river towards **Bruar Lodge**. Turn left immediately over the bridge, on a grass path to rejoin the track just after the lodge. In another 4.5km the track ends at a bridge over a stream.

Ahead, take the clear path slanting up to the right (not the other clear path slanting left). It rises onto moorland and heads north, marked with old, half-mossed cairns many of which are topped off with a lump of white quartz. After running along the moorland hump **Uchd a' Chlarsair** the path dips to a tiny stream. Head uphill for 10 metres to find the next cairn and the clear path again through heather.

The path contours above **Caochan Lub** stream, eventually joining it at a stream junction. The path follows the left-hand sidestream up northwest, before rising onto peaty moorland. Here it finds a strip of grassier ground amid the wasteland of black hags.

The path levels at **Minigaig Pass**. Continue another 300 metres, to a larger quartz cairn where the path dips towards Badenoch. Here head up to the right, on grass, moss and lichen. You could skirt to right of the 902m top, but it's as easy to cross it for the wide views north and the smoother vegetation. A gentle drop east leads to the equally gentle rise to the cylinder trig point on the main 912m summit of **Leathad an Taobhain**.

Another 2.4m of height here would mean a big path, a sprawling cairn, and a couple of sprawling Munro-baggers and their sandwiches... Head down north on short heather and lichen. Quartz lumps mark the path, indistinct at first, down into a col with a stream.

Wheelmarks of a Landrover lead past a ruin for the short climb to **Meall an Uillt Chreagaich**. Here a stony Landrover track runs down north. This could be followed all the way down to Glen Feshie; however, a rougher, softer and much prettier route is available. After 400 metres, as the track bends left, head down right to a stream. Its grassy banks provide an easy descent to a stream junction with the Allt Lorgaidh.

An old stalkers' path on the left bank is just discernable. It runs downstream until the stream dips into a rocky ravine. Now the path contours out to the left, opposite the crags of **Slochd Beag**. The path descends a steep scree slope in gentle zigzags – watch for the sharp bends, or you may find yourself on a sheep path with the true path 20m further down.

At the floor of **Glen Feshie** the path becomes a grass track to a ruin with two pines. Here a stonier track joins from the left. ▶ After 1km, the River Feshie on the right forms a series of braided channels, the best place to attempt a crossing if you are aiming for Ruigh-aiteachain Bothy. Otherwise continue to Carnachuin, where the bridge is due to be rebuilt in summer 2013. Cross to the

The less romantic route came down this track all the way, through the heathery slot with Lochan an t-Sluic.

east bank for pleasant paths up the glen, either alongside the big river or in under the pines. If the bridge at Carnachuin remains obstinately non-existent (its rebuilding was first promised for 2010) continue to a usable bridge 4km downstream.

Paths and grassy tracks east of the river run by **Achleum** to the start of public road at **Auchlean**.

77 Minigaig Pass the ancient way

Length

Difficulty

Start	Blair Atholl station (NN 870 653)
Finish	Ruthven Barracks, Kingussie (NN 764 996, or Auchlean, Glen Feshie NN 853 975)
Distance	45km/28 miles
Ascent	850m/2900ft
Approx time	13hr
Max altitude	Minigaig Pass 850m
Terrain	Tracks, a good hill path, rough, wet hillsides and heather; tarmac track

The ancient drove road between Atholl and Badenoch turned northwest down Allt Bhran to Glen Tromie, joining the following route (Gaick Pass) out to Ruthven Barracks. The descent northwards from Minigaig Pass does not have the surviving path found on the Atholl side. Traces of path among wet grass and heather are overlain in places by the churned track of a quad bike. This recreates the cow-puddled sludge of the 18th century, and on the 'Summer Road to Ruthven' you share in a small way the redcoat soldier's knowledge that whatever happens next is likely to be not nice...

Alternatively, from Allt Bhran you can switch to a Landrover track and east for Glen Feshie; or, for incurable romantics, there's another old path straight ahead.

On-street parking may be found in Blair Atholl village.

WHY TAKE THIS ROUTE RATHER THAN ROUTE 76?

- It is the historical route of the old drovers
- If you're aiming for Glen Tromie rather than Glen Feshie
- It is a legal right of way, usable without restriction in the stalking season

Start as the previous route, from **Blair Atholl** (or House of Bruar) to the **Minigaig Pass**.

From Minigaig Pass, the old path runs down north, faint and intermittent, to a stream junction (NN 806 874). Follow the small stream down to join **Allt Coire Bhran**. After 1km, at the valley floor, is a major stream junction (NN 800 886), with a plantation above and ahead.

Here the 'original Minigaig' route for Ruthven Barracks and Kingussie keeps downstream along **Allt Bhran**. There's a faint heather path about 50–100 metres up to right of the stream. Cross Allt Bhran at an intake dam, for a track on the left bank to the tarred Glen Tromie track (Route 77). At **Glentromie Lodge**, you can divert onto the 'Summer Road to Ruthven', a faint and fairly damp moorland path over the hill to the ruined barracks.

The top of Minigaig Pass, looking north into Badenoch

Alternatively, for Glen Feshie:

Finishing in Glen Feshie option 1
From the major stream junction, keep ahead (north) up the left edge of the plantation. Turn right at its top to find a track that climbs the flank of **Carn Dearg Mor**. The track descends south then runs out to Glen Feshie: or you can bag the Corbett Carn Dearg Mor and descend its north-east ridge, which is pathless and at its foot very heathery.

Finishing in Glen Feshie option 2
For lovers of history and heather, there's an older way to Glen Feshie. It was probably very good a century ago. It is still followable with careful navigation and a little luck. Having left **Allt Bhran** at the major stream junction and headed up the west edge of the plantation, keep north down through a col. The former path is just traceable.

Join **Allt an Dubh-chadha** for 1km. As the stream bends slightly left, the path starts to ease up across the heather slope on the right. It follows the stream valley north for another 1km. Now the stream turns more forcefully left, northwest, with a couple of rock outcrops at the bend. Here the heather path above it keeps ahead, east of north, onto a heather moor. It crosses a very shallow flat col, to join a small stream running down north to the head of **Feith Mhor** stream. Here a track runs northeast to Glen Feshie.

Track (option 2) from Feith Mhor descends to Glen Feshie

78 Gaick Pass

Start	Dalnacardoch Lodge on A9 (NN 721 704)
Finish	Ruthven Barracks, Kingussie (NN 764 996, or Auchlean, Glen Feshie NN 853 975)
Distance	44km/27½ miles
Ascent	200m/600ft
Approx time	11hr
Max altitude	Loch an Duin 500m
Terrain	Tracks, and 4km of path

The Gaick is the Marlene Dietrich of Atholl passes, beautiful and remote. Unlike the German-American bisexual film star, Gaick can be quite easily accessed, by a Landrover track from the south, and an estate road out to Glen Tromie.

The 4km of lochside path at the top can be cycled in parts; the rest can be cycled easily. But for those in boots, the 12km of Tromie tarmac is a bit of a trudge; a more challenging and interesting alternative end is lovely Glen Feshie.

Car parking is by the River Garry at the foot of the hill road to Trinafour. Buses don't officially stop at Dalnacardoch, but may do if you sweet-talk the driver.

Start up the wide, stony track on the north side of the road, past a stalking-season sign. The track enters plantation and after 400 metres forks: keep gently uphill ahead, with a waymark post just after the junction.

The track emerges onto open moor, passing above a quarry. After 2km, a tall cairn stands to left of the track, then it passes the abandoned house **Badnambiast**, Place of the Beast, the beastliness now supplied by sheep who use it for shelter.

The track drops to a bridge over Edendon Water. After 3km the track recrosses the river to pass the ruinous

Sronphadruig Lodge. Keep ahead to where the track fords the stream.

Don't cross the stream, but keep ahead up onto moor, then follow drier ground above the river for 200 metres, until a clear path runs across to the right. Peaty at first, the path soon runs up into heathery ground. The narrow but good path runs along immediately above a fine loch, **Loch an Duin**.

At the outflow, follow the stream for 50 metres, to the start of a new track on the opposite (east) side. It runs down the beautiful valley past **Loch Bhrodainn**. Then it bends round to right of a plantation, and crosses Allt Ghairbh Ghaig, the rough river of Gaick.

Ignore a track on the right here. The track ahead passes **Gaick Lodge** then a third loch, **Loch an t-Seilich**. Pass a plantation, to the loch-foot dam. Immediately beyond, the track becomes tarmac. About 500 metres later, the road bends left above a river gorge, with a gate in a deer fence on the right. ◀ In another 2km, a track turns back up to the right opposite a large new house – this is a longer but easier route to Allt Bhran for Glen Feshie, avoiding a river crossing. But for Ruthven Barracks and Kingussie, just keep north along the tarmac.

This is the start of the diversion to Glen Feshie.

In another 4km **Glen Tromie** narrows, with attractively wooded side slopes. At **Glentromie Lodge**, you can divert onto the 'Summer Road to Ruthven', a faint and fairly damp moorland path. Otherwise, carry on along the tarmac to the B970 at **Tromie Bridge**.

Turn left across the river, and at once look out for a waymarked footpath on the right through Insh Marshes bird reserve, rejoining the road after 2km. Continue for 1km to **Ruthven Barracks**. It's another 1.5km to **Kingussie**.

Finishing in Glen Feshie

Through the deer fence gate (NN 766 888) north of **Loch an t-Seilich**, faint old wheelmarks lead uphill through regenerating pine, then along the edge of swampy ground with heather rising on its right. The track exits the regeneration area through another deer fence gate, then turns downstream beside Allt Coire nan Dearcag to an intake dam on **Allt Bhran**.

Here you must cross the small river, with no bridge. ▸ From the intake dam, mount the riverside bank to find a small heather path on the north bank just above the river. The path follows the bank top above the river's floodplain, after 1.5km dropping to cross a sidestream. It then again runs some 100 metres to left of the stream (not alongside it, as on maps) before descending to a stream junction.

Now head up to the left, with no clear path, to the bottom corner of a plantation just above. A faint, wet path heads up alongside (to left of) this plantation to its top corner. Turn right on a grassy track.

This track passes along the plantation top, then slants up the side of **Carn Dearg Mor**, before descending in zigzags to cross the floor of a boggy valley to a junction. Keep left, down through a heathery hill slot and past a small lochan, to arrive at the little tarmac road in Glen Feshie.

The former bridge at **Carnachuin** has not been replaced, but it's sometimes possible to wade the River Feshie at that point. From there, or from the bridge 4km to the north, very pleasant paths run along the east side of the River Feshie to Auchlean.

If rivers are full, the alternative is to continue down Glen Tromie, for 2km, ignore the gravel track on the right, and cross the Allt Bhran ahead. Traces of old path lead upstream on the north bank.

79 A' Bhuidheanach Bheag by the Crooked Corrie

Length
■ ■ ■ ■ ■

Difficulty
■ ■ ■ ■ ■

Start/finish	Dalnacardoch Lodge on A9 (NN 721 704)
Distance	41.5km/26 miles
Ascent	900m/3000ft
Approx time	12hr
Max altitude	Carn na Caim 941m
Terrain	Tracks, rough paths, steep grass, featureless peaty moorland
Note	Bicycle to Sronphadruig Lodge, 9km each way, saves up to 3½hr

Challenging... exciting... tough. These aren't words heard about A' Bhuidheanach Bheag (the Little Yellowish Item) and Carn na Caim (Curvy Stonepile). Taken from the track above the A9's Drumochter Pass, with a peaty plateau stroll to follow, it takes snow, starlight, or thick mist to add interest to what are sometimes cited as Scotland's dullest Munros.

But on the other side of it all, there's Edendon Water with its 9km of approach track, and the deep, secret Cama' Choire with its gorge and waterfalls. The grassy plateau; but then the plateau of featureless peat, with tricky compass work to the top of the stalkers' path. The lovely lochside path at the head of Gaick Pass; but then the Edendon Water and its 9km of track again. Not everyone will like this alternative route from the east. But nobody can call it dull.

There's car parking (and a usable bus pull-in) at the first lay-by after the start of the dual carriageway on the A9's northbound side: also alongside the River Garry at the foot of the hill road to Trinafour.

Start up the wide, stony track on the north side of the road, past a stalking-season routes sign. The track enters plantation and after 400 metres forks: keep ahead, gently uphill, past a waymark post.

The track emerges onto open moor, passing above a quarry. After 2km, a tall cairn stands to left of the track, then it passes the abandoned house Badnambiast.

Cama' Choire, evening

The track drops slightly to a bridge over **Edendon Water**. ▶ After 3km the track recrosses the river to pass the ruinous **Sronphadruig Lodge**. Keep ahead to where the track fords the stream.

Across the ford, the track runs up into **Cama' Choire**, one of the secret places of Perthshire. If the stream is in spate, don't cross. Otherwise follow the track for 800 metres to a small intake, and recross on the footbridge above the dam. A rough but very useful path now runs upstream on the north bank. Cross the sidestream that flows from waterfalls alongside the crags Bruthach Chiulam.

Here the path becomes indistinct; however, the going is now mostly grassy. The path rises above the stream to cross side-gullies, then contours along the valley side, with the stream in a gorge below. The path fades out at the streamside above the gorge, at the big bend below a sidestream with more waterfalls (NN 684 786).

Above this point the valley narrows with a gorge bottom and very steep sides. So cross to the south side, head upstream a little to view waterfalls in the main stream, then head up the steep grass slope to the south.

Now up on the left, a gentle slope of tufty grass and some heather appears a possible, but dull, route via Ghlas Mheall Mor to A' Bhuidheanach Bheag.

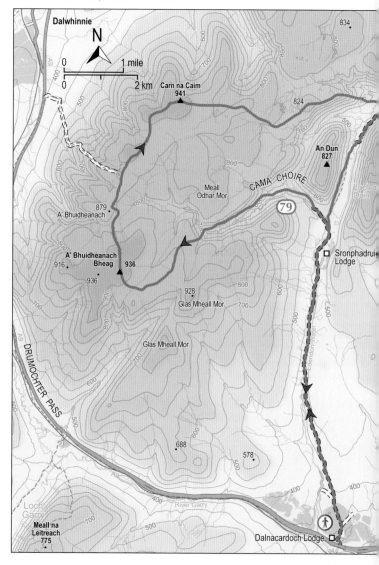

Once on the plateau, you could cross the stream on the left to bag **Glas Mheall Mor**, a Munro Top. Else head up peaty grass southwest, bending right across a shallow col to ascend northwest to the trig point on **A' Bhuidheanach Bheag**.

Head down north, following traces of path and the posts of a former fence. After 800 metres the fencing turns away to the right, but keep ahead, north, down through a wide peaty col. A faint track leads straight up to the quartz-built cairn on **A' Bhuidheanach**.

Here turn east of north, to the right-hand hill hump ahead. On this the Landrover track becomes clear, with fence posts on its right, running north to Point 902m. Here the track bends left, down towards the A9; but keep ahead, northeast, across a peaty col. Fence posts reappear to guide you, and a new (but faint) track arrives from down on the left.

Follow this wheelmark track, with the fencing in sight on your right, as it runs along the smooth hump northeast, then bends left, north, onto the end of **Carn na Caim**. Wheelmarks and fencing lead along the Perthshire boundary to the summit cairn. Big steep drops fall northeast just beyond.

Descent from here is due east – convenient for the compass. In clear conditions, you can wander off the direct line to find less dissected ground. In mist, keep east. Go down grassy slopes to cross a stream that descends northeast. Contour the side of a peaty low ridgeline, then cross its flat top for a slightly steeper descent through grassy peat hags.

At its foot cross another stream that descends northeast, then bear up to the right onto drier ground with short (or fairly short) heather. Keep east onto a moorland hump

Meall Chuaich from Carn na Caim

covered in short heather. It's not named on maps (**824m** on Explorer, NN 713 821).

Head down the rounded ridgeline just north of east. The path appears as a little groove in the heather. At the ridge end, the first of three cairns marks the start of the more visible path. Tiny cairns guide it slightly to right of the crest line to the top of the east-descending steep spur.

The path descends in clear zigzags to the valley floor. It crosses to the river, turning downstream for 50 metres to a footbridge, then rising to join a track. Turn right, following the small track up to its end at a ford of the stream. Head upstream for 150 metres to the outflow of **Loch an Duin**.

A small heather path runs along the steep foot of An Dun just above the loch. At the loch end, the path crosses damp peat to the stream emerging from Cama' Choire. Cross to join the track; or follow the riverbank downstream for 200 metres to join the track as it emerges from its ford.

Retrace your outward steps for 9km down the track to **Dalnacardoch Lodge**.

80 Udlamains and the Sow

Start/finish	Lay-by 79 (parking) at highest point of Drumochter Pass (NN 633 755)
Distance	24km/15 miles
Ascent	1250m/4200ft
Approx time	8½hr
Max altitude	Beinn Udlamain 1011m
Terrain	Heathery ascent to the Sow, then moss and stones with paths; tarmac cycle path to finish

Length

■ ■ ■ ■ ▢

Difficulty

■ ■ ■ ▢ ▢

How often do you drive up the A9, glance at the huge heathery lumps above the road, and feel happy to be on the way to Ben Alder, or the Cairngorms, or Wester Ross... However, the Udlamains are not so harshly heathery as they look from the dual carriageway. And up on the summits, pale stones and moss are also part of the rich tapestry of Munro-bagging. You can get four of them in a day, and with the high start point it's not even a particularly long day.

Short enough, indeed, to add in a bonus Corbett. The Sow of Atholl gives a taste of the heather, before you get onto the established paths over the four Munros to follow.

Start immediately north of the lay-by, taking the old road running below the modern one. Fork right onto a track which passes under the railway. It bends right, and runs up Coire Domhain to right of the stream. About 800 metres into the valley, the track runs close to the water. If you can't cross here, there's a track bridge another 500 metres upstream.

Head straight up the **Sow of Atholl**, on grassy patches among the heather. From the small cairn, head down southwest, with steep drops on your right as you approach the col below.

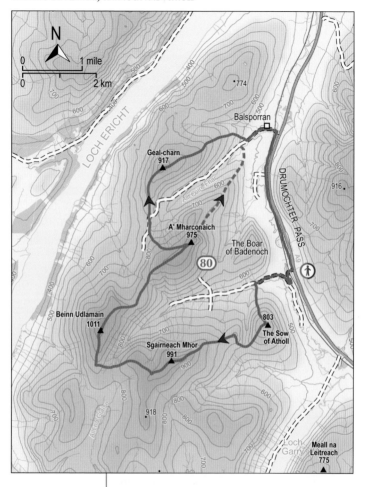

The Sow owes its Corbett status to the **Drumochter Glacier**, and a meltwater lake trapped in Coire Luidhearnaidh. The resulting river flowing northwards has overdeepened this col to give the Sow its required 500ft of drop.

A small path leads up out of the col alongside the drops on the right, then heads left to the shallow col behind the 800m contour ring. A wide but faint path leads up the ridge, with the ground getting stonier and the ridge quite sharply defined as you reach the summit trig point of **Sgairneach Mhor**.

Sgairneach Mhor summit

Between here and Beinn Udlamain is a complex three-way watershed, confusing in mist. Leave Sgairneach Mhor southwest, with a faint path in the moss. After 600 metres there's a lonely cairn with a quartz lump on top. Here turn right, northwest, for the very gentle drop to the wide shoulder at 930m. A larger cairn here marks the turn down just south of west, for the steeper drop to the peaty col below.

The path keeps to right of most of the bare peat in the col, then goes up beside a tiny stream to reach the stony ridgeline of Beinn Udlamain. Old metal fence posts along the Perthshire/Invernessshire boundary mark the way north up the ridge to **Beinn Udlamain**'s large cairn.

The 4km from here to A' Mharconaich are so mossy smooth that you could walk them driving a golf ball. The old fence and a faint path guide northeast across two cols to the preliminary summit. Continue 500 metres almost level to **A' Mharconaich**'s northeast top, which may or may not be the higher of the two but does have the better views and the bigger cairn.

Direct descent from A' Mharconaich to Balsporran Cottages

A' Mharconaich's rounded summit conceals the ridge descending northeast. Head down north, and after a few steps you see the ridge below you, with a clear path forming. The path runs right down to Allt Coire Fhar stream, where you join the surfaced track on the further bank.

This rough track, after ascending very briefly towards Geal-charn, runs down to the right, all the way down Coire Fhar to Balsporran Cottages.

For the **main route** via Geal-charn, from A' Mharconaich's summit, return southwest, skirting to right of that preliminary southwest summit. Don't be in a hurry to slant down right, towards the col far below; the later you leave it, the less rough the ground will be. Various paths converge to lead down into the col, where you join a rough track contouring in from the left. ◄

A broad stony path leads north up the ridgeline to the summit of **Geal-charn**.

Descend east, on a broad path that is often faint on the stony ground. After 1km the ridgeline levels. If you keep east, you reach a tall, square marker cairn (very visible from below) but this stands to south of the true ridgeline and its path, so contour to your left. The path, sometimes peaty and wet, runs down northeast, then east through deepening heather. At the ridge foot it joins a surfaced quad-bike track, running down to the right. This joins the larger track alongside **Allt Coire Fhar**. Follow it out across a level crossing to **Balsporran** Cottages and the A9.

Geal-charn has been a less interesting Munro, at the barely-made-it altitude of 3009ft, whose dull but apt name 'white stony' is shared with four other equally low-status summits. And it's not even in Perthshire. The appropriate comeback for such overt Munro-bagging is the 3.5km walk back into Perthshire, along the tarred cycleway on the west side of the **A9**.

APPENDIX A

Route summary table

	Icon	Distance (km/miles)	Time (hours)	Length rating	Difficulty rating	Page
1 Comrie and Crieff						
1 Meall na Fearna to Ben Vorlich	mtn	26/16½	9	4	4	20
2 Beinn Dearg	mid	13.5/8½	5	2	4	24
3 Water of Ruchill	low	14/9	4	1	2	27
4 Comrie: Deil's Caldron	low	6/3½	2	1	1	30
5 Glen Tarken tracks	low	14/8½	4	2	1	33
6 Ben Chonzie and Auchnafree Hill	mtn	19/12	7	3	4	36
7 Crieff, its Knock, and River Earn	low	13/8	4	2	1	41
8 Glen Almond and the Lochan Slot	low	22/13½	6	2	2	47
2 Killin and Glen Lochay						
9 Looking at Loch Tay: Meall Clachach	mid	10.5/6½	3¾	1	4	52
10 Cam Chreag and Ben Challum	mtn	27/17	9	4	4	55
11 Beinn nan Imirean, Meall Glas	mtn	22.5/14	7½	3	3	60
12 The Tarmachans	mtn	14.5/9	5½	2	5	63
Summit summary: Ben Lawers						
13 Edramucky Burn	mid	2.5/1½	1¼	1	2	71
14 Up and down from the Lairig road	mtn	10/6½	4¼	2	3	73

		Icon	Distance (km/miles)	Time (hours)	Length rating	Difficulty rating	Page
15	Lawers Four from Lawers village	mtn	17/11	8	3	4	75
16	The Cat's Bowl (descent)	mtn	6.5/4*	2*	1	4	78
17	Down via Beinn Ghlas to Lawers village (descent)	mtn	10.5/6½*	3*	1	3	79
18	Glen Lyon: Da-Eig Circuit	mtn	20/12½	7½	3	4	81
3 Glen Lyon							
19	Carn Mairg from Fortingall	mtn	19/12	7¼	3	3	88
20	Back of Schiehallion	mid	23/14½	7½	3	2	92
21	The Black Crag of Glen Lyon	low	7/4½	2¾	1	3	95
22	Beinn Dearg and the Mairgs	mtn	28/17½	10½	5	4	98
23	Meall Ghaordaidh from Glen Lyon	mtn	15/9½	5¾	2	4	103
24	Around Loch an Daimh	mtn	26/16	9½	4	4	105
25	Beinn Heasgarnich and Creag Mhor	mtn	22.5/14	8¼	4	3	111
4 Bridge of Orchy							
Summit summary: Beinn Dorain							
26	Beinn a' Chaisteal and Beinn nam Fuaran	mid	19/12	6¾	3	4	118
27	Beinn Mhanach, the Monk	mtn	20/12½	6½	3	4	121
28	Dorain and Dothaidh from the back	mtn	22/17	9	4	4	123
29	Bridge of Orchy to Beinn Dorain, Beinn an Dothaidh	mtn	13/8	6½	3	4	126
30	Beinn Mhanach long crossing	mtn	18/11	6½	3	4	127
31	Rannoch Edge: Chreachain and Achaladair	mtn	21/13	7½	3	4	130

* as part of a longer route

	Icon	Distance (km/miles)	Time (hours)	Length rating	Difficulty rating	Page
32 Beinn an Dothaidh from Achallader	mtn	11/7	5	2	4	134
33 The Lyon side: Chreachain, Achaladair, Mhanach	mtn	30/19	10½	5	5	136
5 Perth and Dunkeld						
34 Perth and Kinnoull Hill	low	12.5/8	3¾	1	1	142
35 Dunkeld, Birnam Hill and the Tay	low	17.5/11	5½	2	2	147
36 Tracks to Loch Skiach	low	13.5/8	4	1	1	152
37 Craig Lochie	low	15/9½	5	2	5	155
6 Aberfeldy						
38 Farragon Hill from Strathtay	mid	19.5/12	7	3	5	158
39 Aberfeldy: Rob and Rabbie	low	21/13	6	3	1	162
40 Aberfeldy and the Tay	low	14/9	3½	1	1	168
41 Kenmore and the Tay	low	10/6	2½	1	1	171
42 Falls of Acharn	low	8.5/5	3	1	1	174
43 Falls of Acharn to Creag an Sgliata	mid	13/8	5	2	2	178
44 Creagan na Beinne and Ardtalnaig	mid	17.5/11	7	3	4	180
45 Creag Uchdag	mid	19.5/12	6½	3	4	184
7 Tummel and Loch Rannoch						
46 Schiehallion end to end	mtn	12/7½	4½	2	4	188
47 Schiehallion Foot: Limestone and McGregor's Cave	low	8.5/5½	3½	1	5	192
48 Craig Varr and Kinloch Rannoch	low	7.5/5	2½	1	2	194

* as part of a longer route

		Icon	Distance (km/miles)	Time (hours)	Length rating	Difficulty rating	Page
65	Ben Vrackie and the River Garry	mid	17/10½	5½	2	3	244
66	Blair Castle to Glen Tilt	low	17/10½	4½	2	1	248
67	Glen Tilt and Carn a' Chlamain	mtn	29/18	8½	4	2	254
68	Old Bridge of Tilt to Dearg, Mheadhonach	mtn	32/20	10½	5	4	259
69	Bruar Falls and Glen Banvie	low	16/10	4¼	2	1	262
70	Bruar Falls and Blair	low	12.5/8	3½	1	1	266
Summit summary: Beinn a' Ghlo							
71	Around Beinn a' Ghlo (with optional ascent of Ben Vurich)	mid	39/24	11	5	2	270
72	Beinn a' Ghlo from Loch Moraig	mtn	21.5/13½	8	4	4	273
73	Carn nan Gabhar north ridge to Glen Tilt (descent)	mtn	5.5/3*	1½*	4	3	277
74	Glen Tilt to Braigh Coire Chruinn-bhalgain by Carn Torcaidh	mtn	5/3*	2¾*	4	3	279
10 Drumochter							
75	Glen Tilt	low	33.5/21	9	4	1	282
76	Minigaig Pass to Glen Feshie	mid	41/25½	12	5	3	286
77	Minigaig Pass the ancient way	mid	45/28	13	5	5	290
78	Gaick Pass	low	44/27½	11	5	2	293
79	A' Bhuidheanach Bheag by the Crooked Corrie	mtn	41.5/26	12	5	5	296
80	Udlamains and the Sow	mtn	24/15	8½	4	3	301

* as part of a longer route

APPENDIX B

Access (especially in the stalking season)

Since 2005 Scotland has a legal right of access to almost all open country and farmland (the main exceptions being growing crops and land around buildings). Footbridges are explicitly included in the access rights, as are non-damaging cycling, and wild camping – although this doesn't mean roadside camping. Access must be taken 'responsibly', which means with consideration and care for other hill users, land managers and the environment. The full text of the Scottish Access Code is at www.outdooraccess-scotland.com.

In parts of this area, from mid August (sometimes July) to 21 October, responsible access includes avoiding disturbance to deer stalking. Hills managed by NatureScot (formerly Scottish Natural Heritage), the National Trust for Scotland, the John Muir Trust and the Forestry Commission are open to walkers year-round. These include popular routes on Ben Lawers, Meall nan Tarmachan and Schiehallion.

The web-based 'Heading for the Scottish Hills' system can be found at www.outdooraccess-scotland.scot (look under 'Walking and stalking'). Section 6 covers most of the walks in this book; Section 7 covers Glenartney (Routes 1–3); Section 5 covers Atholl and Pitlochry.

The Access Code states: 'If after taking reasonable steps to find out where stalking is taking place... you have been unable to, for example because the estate is not in Heading for the Scottish Hills, it is responsible for you to go ahead with your walk, but take into account reasonable advice given locally or once you have started, such as on notice boards or given by a stalker.' (Such reasonable advice could suggest an alternative route or even an alternative hill.) 'You may also wish to help by using established paths and following ridges.'

Stalking does not take place on Sundays.

1 Comrie and Crieff

Drummond Estates (Glen Artney)
Stalking weekdays 12 Aug–15 Feb. Please keep to recognised paths.
tel: 01764 681257

Glen Turret (East of Scotland Water, Glenturret Estates)
Watch out for shepherds and stalkers and keep clear so as not to disturb their work. Check signboard at Turret dam.

2 Killin and Glen Lochay

Glen Lochay
Glenlochay Estate. Stalking early July to 20 Oct. Sign with stalking information is displayed in the car park and at the entrance to the estate.

tel: 01887 840412 or 07766 816033
manager@pitcastle.com

Ben Lawers
NTS; no restrictions; for north side
see Glen Lyon.

3 Glen Lyon

South Chesthill Estate (south side of the River Lyon)
Stalking between early Sept and 20 Oct.
If further information is needed please
phone 01887 877233 (before 8pm).

North Chesthill Estate (Carn Mairg group)
Occasional stalking from mid Aug,
but particularly from early Sept to 20
Oct. Staying on the ridges, avoiding
the corries and going clockwise from
Invervar round the four Munros will
help prevent deer from being moved
off the estate. If further information is
needed info@chesthill.com.

Meggernie Estate (head of Glen Lyon)
No information given. Look for map
boards in car parks.

Formerly, accepted routes have been:

- Meall Bhuidhe by northwest flank
  of Garbh Mheall
- Meall Bhuidhe from directly above
  Loch an Daimh dam
- Loch an Daimh north shore track
- Stuchd an Lochain from Loch an
  Daimh dam via 888m spot height
- Cam Chreag from Innerwick by
  track Allt a' Choire Uidhre
- Meall nam Maigheach from
  southwest following fence from
  road
- Meall Ghaordaidh from bridge
  west of Stronuich Reservoir, by

Coire Loaghain and southwest
upstream onto north ridge
- Beinn nan Oighreag from Meall
  Ghaordaidh along ridges.

4 Bridge of Orchy

Rannoch side
Blackmount Estate (East). Stalking
between early Aug and 20 Oct. If
further information is needed please
phone 01838 400255 7am–8am.

Main stalking 1 Aug–20 Oct; keep to
established hill paths, ridges and main
watercourses; avoid corries.

Before using a remote or
unconventional route contact Estate
Office tel: 01838 400506; Head Stalker
tel: 07887 901995.

5 Aberfeldy and Loch Tay

Pitcastle Estate (path towards Farragon Hill)
tel: 01887 840412/07766 816033
email: manager@pitcastle.com

Edradynate Estate (descent from Farragon Hill)

Red flags indicate shooting/stalking,
please keep to the tracks.
email: office@elliscampbell.co.uk

6 Tummel and Loch Rannoch

Dunalastair Estate (above Kinloch Rannoch)
Stalking 13 Sept–31 Dec; please keep
to paths, dogs on leads, especially 13
Sept–20 Oct.

Estate manager tel: 01882 632314

7 Rannoch Moor

**Finnart Estate
(Bridge of Gaur, Rannoch)**
Stalking Aug–Feb.

Dunan (Pharlagain)
July to mid Feb. Most stag stalking
from mid Sept, and in Coire Eigheach.
Contact form at www.dunan-estate.
co.uk

Ben Alder
Ben Alder Estate
Stalking 15 Aug–20 Oct,
hind culling 21 Oct–15 Feb.

Chief Stalker tel: 01540 672000

8 Pitlochry and Blair Atholl

Beinn a' Ghlo
Atholl & Lude Estates. Stalking Aug–20
Oct.

Recorded phone message: 01796
481740
julia@atholl-estates.co.uk
tel: 01796 481355

Signboard (updated daily) at Old Bridge
of Tilt.

9 Drumochter
Gaick, Minigaig and Tilt are rights
of way; Glen Feshie is NTS with no
restrictions.

Dalnacardoch
West Grampian Deer Management
Group. Main stalking 12 Sept–21 Oct.

Pass of Drumochter
Drumochter South. Stalking mid
Sept–20 Oct.

tel: 07833 087675 or 01540 673952

Udlamains group
North of Boar of Badenoch: Drumochter
North Estate. Stalking mid Sept–20 Oct.
tel: 01540 670053 (mornings) or
raliaenterprises@aol.com, tel: 07738
100157

South Udlamains: Dalnaspidal Estate.
Main stalking mid Sept–mid Dec.
tel: 01796 483232

Red deer above Rannoch Station

APPENDIX C
Shops, accommodation and transport

Tourist information
VisitScotland Perth
tel: 01738 450600
www.highlandperthshire.org
www.perthshire.co.uk
www.perthshirebigtreecountry.co.uk

Shopping and supplies
Unlike in the wilder Highlands, small towns here have late-opening shops, outdoor gear shops, petrol stations and banks.

Arriving from the south, there's an excellent Graham Tiso gear superstore on the A9 Perth bypass north roundabout tel: 01738 634464 www.tiso.com. There is a monster Tesco on the A85 slip road between the two roundabouts.

Rail travel
Dunkeld, Pitlochry and Blair Atholl are on the busy Edinburgh–Inverness main line. Three trains a day out of Glasgow on the Fort William line pass through Bridge of Orchy, Rannoch Station and Corrour.

Coach and bus
Dunkeld, Pitlochry, Blair Atholl and House of Bruar are on the Scottish Citylink route Edinburgh–Inverness, and Bridge of Orchy is on the Glasgow–Fort William route. Both these have frequent and fast services tel: 0871 266 33 33 www.citylink.co.uk.

Local buses link the smaller towns with Perth or Stirling. They're mostly run by Stagecoach in Perth tel: 01738 629339. Local timetables are on a hidden corner of www.pkc.gov.uk (Perth & Kinross Council).

Weather and snow
The most useful and accurate Internet forecast is at Mountain Weather Information Systems www.mwis.org.uk. There is also a Met Office mountain forecast at www.metoffice.gov.uk under 'specialist forecasts' (click to 'South Grampian'). One or other of them is posted daily in youth hostels and tourist information centres.

The Scottish Avalanche Information Service issues forecasts for Southern Cairngorms of snow conditions and avalanche risk daily December–Easter. Snow conditions in Perthshire will usually (although not always) be rather less serious. The forecast is at www.sais.gov.uk and Be Avalanche Aware app.

There is a webcam pointed at Ben Lawers from Killin at http://webcam.firbush.org.

Computer views from Ben Chonzie, Ben Lawers, Beinn Dorain, Schiehallion, Ben Alder, Ben Vrackie and Beinn a' Ghlo at www.viewfinderpanoramas.org.

1 Comrie and Crieff

Travel
Crieff to Stirling bus 15A;
St Fillans, Comrie and Crieff to Perth
bus 15 several times a day.

Comrie
Croft Farm Hostel and eco camping
tel: 01764 670140
www.comriecroft.com

Two late-opening convenience stores.

Two pubs (Comrie Hotel better for
scruffy hillwalkers) and a neat little
restaurant, the Deil's Caldron.
Chip shop closes 8.30pm.

Crieff
Visitor Centre with tourist shopping
Muthill Road tel: 01764 654014
www.crieff.co.uk

Many cafés and takeaways: café 'No 24'
is friendly and inexpensive.

Crieff Walking Festival, October
www.droverstryst.com (includes Crieff
accommodation).

2 Killin and Glen Lochay

Travel
Killin to Callender bus C60 Kingshouse
Travel tel: 01877 384768, with further
buses to Stirling; or walk 3.5km to
Lix Toll (A82) for Citylink coach to
Glasgow.

Killin
Several hotels, shops; the youth hostel
has long closed.

Folk music festival every June and
Highland Games at the end of July
www.trossachs.co.uk

Petrol from Lix Toll (A82) 8am–6.30pm,
but sometimes closed.

Loch Tay
Ben Lawers Inn is where you have to
eat/drink if you use their car park for
south Lawers routes, but you won't
mind that at all tel: 01567 820 436

Cruachan Farm campsite alongside
Loch Tay tel: 01567 820302
www.cruachanfarm.co.uk

3 Glen Lyon
Fortingall Inn serves very good food.
Post Office café/shop, Bridge of Balgie.

Bus 91 Fortingall to Aberfeldy Sweeneys
Minibuses tel: 01764 681231

For everything else, see Aberfeldy/
Kenmore.

4 Bridge of Orchy
See www.westhighlandway.org

Bunkhouse at Bridge of Orchy on
Bridge of Orchy station platform
www.westhighlandwaysleeper.com

Bridge of Orchy is accessible by
overnight train from London (arrives
8.30am).

Nearby Tyndrum has good cafés, petrol,
shop.

5 Perth and Dunkeld

VisitScotland Perth tel: 01738 450600
www.highlandperthshire.org

Dunkeld has plenty of pubs, shops, B&Bs.

Dunkeld Tourist Infomation
tel: 01350 727688

Jessie Mac's Hostel, Birnam
tel: 01350 727324
www.jessiemacs.co.uk

Wester Caputh Steading farmhouse
hostel (6.4km east) tel: 07977 904198

6 Aberfeldy

Travel

Frequent Stagecoach buses link
Aberfeldy with Perth (bus 23);
Bus 91 Aberfeldy to Kenmore/Acharn
Sweeneys Minibuses tel: 01764 681231

Aberfeldy

Late-opening Co-op, several pubs, chip
shop, late-opening petrol station.

Outdoor shop Munro's
tel: 01887 820008

Café 'Country Fare' with outdoor
seating, hotels, banks, chip shop.
Good inexpensive food at the
Black Watch bar and restaurant.

Short-stay parking only in town square.
Nearest long-stay parking at Moness
Terrace, 300m to east; Birks car park
(Route 39) almost as handy.

Aberfeldy Information Centre
tel: 01887 820276
www.visitaberfeldy.co.uk

Kenmore

Kenmore Hotel, oldest in Scotland, bar
meals and fancy glass-walled restaurant
overlooking river.

Post Office shop 8.30am–5pm
seven days a week.

Loch Tay Paper Boat café
info@paperboatcafe.co.uk

Culdees (somewhat eccentric)
bunkhouse, Fearnan
www.culdeesbunkhouse.co.uk

7 Tummel and Loch Rannoch

Travel

Bus 82 from Pitlochry, five a day –
Elizabeth Yule tel: 01796 472290

Information
www.rannochandtummel.co.uk

Kilvrecht campsite (Forestry
Commission) at Carie car park south
Loch Rannoch Easter–October
enquiries.east@forestryandland.gov.scot
tel: 0300 067 6380

Loch Tummel Inn tel: 01882 634317
www.theinnatlochtummel.com

Kinloch Rannoch

Dunalastair Hotel, cosy afternoon teas
and bar meals tel: 01882 580444
www.dunalastairhotel.com

Waterside Cafe, Kinloch Rannoch
tel: 01882 632333

The Country Store, Kinloch Rannoch,
provisions and some outdoor gear
(Mon–Sat, Sun morning)
tel: 01882 632306

8 Rannoch Moor

Travel
Rannoch Station to Kinloch Rannoch, search 'Demand Responsive Transport' at www.pkc.gov.uk

Rannoch Station Tearoom and railway museum March–October
www.rannochstationtearoom.co.uk
tel: 07557 049543

Moor of Rannoch Hotel and restaurant Feb–Nov, but closed Tuesdays, Wednesdays
www.moorofrannoch.co.uk

9 Pitlochry and Blair Atholl

Pitlochry
VisitScotland iCentre tel: 01796 472215

Munro's outdoor shop, and factory outlets (mountain streetwear).

Late opening convenience stores and small supermarkets.

Three fish and chip shops, uncountable cafés.

Fern Cottage restaurant atmospheric, good food, not pricy
www.ferncottagepitlochry.co.uk

Pitlochry Youth Hostel (SYHA)
Mar–Oct tel: 01796 472308

Pitlochry Backpackers
Apr–mid Nov tel: 01796 470044
pitlochrybackpackershotel.com

Petrol station, late opening.

Golden eagle over Meall Ghaordaidh (Route 23)

Blair Atholl
Convenience store, open till late, country life museum, working water mill; www.blairatholl.org.uk

Several cafés, including the excellently named 'Atholl Browse' and takeaway beside the museum.

Good café at the Bruar Shopping Experience.

10 Drumochter
Nearest village, Dalwhinnie, has hotels, a café and a distillery.

LISTING OF CICERONE GUIDES

For full information on all our guides,
books and eBooks, visit our website:
www.cicerone.co.uk